P9-CBK-338

Bloom's Modern Critical Views

Bloom's Modern Critical Views

TENNESSEE WILLIAMS
Updated Edition

Edited and with an introduction by
Harold Bloom
Sterling Professor of the Humanities
Yale University

BLOOM'S
LITERARY CRITICISM
An imprint of Infobase Publishing

Bloom's Modern Critical Views: Tennessee Williams—Updated Edition

Copyright ©2007 Infobase Publishing

Introduction © 2007 by Harold Bloom

Bloom's Literary Criticism
An imprint of Infobase Publishing
132 West 31st Street
New York NY 10001

ISBN-10: 0-7910-9430-8
ISBN-13: 978-0-7910-9430-3

Library of Congress Cataloging-in-Publication Data
Tennessee Williams / Harold Bloom, editor. — Updated ed.
    p. cm. — (Bloom's modern critical views)
  Includes bibliographical references and index.
  ISBN 0-7910-9430-8 (hardcover)
  1. Williams, Tennessee, 1911–1983—Criticism and interpretation. 2. Southern States—In literature. I. Bloom, Harold. II. Title. III. Series.
  PS3545.I5365Z843 2007
  812'.54--dc22
  [B]   2006032895

Contributing Editor: Pamela Loos

Cover designed by Takeshi Takahashi

Cover photo © Time Life Pictures/Getty Images

Printed in the United States of America

Bang EJB 10 9 8 7 6 5 4 3 2 1

This book is printed on acid-free paper.

Contents

Editor's Note

My Introduction unfashionably first broods on the relative lack of aesthetic eminence in American drama when compared to American poetry and prose fiction. Here, and in this volume's Afterthought, I would now add David Mamet and Tony Kushner to our playwrights of true achievement. Tennessee Williams, more even than Eugene O'Neill, seems to me our most authentic *literary* dramatist, as alive on the page as in the theater.

Jacqueline O'Connor centers upon Williams' representations of madness, while John M. Clum analyzes the dialectic of Williams' heroic females and their inadequate men.

For Nancy M. Tischler, the Romantic tradition of D. H. Lawrence, Wordsworth, Byron, Scott Fitzgerald, and Hart Crane is the domain of Williams' drama, after which Bert Cardullo examines the Romanticism of *The Glass Managerie*.

In a shrewd essay, Linda Dorff qualifies the playwright's Romanticism by way of some of his deliberately grotesque poems, in which Rimbaud is employed to distance Williams from Hart Crane.

D. Dean Shackelford sees Williams' personal and critical essays as intricate fusions of life and literature, while Verna Foster restores the comic element to the tragic *A Streetcar Named Desire*.

The decline in reputation of Williams' later plays is judged by Annette J. Saddik to be partly the consequence of critical expectations founded upon the work of Samuel Beckett.

Camino Real is contrasted sharply to *Streetcar* by Frank Bradley, after which Philip C. Kolin engages Williams' most characteristic personae, his extraordinary Southern belles.

My Afterthought returns to Williams's deep identification with two great homoerotic self-destructive poets, Arthur Rimbaud and Hart Crane.

Introduction

I

It is a sad and inexplicable truth that the United States, a dramatic nation, continues to have so limited a literary achievement in the drama. American literature, from Emerson to the present moment, is a distinguished tradition. The poetry of Whitman, Dickinson, Frost, Stevens, Eliot, W. C. Williams, Hart Crane, R. P. Warren, Elizabeth Bishop down through the generation of my own contemporaries—John Ashbery, James Merrill, A. R. Ammons, and others—has an unquestionable eminence, and takes a vital place in Western literature. Prose fiction from Hawthorne and Melville on through Mark Twain and Henry James to Cather and Dreiser, Faulkner, Hemingway, Fitzgerald, Nathanael West, and Pynchon, has almost a parallel importance. The line of essayists and critics from Emerson and Thoreau to Kenneth Burke and beyond constitutes another crucial strand of our national letters. But where is the American drama in comparison to all this, and in relation to the long cavalcade of western drama from Aeschylus to Beckett?

The American theater, by the common estimate of its most eminent critics, touches an initial strength with Eugene O'Neill, and then proceeds to the more varied excellences of Thornton Wilder, Tennessee Williams, Arthur Miller, Edward Albee, and Sam Shepard. That sequence is clearly problematical, and becomes even more worrisome when we move from playwrights to plays. Which are our dramatic works that matter most? *Long Day's Journey Into Night*, certainly; perhaps *The Iceman Cometh*; evidently *A Streetcar Named Desire* and *Death of a Salesman*; perhaps again *The Skin of Our Teeth* and *The Zoo Story*—it is not God's plenty. And I will venture the speculation that our drama palpably is not yet literary enough. By this I do not just mean that O'Neill writes very badly, or Miller very baldly; they do, but so did Dreiser, and *Sister Carrie* and *An American Tragedy* prevail nevertheless. Nor do I wish to be an American Matthew Arnold (whom I loathe above all other critics) and proclaim that our dramatists simply have not known enough. They know more than enough, and that is part of the trouble.

Literary tradition, as I have come to understand it, masks the agon between past and present as a benign relationship, whether personal or societal. The actual transferences between the force of the literary past and the potential of writing in the present tend to be darker, even if they do not always or altogether follow the defensive patterns of what Sigmund Freud called "family romances." Whether or not an ambivalence, however repressed, towards the past's force is felt by the new writer and is manifested in his work seems to depend entirely upon the ambition and power of the oncoming artist. If he aspires after strength, and can attain it, then he must struggle with both a positive and a negative transference, false connections because necessarily imagined ones, between a composite precursor and himself. His principal resource in that agon will be his own native gift for interpretation, or as I am inclined to call it, strong misreading. Revising his precursor, he will create himself, make himself into a kind of changeling, and so he will become, in an illusory but highly pragmatic way, his own father.

The most literary of our major dramatists, and clearly I mean "literary" in a precisely descriptive sense, neither pejorative nor eulogistic, was Tennessee Williams. Wilder, with his intimate connections to *Finnegans Wake* and Gertrude Stein, might seem to dispute this placement, and Wilder was certainly more literate than Williams. But Wilder had a benign relation to his crucial precursor, Joyce, and did not aspire after a destructive strength. Williams did, and suffered the fate he prophesied and desired; the strength destroyed his later work, and his later life, and thus joined itself to the American tradition of self-destructive genius. Williams truly had one precursor only: Hart Crane, the greatest of our lyrical poets, after Whitman and Dickinson, and the most self-destructive figure in our national literature, surpassing all others in this, as in so many regards.

Williams asserted he had other precursors also: D. H. Lawrence, and Chekhov in drama. These were outward influences, and benefited Williams well enough, but they were essentially formal, and so not the personal and societal family romance of authentic poetic influence. Hart Crane made Williams into more of a dramatic lyrist, though writing in prose, than the lyrical dramatist that Williams is supposed to have been. Though this influence—perhaps more nearly an identification—helped form *The Glass Menagerie* and (less overtly) *A Streetcar Named Desire*, and in a lesser mode *Summer and Smoke* and *Suddenly Last Summer*, it also led to such disasters of misplaced lyricism as the dreadful *Camino Real* and the dreary *The Night of the Iguana*. (*Cat on a Hot Tin Roof*, one of Williams's best plays, does not seem to me to show any influence of Crane.) Williams's long aesthetic decline covered thirty years, from 1953 to 1983, and reflected the sorrows of a seer who, by his early forties, had outlived his own vision. Hart Crane, self-slain at thirty-two, had set for Williams a High Romantic paradigm that helped cause Williams, his heart as dry as summer dust, to burn to the socket.

II

It is difficult to argue for the aesthetic achievement of Tennessee Williams's long, final phase as a dramatist. Rereading persuades me that his major plays remain *The Glass Menagerie*, *A Streetcar Named Desire*, *Suddenly Last Summer*, and the somewhat undervalued *Summer and Smoke*. *Cat on a Hot Tin Roof* was a popular and critical success, on stage and as a film. I have just reread it in the definitive *Library of America* edition, which prints both versions of Act III, the original, which Williams greatly preferred, and the Broadway revision, made to accommodate the director Elia Kazan. Here is the ambiguous original conclusion, followed by the revision:

> MARGARET: And so tonight we're going to make the lie true, and when that's done, I'll bring the liquor back here and we'll get drunk together, here, tonight, in this place that death has come into ... —What do you say?
> BRICK: I don't say anything. I guess there's nothing to say.
> MARGARET: Oh, you weak people, you weak, beautiful people!— who give up.—What you want is someone to—
> (She turns out the rose-silk lamp.)
> —take hold of you.—Gently, gently, with love! And—
> (The curtain begins to fall slowly.)
> I *do* love you, Brick, I *do*!
> BRICK: (*smiling with charming sadness*): Wouldn't it be funny if that was true?

* * *

MARGARET: And you lost your driver's license! I'd phone ahead and
   have you stopped on the highway before you got halfway to
   Ruby Lightfoot's gin mill. I told a lie to Big Daddy, but we can
   make that lie come true. And then I'll bring you liquor, and we'll
   get drunk together, here, tonight, in this place that death has
   come into! What do you say? What do you say, baby?
BRICK: (X to L side bed)
   I admire you, Maggie.
(Brick sits on edge of bed. He looks up at the overhead light, then
   at Margaret. She reaches for the light, turns it out; then she
   kneels quickly beside Brick at foot of bed.)
MARGARET: Oh, you weak, beautiful people who give up with such
   grace. What you need is someone to take hold of you—gently,
   with love, and hand your life back to you, like something
   gold you let go of—and I can! I'm determined to do it—and
   nothing's more determined than a cat on a tin roof—is there?
   Is there, baby?
(She touches his cheek, gently.)

As Williams noted, his Maggie augments in charm between the two
versions; his Brick modulates subtly, and is a touch more receptive to her.
Shakespeare demonstrates how difficult it is to resist vitality in a stage role,
by creating Sir John Falstaff with a vivacity and wit that carries all before him.
There is nothing Shakespearean about Williams: he sketches archetypes,
caricatures, grotesques, and cannot represent inwardness. And yet, with all his
limitations, he writes well, unlike Eugene O'Neill, who is leaden, and Arthur
Miller, who is drab. Thornton Wilder, Edward Albee, and Tony Kushner also
have their eloquences, but Williams remains the most articulate and adequate
of American dramatists up to this moment.

   Yet his inability to dramatize inwardness is a considerable limitation.
What is Brick's spiritual malady? His homoeroticism is palpably less a burden
than is his homophobia: he will not accept Big Daddy's earlier bisexuality,
anymore than he could yield to love for Skipper (or to Maggie). Brick's
narcissism is central to the play, but even more crucial would be his nihilism,
if only Williams could tell us something about it. As a Hamlet, Brick does
not work at all; he hasn't enough mind to express what most deeply torments
him, and I fear that Williams shares this lack. What deprives *Cat on a Hot Tin
Roof* of any authentic aesthetic eminence is its obscurantism, which may be
indeliberate, unlike Joseph Conrad's in *Heart of Darkness*. It is as though both
Williams and Brick were saying: "The horror! The horror!" without ever
quite knowing what they were trying to talk about.

The ultimately benign and loving Big Daddy and the adoring Big Mama are *not* the cause of Brick's despair. Were it not for his nihilistic malaise, it seems likely that Brick eventually would turn into his dying father, and would become pragmatically bisexual or pansexual. Brick's attachment to Maggie is ambivalent, but so was his affection for Skipper. As a pure narcissist, Brick is autoerotic, in the manner of Walt Whitman.

The play's epigraph, from Dylan Thomas's "Do not go Gentle into that Good Night," is a gesture of tribute to Big Daddy, who, with Maggie the Cat, saves the play. Brick, without them, would freeze the audience, particularly now, when homosexuality is no longer an issue for an audience not dominated by Fundamentalists, Reagan Republicans, and assorted other mossbacks. Read side by side with the wistful *Summer and Smoke*, *Cat on a Hot Tin Roof* seems more a film script than an achieved drama.

III

In Hart Crane's last great Pindaric ode, "The Broken Tower," the poet cries aloud, in a lament that is also a high celebration, the destruction of his battered self by his overwhelming creative gift:

The bells, I say, the bells break down their tower;
And swing I know not where. Their tongues engrave
Membrane through marrow, my long-scattered score
Of broken intervals ... And I, their sexton slave!

This Shelleyan and Whitmanian catastrophe creation, or death by inspiration, was cited once by Williams as an omen of Crane's self-immolation. "By the bells breaking down their tower," in Williams's interpretation, Crane meant "the romantic and lyric intensity of his vocation." Gilbert Debusscher has traced the intensity of Crane's effect upon Williams's Romantic and lyric vocation, with particular reference to Tom Wingfield's emergent vocation in *The Glass Menagerie*. More than forty years after its first publication, the play provides an absorbing yet partly disappointing experience of rereading.

A professed "memory play," *The Glass Menagerie* seems to derive its continued if wavering force from its partly repressed representation of the quasi-incestuous and doomed love between Tom Wingfield and his crippled, "exquisitely fragile," ultimately schizophrenic sister Laura. Incest, subtly termed the most poetical of circumstances by Shelley, is the dynamic of the erotic drive throughout Williams's more vital writings. Powerfully displaced, it is the secret dynamic of what is surely Williams's masterwork, *A Streetcar Named Desire*.

The Glass Menagerie scarcely bothers at such a displacement, and the transparency of the incest motif is at once the play's lyrical strength and, alas, its dramatic weakness. Consider the moment when Williams chooses to end the play, which times Tom's closing speech with Laura's gesture of blowing out the candles:

> TOM: I didn't go to the moon, I went much further—for time is the longest distance between two places. Not long after that I was fired for writing a poem on the lid of a shoebox. I left St. Louis. I descended the steps of this fire escape for a last time and followed, from then on, in my father's footsteps, attempting to find in motion what was lost in space. I traveled around a great deal. The cities swept about me like dead leaves, leaves that were brightly colored but torn away from the branches. I would have stopped, but I was pursued by something. It always came upon me unawares, taking me altogether by surprise. Perhaps it was a familiar bit of music. Perhaps it was only a piece of transparent glass. Perhaps I am walking along a street at night, in some strange city, before I have found companions. I pass the lighted window of a shop where perfume is sold. The window is filled with pieces of colored glass, tiny transparent bottles in delicate colors, like bits of a shattered rainbow. Then all at once my sister touches my shoulder. I rum around and look into her eyes. Oh, Laura, Laura, I tried to leave you behind me, but I am more faithful than I intended to be! I reach for a cigarette, I cross the street, I run into the movies or a bar, I buy a drink, I speak to the nearest stranger—anything that can blow your candles out!
> [Laura bends over the candles.]
> For nowadays the world is lit by lightning! Blow out your candles, Laura—and so goodbye....
> [She blows the candles out.]

The many parallels between the lives and careers of Williams and Crane stand behind this poignant passage, though it is fascinating that the actual allusions and echoes here are to Shelley's poetry, but then Shelley increasingly appears to be Crane's heroic archetype, and one remembers Robert Lowell's poem where Crane speaks and identifies himself as the Shelley of his age. The cities of aesthetic exile sweep about Wingfield/Williams like the dead, brightly colored leaves of the "Ode to the West Wind," dead leaves that are at once the words of the poet and lost human souls, like the beloved sister Laura.

What pursues Tom is what pursues the Shelleyan Poet of *Alastor*, an avenging daimon or shadow of rejected, sisterly eros that manifests itself in a further Shelleyan metaphor, the shattered, colored transparencies of Shelley's dome of many-colored glass in *Adonais*, the sublime, lyrical elegy for Keats. That dome, Shelley says, is a similitude for life, and its many colors stain the white radiance of Eternity until death tramples the dome into fragments. Williams beautifully revises Shelley's magnificent trope. For Williams, life itself, through memory as its agent, shatters itself and scatters the colored transparencies of the rainbow, which ought to be, but is not, a covenant of hope.

As lyrical prose, this closing speech has its glory, but whether the dramatic effect is legitimate seems questionable. The key sentence, dramatically, is: "Oh, Laura, Laura, I tried to leave you behind me, but I am more faithful than I intended to be!" In his descriptive list of the characters, Williams says of his surrogate, Wingfield: "His nature is not remorseless, but to escape from a trap he has to act without pity." What would pity have been? And in what sense is Wingfield more faithful, after all, than he attempted to be?

Williams chooses to end the play as though its dramatic center had been Laura, but every reader and every playgoer knows that every dramatic element in the play emanates out from the mother, Amanda. Dream and its repressions, guilt and desire, have remarkably little to do with the representation of Amanda in the play, and everything to do with her children. The split between dramatist and lyrist in Williams is manifested in the play as a generative divide. Williams's true subject, like Crane's, is the absolute identity between his artistic vocation and his homosexuality. What is lacking in *The Glass Menagerie* is that Williams could not have said of Amanda, what, Flaubert-like, he did say of the heroine of *Streetcar*: "I am Blanche DuBois." There, and there only, Williams could fuse Chekhov and Hart Crane into one.

IV

The epigraph to *A Streetcar Named Desire* is a quatrain from Hart Crane's "*The Broken Tower*," the poet's elegy for his gift, his vocation, his life, and so Crane's precise equivalent of Shelley's *Triumph of Life*, Keats's *Fall of Hyperion*, and Whitman's "When Lilacs Last in the Dooryard Bloom'd." Tennessee Williams, in his long thirty years of decline after composing *A Streetcar Named Desire*, had no highly designed, powerfully executed elegy for his own poetic self. Unlike Crane, his American Romantic precursor and aesthetic paradigm, Williams had to live out the slow degradation of the waning of his potential, and so endured the triumph of life over his imagination.

Streetcar sustains a first rereading, after thirty years away from it, more strongly than I had expected. It is, inevitably, more remarkable on the stage than in the study, but the fusion of Williams's lyrical and dramatic talents in it has prevailed over time, at least so far. The play's flaws, in performance, ensue from its implicit tendency to sensationalize its characters, Blanche DuBois in particular. Directors and actresses have made such sensationalizing altogether explicit, with the sad result prophesied by Kenneth Tynan twenty-five years ago. The playgoer forgets that Blanche's only strengths are "nostalgia and hope," that she is "the desperate exceptional woman," and that her fall is a parable, rather than an isolated squalor:

> When, finally, she is removed to the mental home, we should feel that a part of civilization is going with her. Where ancient drama teaches us to reach nobility by contemplation of what is noble, modern American drama conjures us to contemplate what might have been noble, but is now humiliated, ignoble in the sight of all but the compassionate.

Tynan, though accurate enough, still might have modified the image of Blanche taking a part of civilization away with her into madness. Though Blanche yearns for the values of the aesthetic, she scarcely embodies them, being in this failure a masochistic self-parody on the part of Williams himself. His *Memoirs* portray Williams incessantly in the role of Blanche, studying the nostalgias, and inching along the wavering line between hope and paranoia. Williams, rather than Blanche, sustains Tynan's analysis of the lost nobility, now humiliated, that American drama conjures us to contemplate.

The fall of Blanche is a parable, not of American civilization's lost nobility, but of the failure of the American literary imagination to rise above its recent myths of recurrent defeat. Emerson admonished us, his descendants, to go beyond the Great Defeat of the Crucifixion and to demand Victory instead, a victory of the senses as well as of the soul. Walt Whitman, taking up Emerson's challenge directly, set the heroic pattern so desperately emulated by Hart Crane, and which is then repeated in a coarser tone in Williams's life and work.

It must seem curious, at first, to regard Blanche DuBois as a failed Whitmanian, but essentially that is her aesthetic identity. Confronted by the revelation of her young husband's preference for an older man over herself, Blanche falls downwards and outwards into nymphomania, phantasmagoric hopes, pseudo-imaginative collages of memory and desire. Her Orphic, psychic rending by the amiably brutal Stanley Kowalski, a rough but effective version of D. H. Lawrence's vitalistic vision of male force, is pathetic rather than tragic, not because Stanley necessarily is mindless, but because she unnecessarily has made herself mindless, by failing the pragmatic test of experience.

Williams's most effective blend of lyrical vision and dramatic irony in the play comes in the agony of Blanche's cry against Stanley to Stella, his wife and her sister:

> He acts like an animal, has an animal's habits! Eats like one, moves like one, talks like one! There's even something—subhuman—something not quite to the stage of humanity yet! Yes, something—ape-like about him, like one of those pictures I've seen in—anthropological studies! Thousands and thousands of years have passed him right by, and there he is—Stanley Kowalski—survivor of the stone age! Bearing the raw meat home from the kill in the jungle! And you—*you* here—*waiting* for him! Maybe he'll strike you or maybe grunt and kiss you! That is, if kisses have been discovered yet! Night falls and the other apes gather! There in the front of the cave, all grunting like him, and swilling and gnawing and hulking! His poker night!—you call it—this party of apes! Somebody growls—some creature snatches at something—the fight is on! *God!* Maybe we are a long way from being made in God's image, but Stella—my sister—there has been *some* progress since then! Such things as art—as poetry and music—such kinds of new light have come into the world since then! In some kinds of people some tenderer feelings have had some little beginning! That we have got to make *grow!* And *cling* to, and hold as our flag! In this dark march toward whatever it is we're approaching.... *Don't—don't hang back with the brutes!*

The lyricism here takes its strength from the ambivalence of what at once attracts and dismays both Blanche and Williams. Dramatic irony, terrible in its antithetical pathos, results here from Blanche's involuntary self-condemnation, since she herself has hung back with the brutes while merely blinking at the new light of the aesthetic. Stanley, being what he is, is clearly less to blame than Blanche, who was capable of more but failed in will.

Williams, in his *Memoirs*, haunted as always by Hart Crane, refers to his precursor as "a tremendous and yet fragile artist," and then associates both himself and Blanche with the fate of Crane, a suicide by drowning in the Caribbean:

> I am as much of an hysteric as ... Blanche; a codicil to my will provides for the disposition of my body in this way. "Sewn up in

a clean white sack and dropped over board, twelve hours north of Havana, so that my bones may rest not too far from those of Hart Crane ..."

At the conclusion of *Memoirs*, Williams again associated Crane both with his own vocation and his own limitations, following Crane even in an identification with the young Rimbaud:

A poet such as the young Rimbaud is the only writer of whom I can think, at this moment, who could escape from words into the sensations of being, through his youth, turbulent with revolution, permitted articulation by nights of absinthe. And of course there is Hart Crane. Both of these poets touched fire that burned them alive. And perhaps it is only through self-immolation of such a nature that we living beings can offer to you the entire truth of ourselves within the reasonable boundaries of a book.

It is the limitation of *Memoirs*, and in some sense even of *A Streetcar Named Desire*, that we cannot accept either Williams or poor Blanche as a Rimbaud or a Hart Crane. Blanche cannot be said to have touched fire that burned her alive. Yet Williams earns the relevance of the play's great epigraph to Blanche's terrible fate:

And so it was I entered the broken world
To trace the visionary company of love, its voice
An instant in the wind (I know not whither hurled)
But not for long to hold each desperate choice.

JACQUELINE O'CONNOR

Babbling Lunatics:
Language and Madness

Tell all the Truth but tell it slant—
—Emily Dickinson

Lion's View! State asylum, cut this hideous story out of her brain!
—Violet in *Suddenly Last Summer*

The final exit of Blanche DuBois in the celebrated original production of *A Streetcar Named Desire* on Broadway was a familiar image to Americans of the late 1940s: not only to those who saw that first production but to anyone who read about the play in newspapers or magazines. Blanche's departure on the doctor's arm, depending on his kindness, his gallantry contrasted with the severity of the matron, was reproduced in many articles and reviews about the play and its playwright. A number of factors make this an excellent choice for publicity: all the principals are present, along with the important supporting players; the still makes excellent use of the features of the set, with its interior/exterior design, for we are able to see Blanche departing as well as the card game inside the flat; Stanley and Stella's reconciliation scene occupies the other end of the stage, farthest from Blanche, emphasizing the separation that has occurred between the sisters.

This photo deserves commentary for another reason, however, since it captures an image of Blanche that represents what has happened to her

---

From *Dramatizing Dementia: Madness in the Plays of Tennessee Williams*: pp. 61–75 © 1997 by Bowling Green State University Popular Press.

11

in the play: she has been effectively silenced and removed from the group. Blanche's dialogue during the last scene has led progressively toward this final muteness, for her speeches are substantially shorter and less frequent here than elsewhere in the play. Her only extended dialogue in this scene is the speech in which she imagines her death at sea. Immediately afterwards, the Doctor and Nurse appear, and Blanche's disorientation about the turn of events dominates her remaining lines: "I—I—" and "I don't know you— I don't know you. I want to be—left alone—please!" (I, 415). Only in her famous exit line does she regain her composure in response to the Doctor's gentlemanly overture. "Whoever you are—I have always depended on the kindness of strangers," are her last words, and although this line has attained a stature awarded only to the most memorable lines in theater history, our last visual image of Blanche is her mute exit. In this final picture she is ignored by most of the other characters, who continue activities of life in the Quarter.

Blanche's journey toward this silent leave-taking at the corner of the stage is at the center of this drama, and the streetcar of the title foreshadows the mobility of her life. But we are not well prepared for her muteness, since her "garrulous" personality, to quote Ruby Cohn, has so dominated the stage (Cohn, *Dialogue* 97). Ironically, however, her excess of speech, her incessant storytelling, her insistence on holding the center of attention, underline her forced silence at the end of the play. Stanley's fury during the first poker scene arises in part from the chatter of the two sisters. Blanche asks if she can "kibitz," seeking to gain the players' attention; after she and Stella retire to the bedroom, Stanley attempts to silence their speech, shouting, "You hens cut out the conversation in there!" (I, 294). When the women turn on the radio, Stanley again shouts for silence: "Turn it off!" (I, 295). The noise continues as Mitch joins Blanche in the bedroom, and Blanche turns on the radio again: this time Stanley reacts with violence, storming into the bedroom, and tossing the radio out the window. This display not only demonstrates the force of Stanley's reaction to Blanche's earliest attempt to corner Mitch, it shows his response to unwanted noise: he disposes of it.

The next scene reinforces Stanley's convictions that Blanche talks too much, for he overhears one of her most extended speeches of the play; this lecture consists of a detailed condemnation of Stanley, in which she implores Stella not to "hang back with the brutes!" (I, 323). When Stella reminds Stanley in scene seven that "Blanche and I grew up under very different circumstances than you did," Stanley retorts, "So I been told. And told and told and told" (I, 358). During the birthday party scene, Stanley's second fit of destructive behavior is a reaction to the sisters' criticism of his habits. Apparently influenced by Blanche, Stella remarks that Stanley is "making a pig of himself," and tells him: "Go and wash up and then help me clear the table" (I, 371). Throwing a plate to the floor, he seizes Stella's arm: "Don't ever talk that way to me! 'Pig—Polack—disgusting—vulgar—greasy!'—them kind of words have been on your tongue and your sister's too much around here!" (I, 371). This speech emphasizes Stanley's resentment of the terms which Blanche (and now Stella) apply to him. In the first poker night scene, and in the one above, his physical violence is directed at Stella: in the former scene, he strikes her, and in the latter, he "seizes her arm" (I, 371).

Stanley reacts strongly to the character insults because he senses their truth; shortly after throwing the dishes, he admits to Stella to being "common as dirt." While he only begrudgingly admits to the truth about himself, however, he insists on knowing and exposing the truth about Blanche. Suspecting the counterfeit nature of her life's story, Stanley sets out to prove her a liar. Laura Morrow and Edward Morrow argue that "Stanley is passionately devoted to truth-seeing and truth-telling"; Blanche goes mad "when Stanley confronts her with the truth" (Morrow 59). Because she has embellished and glossed over the facts of her past, no one is compelled to believe her story about the rape; it is this story that precipitates her institutionalization.

In scene seven, when Stanley reveals his findings about Blanche to Stella, the latter denies the information about her sister's expulsion from Laurel. She calls Stanley's accusations "contemptible lies" and "pure invention." Having heard all of it, however, Stella does admit: "It's possible that some of the things he [the salesman] said are partly true" (I, 364). With her concession that Blanche's version of how and why she left Laurel may not be entirely accurate, Stella opens the floodgates for her final rejection of Blanche. Blanche tells one final story, that Stanley raped her on the night of the baby's birth; Stella rejects this account, having already acknowledged that Blanche has been fabricating other tales. The story of the rape, which Stella tells Eunice she cannot believe if she is to continue to live with Stanley, convinces Stella that she must participate in the act of Blanche's institutionalization. Although the audience/reader knows that this time Blanche does not lie, the conscience of the community, represented by Stella and Eunice, judges this story to be a falsehood. When the conscience of the community makes its verdict, then the confinement can take place without delay.

Blanche's insistence, therefore, on changing the past to agree with her image of herself as a proper gentlewoman, establishes the necessary precedent for Stella's denial of the rape. It is impossible to know what parts of Blanche's own character analysis are lies, and what stories result from self-delusion. When Mitch confronts her about her lies, she claims: "Never inside, I didn't lie in my heart" (I, 387). Although she insists that she has never been guilty of deliberate cruelty, she admits to Mitch that she prompted Allan's suicide by telling him, "You disgust me" (I, 355). Contradictory assertions seem to be symptomatic of her emotional disintegration; as all stability slips away from her, the statements she makes conflict with one another.

In *Streetcar*, Blanche's mental decline is apparent throughout the play; in the opening of scene ten, advanced deterioration is visible, only in part connected to her extreme drunkenness. As Stanley enters, she speaks "as if to a group of spectral admirers" (I, 391). Perhaps her confession to Mitch about her life in Laurel has propelled Blanche to the very brink of sanity; significantly, the former scene marks the first time that she tells the entire truth about her past. This combination of circumstances provides further evidence that telling the truth contributes to her downfall. Whatever the causes of this latest break with reality, she has succumbed to the illusion about Shep Huntleigh's rescue of her, and imagines that she is preparing to take a cruise. Although her loss of sanity seems evident, however, her departure to the state hospital is not made final until she exposes Stanley's violent act. Stanley has already proven to Stella and Mitch that Blanche lied about her life in Laurel; when the truth of the rape becomes an issue, they choose Stanley's story over that of Blanche.[1]

This predicament, the determination to choose one story over another, as well as the defensiveness of the one deemed mad because of the content of the account, is a source of tension in other plays as well. Although the process is reversed in *Suddenly Last Summer*, once again the sanity and the confinement of the presumed mad person depends on the story that is central to the play. An early draft, in which Catharine is named Valerie, focuses on her propensity to chatter, for she tells the sister who accompanies her from the institution: "I can't stop talking, I never could when I'm nervous."[2] Immediately after this, she informs the doctor that her nails have been cut to keep her from hurting herself during the convulsions that occur after shock treatment. The doctor then asks the sister, "Isn't she off shock now?" and Valerie replies: "You can ask me, I can answer. I'm off it now." This version emphasizes that the girl is ready and anxious to talk about her treatment, and to tell the story that has been her undoing; indeed, she will persist in telling her version of the truth no matter what: "They can't cut the true story out of my brain." Also: "I'm going to get the truth serum again I know. But it doesn't change the story." A longer speech about the story she is prepared to tell reveals her inner wrestling with the narrative of her cousin's fate:

> I can't falsify it ... It's no pleasure having to repeat the same story over and over, but even if I wished not to, even if I wished to falsify it, what could I say? ... I just can't help repeating what actually did happen, it just—spills out!—each time!—the truth about what happened.[3]

Although Williams deletes these comments from the final version, he retains the concentration on truth; the word "truth" is repeated fifteen times, mostly by Catharine, and it is echoed by the doctor in the final line of the play: "I think we ought at least to consider the possibility that the girl's story could be true" (III, 423). Truth has "the last word." Its constant recurrence emphasizes its significance. Defining the truth may well determine Catharine's future.

In the earlier version, Valerie [Catharine] sums up the major conflict of the play when she tells the doctor, "I'm not mad. It's just that I witnessed something no one will believe and they'd rather think I'm mad than to believe it."[4] Her statement illustrates one of the most common determinations of madness in Williams's plays: whether an implausible story is accepted by the other characters. The predicament she describes could be that of either Blanche (although Blanche is more than a witness to the violent act in *Streetcar*), or Valerie [Catharine], for the latter assesses the truth as unbelievable; the only option for those who deny this truth is to proclaim the teller mad. In both plays, the madwoman insists on telling a story whose premise is unacceptable, thus resulting in that woman's expulsion from society. Allan Ingram in *The Madhouse of Language* writes: "one prime feature of the madman's discourse is obsession, the returning always to one subject of conversation" (38). Catharine's obsession with the story of Sebastian's death causes her to return to that subject incessantly; as Violet tells the Doctor, Catharine "babbles" it at every opportunity. Although we wonder about her sanity, we cannot deny her obsessive discourse.

In a review of the original production of *Suddenly*, Richard Watts describes the action as "in large part a drama of two speeches, the first by the mother of a dead poet, who is certain that a young woman has caused his death, and the other by the possibly insane girl, who gives her own version of what happened."[5] Like the rape in *Streetcar*, Sebastian's death is also a story of violence, as well as a narrative that maligns the character of the central male figure of the play. In *Suddenly*, however, Sebastian is dead, and cannot refute the tale's truth, as Stanley does. At *Suddenly*'s opening, Catharine is already confined for telling the story, and so the action contrasts with that of *Streetcar*: it moves toward the possible release of Catharine at the end of the play. The account that Catharine gives of Sebastian's death unequivocally provides the only reason for Catharine's confinement, although she does exhibit peculiar behavior: she causes a scene at a Mardi Gras ball, and she shows unusual distance from her own feelings by using the third-person in her diary. But her horrifying tale, with the aspersions it casts on Sebastian's character, sends her to the asylum and results in her receiving various treatments for memory suppression, attempts designed to prevent her from repeating her version of his murder.

The story prompts Violet Venable to seek the assistance of Doctor Cukrowicz, who performs lobotomies. If he can determine that Catharine has fabricated the story, he will perform the operation. In this play, two men represent the deciding consensus of the community: the doctor, and Catharine's brother, George. Unlike *Streetcar*, in *Suddenly* we do not know if the story is true, but we do get to hear Catharine tell it, and we also witness the reaction of her audience. In *Suddenly*, the story has strikingly different effects on the characters who hear it: Catharine's narrative sends Violet into a rage, demanding that the story be excised from her niece's brain; however, it seems to convince the doctor, who is at least ready to accept the possibility of its truth. George seems more convinced, even though his position throughout the play has been on the side of his aunt, since he wants the money from the inheritance.

These two plays make clear, in different ways, that the characters' ability to convince others of the truth of certain situations does not depend on whether these events actually occurred. Ultimately, this is because the line between truth and fiction often blurs. Tom Wingfield's description of the play he narrates gives a hint of this, when he claims it to be "truth in the pleasant guise of illusion," and Blanche provides another twist when she speaks of telling "what ought to be truth." Both *Streetcar* and *Suddenly* raise the possibility of confinement for a major character; what becomes clear, however, is that the confinement is decided in part because these women have forced others to consider how the truth might be determined.

One important distinction is noteworthy in a comparison of the storytelling aspects of the plays. We might contrast their dramatic progression by saying that Blanche moves toward madness, and Catharine moves away from it toward her possible release. Blanche's last long speech is not about the past, as the others have been, but about the future, a virtual prediction of her own death. In contrast, Catharine's longest speech occurs at the end of the play; she does not appear in the first scene, and in that scene Mrs. Venable controls the doctor's perceptions of Sebastian's character and life. Violet makes a reference to "talking the ears off a donkey," indicating an awareness of her verbosity. When the group has gathered to hear Catharine's version of the events in Cabeza de Lobo, Violet repeatedly interrupts Catharine's speeches, attempting to adjust or deny the girl's declarations. Finally the doctor halts the interruptions, and demands that Catharine be allowed to continue her narrative without interruption. Not only is the monologue the dramatic climax of the play, it allows the revelation of the story that has caused Catharine's confinement, a narrative that Violet seeks to silence. The release of this story to the ears of the family and the doctor (and the audience) thwarts Violet's effort to suppress it, and may lead to Catharine's release.

This situation contrasts with Blanche's circumstances in *Streetcar*. Although we see the rape, or at least its commencement, we do not hear Blanche tell of it later; all we know of Stella's reaction to it is that she rejects it, deciding to send her sister to an institution. Blanche's inability to find a sympathetic audience suggests that she is being sent away because she spoke of the rape, and broke the silence with her accusation against Stanley.

In both plays the confinement hinges on a story of an unmentionable act, a violation of an accepted societal taboo. Beyond the shock value of these acts, they have a common ground in violence and in their taboo elements. Their similarity implies that madness has connections to the unmentionable, that society seeks to suppress the language of madness because that language speaks of prohibited acts of sex and violence. Lucretia's confinement in *Portrait of a Madonna* can be seen in this light as well: although we are quite convinced that she fabricates her story about Richard's visits to "indulge his senses," the narrative has the taboo quality of the others, with its subject matter of rape and illegitimate conception. The madwomen in these three plays are put away in part because of the shocking stories they tell, which reveal unspeakable elements of human behavior. As Catharine claims of her narrative, "it's a true story of our time and the world we live in" (III, 382); this may be so, but the other characters refuse to admit it.

The situations that instigate the madwomen's confinement reveal a pattern that can be traced through some other Williams's plays. In *The Night of the Iguana*, Shannon tells his own version of the "forbidden act"; his act, like the others, is inextricably tied to his first confinement. Once more, a story of unacceptable behavior alarms the community, and they confine the person responsible for shocking them. Shannon's conduct with her young charge prompts Miss Fellowes to investigate his past. Shannon denies her accusations that he has been defrocked, even attempting to convince those around him of his current ministerial status. He insists to Hannah that he must wear his collar because, "I've been accused of being defrocked and of lying about it. I want to show the ladies that I'm still a clocked—*frocked!*—minister of the ..." (IV, 300).

When questioned further on the subject by Hannah, he admits to being "inactive in the Church for all but one year since I was ordained a minister of the Church" (IV, 301). Her response: "Well, that's quite a sabbatical, Mr. Shannon," signifies that she will accept his version of his discharge. This tactic draws the story out of him, and he tells of his sexual transgression with a young Sunday-school teacher: "the natural, or unnatural, attraction of one ... lunatic for ... another" (IV, 303). His behavior elicits disapproval from the parishioners, to which he responds with a shocking sermon on "the *truth* about God!" [my emphasis] (IV, 304). Despite a difference in magnitude, perhaps, Shannon's story shares qualities with the others in Williams's plays. Most important for this analysis, Shannon's attempt to warn his parishioners results in his confinement: "Well, I wasn't defrocked. I was just locked out of the church in Pleasant Valley, Virginia, and put in a nice little private asylum to recuperate from a complete nervous breakdown as they preferred to regard it" (IV, 304).

Although Shannon's affair with the young woman earns their "smug, disapproving, accusing faces," his attempts to enlighten them about the Western concept of God as a "senile delinquent," an "angry, petulant old man," brings about his institutionalization.

As these plays illustrate, honest expression threatens those who reveal what they consider the truth, when that expression affronts the members of society who are considered normal. Only Lucretia's story about Richard is quite clearly false; what it explains about her lonely, isolated life, however, is undeniably revealing. What the reception of these narratives explains about the fear and narrowness of the communities who reject the tellers is as crucial to our understanding of the plays as our attempt to analyze the emotional instability of the characters deemed mad. Viewed this way, madness becomes the social category created for dealing with these rebels; the confinement which results from this labeling provides a method for insuring their silence. The play's form, however, contradicts this silence: in most cases, the audience witnesses the release of the truth. The community of the play denies the story, but from our vantage point outside the action, we see its effect on the society of the drama. Although the characters deemed mad speak of their weaknesses, their frailties, they prove stronger than their "normal" counterparts, for they willingly face the unpalatable. *Iguana* stands apart from the other plays, for in Hannah Jelkes, Shannon finds a sympathetic audience who does not spurn his story.

The Two-Character Play provides another example of the taboo narrative, for Felice and Clare of the play-within-the-play have a sordid tale of their own to tell, or to hide. Their father's murder/suicide of his wife and himself constitutes their story of family horror; like the other characters I have discussed, they cannot help but be obsessed by the incident, even though they are aware of its part in isolating them from the community of New Bethesda. Clare insists on mentioning the "terrible accident" when she calls the Reverend Wiley, and Felice accuses her of "babbling" to him. They cannot find a way to reconcile the story with their relationship in the world, specifically to the insurance company that will not honor their father's insurance policy.

With this dilemma, *The Two-Character Play* highlights another issue of language and madness: the brother and sister struggle constantly with certain kinds of language. When they discuss the insurance policy that has been forfeited because their father killed his wife, then himself, Clare cannot find the correct language, the official language to describe the rejection of their claim. The Acme Insurance Company has notified them by mail about the denial:

> Clare: —what's the word? Confiscated?
> Felice: Forfeited.
> Clare: Yes, the payment of the insurance policy is forfeited in the—what is the word?
> Felice: Event.
> Clare: Yes, in the event of a man—[*She stops, pressing her fist to her mouth.*] (V, 343)

Clare lacks the proper official language of the insurance company, the bureaucratic language with which they deny payment. Beyond that, she finds it impossible to tell the horrible story with which she and her brother are obsessed.

Williams states in the author's notes of the 1970 manuscript version: "'Grossman's Market' (and its proprietor) and 'The Acme Insurance Company' represent formidable and impersonal forces in the lives of the two characters."[6] Williams also points out in his notes that the "Acme" responds to a twelve-page written and rewritten letter of appeal with only three typewritten sentences. The "Acme" speaks with the voice of authority, the voice of reason: it follows strict guidelines about paying claims. When Felice and Clare speak of the insurance company's response, Felice argues: "[T]here are situations in which legal technicalities have to be, to be—disregarded in the interests of human, human—"; however, Clare rightly answers him, "You under-esteem the, the—power of a company called *The Acme*."[7] Clare notes the disparity between the twelve-page appeal and the three sentence response, which indicates that the emotional language of the disturbed and isolated survivors, holds no weight for the businesslike approach of the company.

Felice and Clare speak of lying to the insurance company, and likewise, about lying to Mr. Grossman about whether they will be paid the money from Acme. Once more we see that the truth becomes a barometer of insanity; if Felice and Clare relate the true circumstances of their parents' death, the insurance company can label the family disturbed and be rid of them with a terse, official note. Its opinion will then influence other institutions, such as Grossman's market, spreading outward to the members of the community. If the surviving siblings can convince "Acme" of a more acceptable version of the circumstances that justify the claim, they might be entitled to some monetary compensation that would allow them once more to be paying customers at the market. Like the characters of the other plays, however, Felice and Clare cannot alter their story in order to accommodate the norms of the community.

This is just one case of the brother and sister's failure to use language to their advantage. Felice and Clare are constantly stymied by the absence of the language that they need to convince others to help them. When they receive the telegram from their theater company, accusing them of being insane, they cannot respond to these accusations, because the company chooses a one-sided method of communication to state their grievances. During the play-within-the-play, the other Felice and Clare often argue about the effects that their cries for help may have on those they ask. When the representatives from "Citizens Relief" come calling, Felice and Clare cannot face them, so they do not answer the door. When they speak afterward of the possibility of asking the group for help, they are hesitant because of what they might have to say to them:

> Clare: Oh, but all the questions we'd have to—
> Felice: Answer.
> Clare: Yes, there'd be interviews and questionnaires to fill out and—
> Felice: Organizations are such—
> Clare: *Cold!*
> Felice: Yes, impersonal things. (V, 333)

They are afraid of what they might have to tell the group in order to receive help, and as in the case of the insurance company, they know enough not to expect human warmth from an organization. They cannot make their needs known to anyone lacking compassion for their troubled and battered psyches.

Clare suspects that this kind of compassion may be available from the Reverend Wiley, although his name alerts us that this is rather doubtful. Sy Kahn notes the comparison between the names of the stage manager (Fox) and the minister, suggesting that both might be "wily foxes" (50). Clare's call to the minister is the first and only time the brother or sister make outside contact with anyone, although they speak of doing so throughout the inner play. Felice does not want Clare to call the Reverend, for when she tells the operator to put her through to him, "Felice tries to wrest the phone from her grasp, and for a moment they struggle for it" (V, 337). Clare insists that Felice let her talk: "You'll have to let me go on or he'll think I'm—" (V, 337). Clare speaks to the Reverend about the charges against her father, and the subsequent results of these charges on the lives of his children. Insisting on the false nature of these accusations, she speaks of their struggles to exist "surrounded by so much suspicion and malice" (V, 337). Felice grabs the phone from her, makes an excuse of illness to Wiley, and hangs up. He complains to Clare that "our one chance is privacy and you babble away to a man who'll think it his Christian duty to have us *confined* in—" (V, 338). Clearly, Felice believes that any talking they might do will only decrease their chances of remaining free; communication with others will not help them, but will contribute to their doom.

After Felice and Clare have abandoned hope of taking a trip to Grossman's market, not only because they cannot go out, but because they cannot face speaking to Grossman about their need for more credit, they consider asking for assistance from "Citizens' Relief." The name suggests the impossibility of this idea, for they are no longer citizens. They do not belong to the community, but are set apart from them, and can expect no aid; they cannot even request it. If they could, they might still be part of the community. Once they decide to attempt such a plea, their phone is dead. Felice suggests that Clare go next door and ask to use the neighbors' phone, and tells Clare to call out to the neighbor woman, who is in the yard. Clare attempts to address her, but cannot speak loudly enough to be heard. Her "outcry" does not go out, and when Felice tells her: "Not loud enough, call louder," she turns from the window. She sums up the impossibility of their situation: "Did you really imagine that I could call and beg for Citizens' Relief in front of those malicious people next door, on their phone, in their presence?" (V, 355).

Although Felice and Clare have lost the ability to communicate with others, they can speak to each other. The whole play consists of the communication between these deranged characters. By peopling this play with only two characters, whose sanity is questionable, Williams concentrates on creating a private language between people who need not worry about outside interference. In this play, Williams employs his common tactic of frequent dashes, marking incomplete sentences; here it does not signify a difficulty of communication, but the opposite, since Felice and Clare are close enough to interpret one another's unspoken words. An element of theatrical self-consciousness complicates this impression; when Felice and Clare act out the inner play, they are aware of each other's words because of the script they have memorized. The script is in a state of flux, however, because of Clare's insistence on improvisation, and even when they "come out" of the play, they anticipate each other's words.

The unfinished sentences and emphasis on the unspoken word appear in another play of this period, *In the Bar of a Tokyo Hotel*. By comparing the two, we see the way that Williams has used this technique with effectiveness in *The Two-Character Play*, while in the other work the same half-sentence construction lends only incoherence to the text.[8] Throughout *In the Bar of a Tokyo Hotel*, everyone speaks in incomplete sentences, although only Mark, the ravaged artist, appears to suffer from psychological problems. The reader or audience is puzzled, then, about why the characters stop mid-sentence or why another character jumps in to finish another's thoughts. In both plays, the device seems to indicate the verbal incapacity of the characters, as well as the inadequacy of language to express their state of emotional turmoil. Williams achieves more consistency, as well as more significance, when he uses this verbal technique in *The Two-Character Play*. When Felice and Clare cut short their sentences, they exhibit their fears of the things they dare not speak; they demonstrate their frozen psychological state; they convey the unspeakable terror of their situation. Likewise, when they help each other finish sentences, they indicate their interwoven lives and personalities, and their limited ability to aid each other in communication. Although they have been cut off from the world, both in the outer play and the inner one, communication may be difficult, but it is still possible between them.

Discussion of this linguistic feature of *The Two-Character Play* suggests that consideration of other features of language might be appropriate to an analysis of madness in the texts of this study. Allan Ingram writes on the writing and reading of madness in the eighteenth century:

> We should not deny the existence of madness as something that is also beyond the framework of a linguistic construct. The experience of pain and of mental suffering must always proceed in a region that is remote from language, even if the sufferer attempts to retrieve that experience through the medium of language. (8)

In looking at Williams's plays, then, we might consider how the playwright overcomes the obstacle of language in relation to madness: can madness be expressed through a language governed by principles of reason? Is it possible for the mad to reach across the division that separates them from the sane and express the experience of madness? What's more, can the characters of a drama present themselves as mad, and still speak in a language comprehensible to the audience? Perhaps Williams's isolation of Felice and Clare in *The Two-Character Play* represents an attempt to set their language apart: as long as no other characters interact with the deranged brother and sister, their communication exists apart from the world. Although Felice and Clare show confusion and fear in their speeches, we do not hear lunatic ravings. This holds true for all the mad characters of Williams's plays, leading to the conclusion that Williams by and large does not succeed in dramatizing madness at the level of language use.

This being said, however, we may still examine the linguistic features that the playwright employs to invoke the nervousness and levels of delusion that we recognize as his attempts to have his characters vocalize their emotional instability. Williams's early characters often speak in an artificial manner: Alma Winemiller is accused by others as being affected and self-consciously pretentious in her speech. Blanche also uses the flowery language of a past age, in part an attribute of these women's southern heritage. Both Alma and Blanche, however, are noted for their nervous, hysterical characters; their tendency towards hyperbole is intertwined with southern gentility and emotional extremity. Thus, in *Eccentricities of a Nightingale*, Alma's father tells her: "The thing for you to give up is your affectations, Alma ... that make you seem—well—slightly peculiar to people! ... You, you, you—*gild the lily*! ... you—stammer, you—laugh hysterically and clutch at your throat!" (II, 32). Exaggeration is a trait of eccentricity, and Alma's strangeness cannot be separated from her verbal mannerisms.

Blanche also exaggerates, but while her verbal extravagance is, like Alma's, a plea for attention, her extreme comments about herself tragically foreshadow her fate. She tells Stella: "I was on the verge of—lunacy, almost!"; "Daylight never exposed so total a ruin!"; "I want to be *near* you, got to be *with* somebody, I *can't* be *alone!*" (I, 254, 257). However, Blanche's ability to describe her mental condition deteriorates at the play's ending, when, mute and lost in illusion, she is led off by the Doctor.

The faltering quality of the dialogue is another feature distinctive of Williams. Rarely has a playwright employed more dashes or ellipses to demonstrate nervousness, indecision, and hesitation. These traits are attributable to the characters who find themselves at the end of their rope, and are confused or lost about where or how to proceed. The verbal hesitations signify the inner hesitation, and convey to the audience the loss of purpose or direction that marks the wandering mind. Williams's use of this kind of verbal reluctance represents his version of loss of expression. The mad characters in Williams's plays are rarely silent, as Blanche is at the conclusion of *Streetcar*; on the contrary, they have ways of illustrating their mental incapacities.

Clothes for a Summer Hotel marks both similarities and differences with the earlier plays about madness. In this late play, Williams writes of the Zelda Fitzgerald who has been institutionalized; yet, of all the characters in the play, she is the most perceptive and the most vocal about human failings and the limitations of relationships. Scott, the "sane" partner in their marriage, comes to the hospital "dressed as if about to check in at a summer hotel" (*Clothes* 9). He becomes excited and disturbed when unrecognized, then presumed drunk, by Dr. Zeller; Scott suffers further indignities in Act Two, when he has another conversation with the doctor, the latter insisting on the superiority of Zelda's novel: "Zelda has sometimes struck a sort of fire in her work that—I'm sorry to say this to you, but I never quite found anything in yours, even yours, that was—equal to it" (55). Scott, the successful writer, master of language, does not measure up to his wife's abilities to lure this reader.

In the couple's verbal matches, Zelda more often emerges superior as well as more honest. She speaks truthfully of her estrangement from Scott, while he "draws back wounded" when she pointedly describes their embrace as a "meaninglessly conventional—gesture" (10). She acknowledges that her continued confinement depends on society's labeling of her: "I only come back here when I know I'm too much for Mother and the conventions of Montgomery, Alabama. I am pointed out on the street as a lunatic now" (11). Voicing her belief that she did not provide the best atmosphere for Scott's work, she confesses to him that he "needed a better influence, someone much more stable as a companion on the—roller-coaster ride which collapsed at the peak" (15). In all these statements about her illness and the collapse of their marriage, Zelda speaks with perceptive self-knowledge and brutal honesty. Near the close of the first scene, Williams's stage directions indicate what we have come to suspect: according to him, madness is a social category, highly ambiguous and questionable. The playwright does so with a slight, almost imperceptible gesture, which gains significance upon close examination of Zelda's character. When Zelda speaks of life in the asylum, Williams notes that "Zelda must somehow suggest the desperate longing of the 'insane' to communicate something of their private world to those from whom they're secluded" (26). By placing quotation marks around the word "insane," Williams calls into question the label he has used to define his most memorable characters. This note likewise highlights the aspect of communication that is so crucial to the understanding of the verbal struggles of those who are called mad. Finally, Williams insists that Zelda's words in this section are not crucial, "mostly blown away by the wind," but her eyes and her gestures "must win the audience to her inescapably from this point in the play" (26). As with Blanche's mute exit, when her image replaces her verbal power to convince us, Zelda's presence must argue her position.

While Zelda's words are swallowed by the wind here, however, she remains the most vocal character in the play, explaining her life and her destiny. Her eloquence in the final scene, where she speaks of madness, art, life, and death, reveals her superior vision, having been "purified by madness and by fire" (9). Zelda places herself in the tradition of the mad seer, telling Scott of her death by fire, aware of this because "the demented often have the gift of Cassandra, the gift of—Premonition!" (15). Her perceptive outlook on the past and the future reveals her more capable than Scott of acknowledging the truth about their marriage and his career.

Finally, the play resembles the others in this discussion, with its use of the sexual transgression as secret and truth revealed. Zelda's affair with Edouard, a French aviator, dominates the action of the two middle scenes, with the intern from the asylum doubling as Edouard; this tactic blurs the boundaries of past and present. Although Scott knows of the affair, Edouard worries about her husband's reaction; as the intern, he speaks of Scott: "*Pauvre homme.* I was always concerned. Wondered what effect the indiscretion—" (25). The affair lacks the violence, the horror of narratives from the other plays, but it has its part in Zelda's institutionalization. She claims her infidelity sets off her madness, for the end of the affair prompts her to attempt suicide; she tells Scott that when Edouard rejected her, "I think my heart died and I— went—mad" (59). Given Zelda's clear-headed responses to all that happens around her, her madness is questionable. Perhaps, however, this is as it should be: her institutionalization provides the consummate example of the fate of the sensitive individual who cannot find a suitable outlet for her passions. Although confined, she remains cognizant of her situation; like Catharine Holly, she cannot keep from protesting the truth of her experience.

In creating characters who persist, despite great difficulty, in proclaiming "true stories of our time and the world we live in," Williams demonstrates his conviction that American society seeks to silence those who shock or outrage with stories of the unmentionable. By establishing these narratives as intrinsic parts of the action, by hanging the fate of the characters on the telling of these tales, the playwright creates situations in which those who bear witness to the atrocities of human action find their sanity questioned, their words muted. Like the fools in Shakespeare's plays, these characters and their truths are disregarded or disbelieved. Unlike Shakespeare, however, where the fools' warnings predict the downfall of the characters who ignore them, Williams's "fools" and their babbling affect their own destiny, usually adversely.

NOTES

1. We do not know whether Mitch believes Blanche about the rape; it is possible that the truth of it would only confirm his decision about Blanche, that she is "not clean enough to bring in the house" with his mother. His presence at the second poker game, even though he makes an ineffective move to protect Blanche from the Matron's attempts to subdue her, shows that he goes along the path of least resistance.

2. Tennessee Williams, *Suddenly Last Summer*, ts., Humanities Research Center, U of Texas, Austin, undated. All quotations from *Suddenly* are from this manuscript, unless otherwise noted in the text.

3. Williams, *Suddenly Last Summer*, ts.

4. Williams, *Suddenly Last Summer*, ts.

5. Richard Watts, Jr., "Two Dramas by Tennessee Williams," rev. of *Suddenly Last Summer* and *Something Unspoken* by Tennessee Williams, *New York Post*, 8 Jan. 1958: 64.

6. Tennessee Williams, *The Two-Character Play*, ts., Humanities Research Center, Austin, 1970: Author's notes.

7. Williams, ts., 1970.

8. David Savron argues that *In the Bar of a Tokyo Hotel* has been misunderstood by its critics, and that the play marks an important development in Williams's writings: "an insistent and radical fragmentation of discourse, character, and plot that is far more aggressive and overt than that which marks even the most surrealistic of his earlier plays." See David Savron, *Communists, Cowboys, and Queers: The Politics of Masculinity in the Work of Arthur Miller and Tennessee Williams* (Minneapolis: U of Minnesota P, 1992): 135.

JOHN M. CLUM

The Sacrificial Stud and the Fugitive Female in Suddenly Last Summer, Orpheus Descending, *and* Sweet Bird of Youth

CATHERINE: I tried to save him, Doctor.

DOCTOR: From what? Save him from what?

CATHERINE: Completing!—a sort of!—*image!*—he had of himself as a sort of!—*sacrifice* to a!—*terrible* sort of a—

DOCTOR: —God?

CATHERINE: Yes, a *cruel* one, Doctor!

Suddenly Last Summer

Tennessee Williams's Val Xavier, the itinerant sexual magnet of *Orpheus Descending* (1957), is immolated with a blowtorch on the night before Easter. Chance Wayne, the hustler hero of *Sweet Bird of Youth* (1959), is castrated on Easter Sunday. In between these two plays and acting as a queer gloss on them is the grotesque parody of the Eucharist in Sebastian Venable's crucifixion and consumption by the street urchins he has tasted in *Suddenly Last Summer* (1958). These three martyrs, Sebastian Venable, Val Xavier, and Chance Wayne, are sacrificed for violating their proscribed roles in the patriarchal sex/gender system. The possibility of a new sex/gender system is seen through the two central female characters in each play, one mutilated, the other healed. These plays, then, make a kind of trilogy, developing themes and characters seen in earlier plays and resolving in Williams's next dyad of quasi-religious acceptance, *The Night of the Iguana* (1961) and *The Milk Train*

From *The Cambridge Companion to Tennessee Williams*, edited by Matthew C. Roudané: pp. 128–146 © 1997 by Cambridge University Press.

27

Doesn't Stop Here Anymore (1963–64). I want to focus here on the beautiful male as sexual martyr in these three plays, on the dynamics and erotics of the martyrdoms, and on the ways in which his relationship to the fugitive woman suggests a liberating possibility. To discuss Williams's depictions of the sex/gender system, one must also examine the relationship of homosexuality and heterosexuality in Williams's work.

THE TRAFFIC IN WOMEN / THE TRAFFIC IN MEN

In her groundbreaking essay, "The Traffic in Women: Notes Toward an Anthropology of Sex," Gayle Rubin defines the way in which gender (socially constructed masculine/feminine as opposed to the biological male/female) is determined (by heterosexual men, of course) and the ways in which women's roles are determined by negotiations between men.[1] For instance, women are married to allow men to form tribal or national alliances. This system makes the woman the currency of masculine transactions. The system of heterosexual marriage also ensures the policing of compulsory heterosexuality by means of official homophobia, which never succeeds at the impossible task of eliminating homosexual desire or behavior. It may even find a limited space for such behavior within a system so long as heterosexual marriage is privileged.

Eve Kosofsky Sedgwick goes a step further than Rubin to show that the homosocial bonds between men—what is often called male bonding—for which women are the currency—contain elements of homophobia to "protect" them from the very real potential of homosexual desire often denied but inherent in such bonds.[2] Recently critics have been writing about the ways in which women forge potentially subversive bonds within this system and the ways in which those bonds are subverted by marriage.

In Williams's work, there is from the outset a different formulation. Instead of the woman being the apex of a triangle, with a bond between two men at its other poles, a man is at the apex, with a tentative bond or conflict between two women negotiated by them in order to establish a bond with the man. We see this in the scenes between Blanche and Stella in *A Streetcar Named Desire*. There the two sisters argue about Stanley. His sexual attractiveness is not questioned, but his worthiness as a marriage partner is. The conflict here is between Blanche's romantic, essentially asexual view of marriage, which may have led her to marry a homosexual but is hardly consonant with her subsequent promiscuity, and Stella's understanding that marriage is one avenue for sexual fulfillment, a channel for her healthy sexual appetite. Ostensibly Stella and conventional heterosexual marriage win, but only through Stella's denying the truth about Stanley's rape of Blanche. For all Stanley's macho posturing, it is Stella's denial that sends Blanche to the asylum, not Stanley's rape. When Blanche goes, so also goes the possibility of homosexuality which she brings into the play through the story of her husband and through her own camp behavior. At the end, Stanley does not stand triumphant. Rather, he kneels before Stella in a final tableau which shows her as the powerful figure in this heterosexual unit.

In *Suddenly Last Summer*, *Orpheus Descending*, and *Sweet Bird of Youth*, two women form a triangle with a man who is martyred, yet no relationship between a man and either of the women can be sustained. While the martyred men represent some violation of the socially acceptable principle of masculinity—that is, they are threats to marriage and patriarchy—it is the women who define the meaning of the martyrdom and who really offer the potential for change in the sex/gender system. In essence, as in the epigraph from *Suddenly Last Summer*, the women voice and define the men.

Though the focus is on the violence done to the male figure, the women are also in danger of mutilation and death. Catherine in *Suddenly Last Summer* is in danger of being lobotomized, Lady in *Orpheus Descending* is killed, and Heavenly in *Sweet Bird of Youth* has her womb surgically removed. Yet, for one of the women, there is also a healing process.

MARTYRS, HOMOSEXUALITY, AND ATONEMENT

Of these three martyrs, Sebastian Venable is the one who is most closely related to characters in earlier Williams plays. Like Blanche DuBois's husband, Allan Grey, in *A Streetcar Named Desire*, and Brick Pollitt's friend, Skipper, in *Cat On a Hot Tin Roof*, Sebastian is a dead gay man whose story is relegated to exposition, but he is the focus of the play from its first line, "Yes, this was Sebastian's garden" (350),[3] to Catherine's description of his gruesome death and its aftermath. Sebastian is another invisible homosexual, impossible to show on stage in the 1950s, though from the very beginning of his career, Williams insistently forged a space, however tentative, for the presentation of the homosexual. But these homosexuals in Williams's plays and stories always die a grotesque death, not so much as the expected punishment for their proscripted desire, but as the victim of rejection by those closest to them. Allan Grey shot himself after being publicly exposed and humiliated by his wife. Skipper drank himself to death when he became convinced of his homosexuality and when his best friend deserted him. One has to remember that *Cat On a Hot Tin Roof* takes place in the bedroom of a gay couple (dead, of course) who represent the play's only model for a long-term loving relationship.[4]

Sebastian Venable does not kill himself as Allan and Skipper do. In an aria of violence worthy of Euripides, his cousin Catherine relates how he was killed, stripped, and partially devoured. Understanding this primal scene is crucial to understanding the meaning of martyrdom in these plays of the late 1950s. As usual in Williams, the starting point for such an understanding is in Williams's stories, where we often find the first sketches of some of the plays and the crucial themes of the plays presented in more openly homosexual terms. Sebastian's bizarre death has its roots in Williams's short story, "Desire and the Black Masseur" (1946).

Anthony Burns, thirty years old, but still with the unformed face and body of a child, had a lifelong desire "to be swallowed up" which was only realized at the movies "where the darkness absorbed him gently so that he was like a particle of food dissolving in a big hot mouth" (105).[5] Anthony's life becomes devoted to attaining his desire.

In the story written just before *A Streetcar Named Desire*, Williams defines that favorite word of his—desire—more cogently than he does in any of his other works and relates it to Christian notions of guilt and atonement. We are told in one paragraph that "Desire is something that is made to occupy a larger space than that which is afforded by the individual being" (206), and in the next paragraph that "the sins of the world are really only its partialities, its incompletions, and these are what sufferings must atone for" (206). Man's weakness is that he is too small for his overwhelming desire. Atonement, the "surrender of self to violent treatment by others with the idea of thereby clearing one's self of his guilt" (206), is one compensation for one's smallness, one's inability to contain one's desire.

Anthony Burns discovered his sought-for compensation, atonement, in the baths. There a giant Negro masseur, who hated white men for their assaults on his pride, provided Anthony with violent massages which provided both sexual release and atonement. This transaction, like the transaction between hustler and john, seems to place desire in a loveless, materialistic framework, but Williams is always aware of the slippages in such a rigid formulation. For him, love can be found in any sexual connection, however brief or ostensibly cynical. In Williams's world, money is usually a factor in sexual transactions. If the ideal is a passion which transcends a world in which "there's just two kinds of people, the bought and the buyers," that is seldom and only briefly attained. The violent, paid transactions between Anthony and the masseur allowed both to enact their deepest desires and became for both, acts of love: "The giant loved Burns, and Burns adored the giant" (109). When Anthony's cries of pleasure/pain became too loud and the manager discovered his bruised, broken body, the Black masseur was fired. He carried the battered, but sated Anthony to his house in the Black section of town to continue their passion. The move from the place of business to the masseur's home is a move from a system of cash exchange to another system of consumption and a move into the world of the racial other.[6] Their final week together was at the end of Lent, Passion Week, within earshot of the services of atonement from the church across the street: "Each afternoon the fiery poem of death on the cross was repeated. The preacher was not fully conscious of what he wanted nor were the listeners groaning and writhing before him. All of them were involved in a massive atonement" (210), but none so massive as that of Anthony Burns, who died willingly and contentedly at the hands of his Black masseur. His last wish was also enacted when the giant masseur ate his body: "Yes, it is perfect, he thought, it is now completed" (211), a parody of Christ's last words on the cross, "Consumatum est."

Peace, perfection, serenity, completion, from this violent communion and literal consumption of the flesh. "Take, eat, this is my body which is given unto you," Christ said at the Last Supper, but he only spoke metaphorically. Always the pagan, Williams believed that true fulfillment of desire will come only from such a complete communion as that of Anthony Burns and his Black masseur. It is typical of Tennessee Williams that this story offers such a multiplicity of meanings. Here, unlike his plays, he can openly offer his vision in its original homosexual terms, though homosexuality only offers release in a brutal, final masochistic relationship. Here is not Blanche's belief that "The opposite of death is desire"; rather the fulfillment of desire is death and the only total relationship is a literal enactment of the Eucharist. Christianity offers a pale, symbolic approximation of the Dionysian sacrifice at the heart of real passion. But this passion also has a racial dimension, a joining of undeveloped white self with the gigantic, overwhelming Black other, yet this was love. Here is an allegory of race relations where perfection, communion, can only come through ritual violence, where cultures meet and atone. Here also is Williams's vision of religion, of guilt, and the need for atonement at the heart of our most basic needs. Sex and atonement are inextricably linked in a perversion of *imitatio Christi* which no one can escape. Those who act on their sexual desire contain their own policemen.

Anthony Burns and the Black masseur connected through simultaneous fulfillment of their separate desires, not through a romantic, spiritual joining. This idea is central to Williams's work: love, insofar as it exists at all, is the transient joining of two different desires contained in individuals who will always remain isolated, separate. This is why romantic love and marriage, straight or gay, seem to be impossibilities in Williams, or, at best, uneasy compromises. Williams's stories and dramas are sagas of solipsism. People may occasionally and briefly break through and connect with others, but their real dramas, passions, are enacted within. People may be the victims of awful violence, but they are often willing victims. This is why in Williams liberation can only come with death. One's self—body, mind, desires—is a turbulent drama from which one only exits through death. Religion is one language for defining this combination of isolation, desire, and atonement. This formulation supports the idea that for Williams, despite his vaunted revolutionary politics, politics is contained within the individual, not in the relationship of individual to others and to the body politic.

While these principles are basic to all of Williams's work, we see them dramatized most vividly in this homoerotic, if not consistently homosexual, trilogy of male sacrifice and martyrdom written in the late 1950s. The aristocratic poet Sebastian Venable in *Suddenly Last Summer* is, like Anthony Burns, devoured by "the other" with whom he has been engaged in paid acts of sex. While Anthony Burns has desired anonymity, Sebastian has carefully, with the help of his doting mother, maintained an image of aristocratic superiority and artistic sensibility. When mother can no longer serve as policeman of the image, denying the homosexual reality underneath, Sebastian runs amok with starving Mediterranean urchins, revealing the underside of the image of old world pomp he and his mother have nurtured. When he decides he will no longer sexually consume these hungry boys, they literally consume him.

Suddenly Last Summer offers Williams's version of meaningful martyrdom. Its violence is tied up in complex ways with homosexual desire, which is described as voracious appetite: "Fed up with dark ones, famished for light ones: that's how he talked about people, as if they were—items on a menu" (375). It is far too easy to see, as some have done, Sebastian's death as poetic justice, the queer consumer consumed. Or, in a sexy replaying of the French Revolution, the predatory aristocrat torn asunder and eaten by the exploited peasantry. However, nothing in Williams is as simplistic as poetic justice, nor would Williams ever present a story so supportive of Puritan policing of desire. Sebastian's death is a working out of the connection of hunger and desire. Clearly Williams connected sex, at least homosex, and feeding, sating of appetite. As I have noted elsewhere, he was known to talk like this himself.[7] Here this connection of feeding and desire is clearly connected to religion, to Sebastian's search for God. *Suddenly Last Summer* is another expression of Williams's paganism in Christian terms, another blasphemous Eucharist. Sebastian's garden, the true expression of his vision of the fallen world, is filled with carnivorous plants. His vision of God is of birds of prey devouring the baby turtles as they rush toward the sea on the Galapagos Islands. His death is consonant with his own vision: the human birds of prey feast on his corpse as he sexually feasted on their bodies. Not divine justice, but divine economy. Hunger—hungers—desire—the operative principle. Nor is the sating of desire without its consequences. Sebastian does not seek atonement, but he gets it nonetheless. We are to see the cosmic meaning in this violent act as we see the inevitable failure of policing and silencing it.

INTERSECTING TRIANGLES

Suddenly Last Summer is structured as two conflicting narratives of Sebastian which represent the conflict between Catherine, who has seen "the truth" of Sebastian's life and death, and Sebastian's mother Violet (the color of penitence, atonement), who ruthlessly protects the eternally young, eternally chaste, image of her too-beloved son. To allow his image to age would be to admit age and mortality exist. To allow him sexuality would be to lose her primacy in his life. To acknowledge the ramifications and consequences of his vision would be to acknowledge an unbearable truth. Violet Venable wants her son to be a work of art, carefully tended like his carnivorous garden. Yet the "real" story Catherine tells is far richer, more interesting, more terrifying, than Violet's chaste version of Sebastian. To protect her version of Sebastian, Violet will order an act of violence as brutal as anything her son could conceive of: the destruction, the literal cutting apart, of a mind.

The competing agents of truth in this story are both women, the Solomonic arbiter an agent of the ultimate thought police, psychiatrists, who in America have a particularly bleak record in the immoral, impossible policing of homosexual desire. The blond, handsome "Dr. Sugar" is offered a large bribe to keep Violet's memory of Sebastian sweet. Catherine, who admits she "came out" sexually in the bohemian French Quarter before she "came out" as a debutante in the aristocratic Garden District, cannot deny what she has seen and experienced, despite the wishes of her poor family, desperately in need of Violet's largesse, or the threat of mental castration, lobotomy. Nor can Dr. Sugar honestly fulfill his function of denying what Catherine has seen. The ultimate, religious truth of Sebastian's death and devouring, as voiced by Catherine, is too powerful to be denied even by a psychiatrist.

While Dr. Sugar, both alien to this aristocratic hothouse through his Polish origins and rendered ineffectual by his sweet nickname, decides the outcome of the conflict between the two women, he is little more than a plot device. The women dominate the play as even Sebastian only exists as voiced by them. One question intrigues me: why must the "young, blond" Dr. Sugar be "very, very good looking"? Why couldn't Dr. Sugar look like ... Sigmund Freud? Is the "glacially brilliant" doctor with his "icy charm" potentially homosexual? In fifties dramas, very good looks are often a sign of homosexuality. The only sign of Mr. Harris's homosexuality in Robert Anderson's *Tea and Sympathy* is that he is described as "good looking." The beautiful blond man, Rodolpho, in Arthur Miller's *A View From the Bridge* is accused of being homosexual. Being too good looking, thus being looked at, was a sign of being not totally masculine, thus homosexual. Dr. Sugar is neither responsive to Mrs. Venable's steel magnolia charm nor to Catherine literally throwing herself at him: "*She crushes her mouth to his violently. He tries to disengage himself*" (403). This hint of a remaining homosexual potential after Sebastian's death means that there is no realistic closure to homosexuality in the play. Sebastian is not killed to remove homosexuality from the scene—only a heterosexual writer could maintain that formula—rather the narrative of his death keeps his vision and his sexuality alive, aided visually by the presence of that very, very good-looking man in a white suit just like the one Sebastian was wearing![8]

In "Desire and the Black Masseur" and *Suddenly Last Summer*, we see the daring of Williams that makes him our greatest playwright, the willingness to go to extremes beyond even the absurdities of melodrama to share his frightening vision with his reader and his audience. Like the mad extremes of Euripides' *The Bacchae*, these works offer a Dionysian vision of human experience, made more vivid by the contrast with the mundane "reality" of modern American life and the futile attempts to deny those acts which are most human and most godlike. But to what end? At the conclusion of *Suddenly Last Summer*, Catherine's story has freed her from the threat of a lobotomy, but the characters move off in different directions, disconnected. The truth of Sebastian's story is also the truth of isolation. At the end of the play Violet and Catherine leave the stage separately and alone with their memories of Sebastian.

THE MARTYRDOM OF THE PASSIVE STUD

In Williams's early plays, the sexually transgressive figure was the woman. In *A Streetcar Named Desire* (1947), Blanche DuBois can play the prim Southern belle, but her proudest moment is ravishing the soldiers from the nearby base, leaving them spent on the grass where "later the paddy wagon would gather them up like daisies" (389). Blanche is a wild card in the seven card stud game that is the sex/gender system. For that the men in the play must humiliate and punish her, but Williams is on the side of queer, if not gay, Blanche. The parodic image of the heterosexual family that ends the play does not provide a final resolution. The Blanches of the world endure if they do not yet prevail. Alma Winemiller in *Summer and Smoke* (1948) moves from being a prim, hysterical, preacher's daughter to a sexually liberated woman willing to find her transient fulfillments in occasional sex—the kindness of strangers—but Alma is not punished. Her liberation is her triumph, her cavalier's plume. It is her beloved John, who moves from wildness to conventional marriage, who is crying when we last see him.

There are three sexually transgressive figures in *Orpheus Descending*: Carol Cutrere, Val Xavier, and Lady Torrance. Carol, the wayward daughter of the richest family in town, is a self-confessed exhibitionist and "lewd vagrant." Strangely made up like a punk before her time, Carol is the only true rebellious spirit in the small Southern town in which the play takes place. Like her predecessors in Williams's plays, she asks for the pleasure she craves. She sees herself as a remnant of an earlier, less civilized time: "This country used to be wild, the men and women were wild and there was a wild sort of sweetness in their hearts, for each other, but now it's sick with neon, it's broken out sick with neon, like most other places" (327).[9] Carol is often accompanied by an old Black Conjure Man whom she pays to give a wild Choctaw Indian cry from another place and time. The sexual energy, the wildness of the past, is heard in the cry of racial otherness, Native American and Black. But Carol's wildness is no threat to the Southern patriarchal order. She is a remittance relative, paid to get out of town, but not in danger when she breaks her contract and appears. She is an embarrassment to her family and an outrage to the women, but nothing more. Yet only Carol understands the threat Val represents to the community, and his mythic status as well as his sexual attraction. It is she who warns him of the danger he is in and it is she who remains to define him at the end of the play.

Val Xavier is mutilated and sanctified for his sexual potency, which is a threat to other men because the sexual free agent is a magnet, drawing women outside the boundaries of patriarchal authority and marriage. Val first appears as if summoned by the Conjure Man's wild Choctaw cry. The stage directions tell us that Val "*has the kind of wild beauty about him that the cry would suggest*" (240). He wears a snakeskin jacket, a kind of Dionysian remnant of his link with the wildness of nature and human desire, but also connoting the Judeo-Christian notion of temptation. He also carries with him a guitar, his version of Orpheus's lyre, but Val's guitar connects him to the blues, and through them to the racial other, the Black. On his guitar are inscribed the names of great Black musicians: Leadbelly, Bessie Smith, King Oliver, and Fats Waller.

Val has lived the life of a vagabond, singing and playing in New Orleans bars, but the day he appears in this small-town general store is his thirtieth birthday, "and I'm through with the life I've been leading. I lived in corruption but I'm not corrupted" (261). Val does not lament the loss of youth as many of Williams's characters do, but he wants to retain the freedom of youth. He wants to remain "uncorrupted" which for him means remaining outside the materialistic system of ownership. He tells Lady Torrance:

> VAL: Lady, there's just two kinds of people, the ones that are
> bought and the buyers! No!—there's one other kind ...
> LADY: What kind's that?
> VAL: The kind that's never been branded. (265)

The only way to remain uncorrupted is to be like "a kind of bird that don't have legs so it can't light on nothing but has to stay all its life on its wings in the sky" (265). Such freedom may be an impossible goal, but the free bird is also isolated, as all beings are: "We're all of us sentenced to solitary confinement inside our own skins, for life!" (271). The impossibility of the freedom Val so eloquently describes, and the inevitability of the isolation he laments are borne out by the action of the play.

Val takes a job working in the general store Lady runs for her terminally ill husband. Lady, the other figure in this female-dominated triangle, is an Italian-American whose father ran a wine garden where young couples came to have sex. The garden was burned down and Lady's father burned up when a Ku Klux Klan-like group discovered that he sold liquor to Blacks. Eighteen-year-old Lady had been left by her lover, David Cutrere, Carol's brother, who married for money to save the family home. David and Lady had had an extraordinarily passionate relationship, "Like you struck two stones together and made a fire!—yes—fire" (230). Broke and bereft, Lady is "sold cheap" to Jabe Torrance who, unbeknownst to her, led the gang that killed her father. Now Lady lives for the moment she turns part of the general store into a recreation of her father's wine garden, recreating the sexually free past the men in the town destroyed and the site of her moment of passion and happiness.

We are told by the women who form a kind of Greek chorus—while patriarchy may be conditionally restored, women have the dominant voices in this play—that Lady's marriage is sexless and barren, that she and her husband live in separate rooms on opposite sides of the dark second floor of the general store, that her only previous passion was with David Cutrere. David had to give up their relationship for economic survival and Lady had to marry, to sell herself, for economic survival. The store represents the barren world of commerce, of people bought and sold, that Val tries to rise above. The minute he literally moves into that store, he places himself at great risk, for he makes himself vulnerable to a dehumanizing system. The system, itself barren, will not allow Lady fertility. Twice she is robbed of motherhood.

Val may be able to resist Carol Cutrere, but his sexual magnetism is still his undoing. Val becomes the one person who will listen to the blind visionary sheriff's wife, Vee, but twice the sheriff catches them in moments of innocent physical contact, a result of their spiritual understanding. The sheriff delivers an ultimatum to Val: "Boy, don't let the sun rise on you in this county" (321), an echo of a common Southern threat, "Nigger, don't let the sun go down on you in this county" (320). Val's perceived threat to a powerful man's property—his wife—turns him into a "Nigger." Val has also, somewhat reluctantly, slept with and impregnated Lady Torrance. There is no conventional love scene. Like Blanche, Alma, and Carol Cutrere, Lady takes what she wants and needs to bring herself back to life. Once Lady realizes that she is pregnant, that she has life within her, she can let Val go. The man who wants to avoid being seen merely as the stud has been just that.

However strong the women are, the men of the town provisionally restore the sex/gender system. On Easter eve, Lady's dying husband comes down the stairs from his bedroom with a gun, shoots Lady and shouts that Val has killed his wife and robbed his store. The townsmen, probably the same ones who killed Lady's father and burned down his wine garden, take a blowtorch and incinerate Val.

The primary images in *Orpheus Descending* are heat and fire. Val's body temperature is two degrees warmer than most humans, a reflection of his sexual energy. In a strange sex reversal, Val is in heat and arouses all the females who come near him. But Val's heat is countered by the fire that destroys all signs of sexual energy, the orgiastic wine garden and Val himself. The fire is the fire of a human hell and Val, like Orpheus, has the power to bring the woman he loves out of the abyss: "I guess my heart knew that somebody must be coming to take me out of this hell! You did. You came. Now look at me! I'm alive once more!" (333). But, like Orpheus's Eurydice, Lady's rescue is temporary. Characteristically, Williams mixes pagan mythology with Christian. This Orpheus is killed on Easter eve. Val is Christ, Dionysus, and Eros combined, the spiritual principle and the sexual principle, or rather the sexual principle made spiritual, seeking an impossible freedom.[10]

In essence, Val is killed for bringing life to the town. He literally brings life to the imprisoned, embittered Lady. He also enables the visions that inspire Vee's religious paintings. He is killed by men who can only bring death and destruction. Val, the disseminator of Black culture through his music, the rebel who will not conform to patriarchal order, threatens the social order by bringing life and a measure of autonomy to the women. The men do not win, however. At the end, Carol has Val's snakeskin jacket: "Wild things leave skins behind them, they leave clean skins and teeth and white bones behind them, and these are tokens passed from one to another, so that the fugitive kind can always follow their kind" (341). Carol refuses to obey the sheriff's order to stop and walks past him as if she hasn't seen him. The old Black Conjure Man is alone on stage as the curtain falls. The victory of the white patriarchy is temporary at best. The spirit embodied in

Val still exists and prevails, but through the body and voice of a transgressive, isolated woman.

Ironically, Val, the reluctant stud, is a relatively passive character. He attracts women but tries to resist their attempts to take what they want from him. Freedom for him means freedom not only from the world of people being bought and sold, but freedom from women. He will not have sex in the graveyard with Carol Cutrere (another mix of death and desire), and he tries to leave when he realizes that Lady wants to set him up as live-in lover as well as employee: "A not so young and not so satisfied woman that hired a man off the highway to do double duty without paying overtime for it ... I mean a store clerk days and a stud nights, and—" (304). When Lady cries out her need for him, he walks into the alcove where he sleeps. Lady must be the aggressor and go in and take him. The sheriff may see Val's hand on his wife's bosom, but she put it there.

Williams transfers to his heterosexual redeemer the qualities of his earlier homosexual martyrs: Oliver Winemiller, the beautiful one-armed hustler who is electrocuted with the letters of his male admirers shoved between his legs; the beaten and eaten Anthony Burns (note the last name!). As these beautiful men, straight or gay, are erotic fantasies for Williams, so their mutilation is an erotic fantasy, the ultimate communion with them. There is a book to be written on physical mutilation as a sign of homosexuality in gay drama, the mark of a vindictive heterosexist society. In some of Williams's plays, the mutilation is a sign of a potential gay reading of the straight body.

Why the move from the homoerotics of the stories to the heterosexuality of *Orpheus Descending*? One could make a case that this is Williams presenting what he thinks his audience will tolerate, but there were references to homosexuality all through the highly successful *Cat on a Hot Tin Roof*. Moreover, as Rory B. Egan points out, "The homosexuality of Orpheus is a feature of several ancient versions of the story, including Ovid's, and it is usually a concomitant of his attractiveness to women and their resentment at his hostility or indifference."[11] Is Val necessarily exclusively heterosexual? He has bummed around the French Quarter, and throughout the play he tries to avoid sexual contact with the women who pursue him. Williams came out at a time when there was less delineation between straight and gay, when the secrecy surrounding homosexuality made it possible for men to have sex with other men without fear of being branded as homosexual. Seeing a straight "stud" as sexually attractive and available was a reality as well as a fantasy in the pre-Stonewall years in which Williams spent his young manhood.[12] Indeed, Val's reluctance and passivity suggest a sexually ambiguous figure. This is not the aggressive stud, a cousin of Stanley Kowalski. Val is more akin to Doctor Sugar. It is the women who are active, taking what they want from the men.

The world of *Orpheus Descending*, like that of *Suddenly Last Summer*, is one of powerful women and sexually ambivalent men. The patriarchs seem impotent, capable of killing but not of creating life. There is no place for marriage in this Amazon society in which the man's basic function is to be, however reluctantly, "stud at bay." In killing Val and Lady, the men kill part of the potential for a new, non-patriarchal gender order. But at the final curtain, there is still Carol, Val's snakeskin jacket, and the wild Choctaw cry. Carol represents freedom and isolation in a play that denies all human connection except brief sexual encounter. As Val declares: "Nobody ever gets to know *no body*! We're all of us sentenced to confinement inside our own skins, for life!" (271).

THE STUD CORRUPTED

In all three plays of male martyrdom, we are in symbolic landscapes: from the carnivorous creation of a malevolent God in *Suddenly Last Summer*, to the Southern Hades of *Orpheus Descending* where fire reigns, to the heavenly world of St. Cloud on the "gulf of misunderstanding," the setting of *Sweet Bird of Youth*, where impotent men emasculate those who threaten their power. *Sweet Bird of Youth*, like its companion pieces, is comprised of intersecting triangles: Chance, Heavenly, and Heavenly's father, Boss Finley; but far more important, Chance, Heavenly, and Alexandra del Lago. The two women never meet, but offer the two sexual and emotional possibilities Chance experiences in the play. Heavenly is a mirage, the shell of the girl Chance loved, but Chance, denying the power of time, believes that regaining her is regaining his youth and his purity. The aging star Alexandra del Lago is very real, complete with grand neuroses and the means to temporarily forget them. She is also, like many of Williams's heroines—Alma, Maggie the Cat, Catherine—an agent of truth forcing a weak man to confront reality.

Chance, figuratively, is the black-sheep brother of Brick Pollitt in *Cat on a Hot Tin Roof*. Like Brick, he wants his world to be what it was when he was a teenager, but Brick had real athletic ability while Chance never had much more than his looks to depend on. Brick's one experience of ideal beauty was his asexual friendship with Skipper. His desire to live stopped when he realized that friendship was not as ideal as he thought. Chance had one glorious moment of beauty in bed with Heavenly on a speeding train and lives to recreate that moment. There is purity in Chance's futile dream, but Chance's link with reality is more tentative than that of most Williams characters, male or female.

If Val Xavier resists entering the world of buyers and bought, Chance is totally absorbed into that world. Chance is a gigolo, a man who lives off the money of the women who hire him for sex and companionship. The gigolo is the most fascinating case of reversal of the sex/gender system. The woman is in financial control and pays the financially dependent man to service her physically and emotionally. His looks and his sexual prowess are his most important assets. Williams, no stranger to hiring men for sex, used the related (sometimes identical) figures of the male hustler in a number of works, particularly the story "One Arm," the novel *The Roman Spring of Mrs. Stone*, and the plays *Sweet Bird of Youth* and *The Milk Train Doesn't Stop Here Anymore* in which the paid companion, Christopher Flanders, functions symbolically as the angel of death.

To the men in power in St. Cloud, Chance is a "criminal degenerate," a phrase usually applied to homosexuals. *Sweet Bird of Youth* is one instance of a Tennessee Williams play which was first intended to present a homosexual relationship, then "heterosexualized." In his study of the sketches and manuscripts of *Sweet Bird of Youth*, Drewey Wayne Gunn explains:

> In most early versions, including the ones which led directly to Act I of *Sweet Bird*, "she" is Artemis Pazmezoglu, a plump but spiritually attractive man vaguely connected in Hollywood. In some drafts, Art is in retreat in Phil's [the early name for Chance] home town, and Phil searches him out for help with his faltering acting career. But in the most important draft of this series, Art has picked Phil up in Miami, fallen in love with him on a nonphysical basis (he is too old for sex, he says), passed out drunk, and been driven by Phil to his home town to search out the old girlfriend ... the daughter of Boss Finley.[13]

Williams was right: a sexual relationship with a woman had more dramatic interest than a one-sided nonsexual homosexual crush (all the 1950s would allow). Yet, oddly, Chance considers himself metaphorically "castrated" for being treated as what he is, a gigolo (120). When in the first scene Alexandra del Lago scoffs at his attempts to blackmail her and orders him to perform in bed, Chance turns puritan:

> PRINCESS: Chance, I need that distraction. It's time for me to find out if you're able to give it to me. You mustn't hang onto your silly little idea that you can increase your value by turning away and looking out a window when somebody wants you ... I want you ... I say now and I mean now, then and not until then will I call downstairs and tell the hotel cashier that I'm sending a young man down with some traveler's checks to cash for me ...

CHANCE [*turning slowly from the window*]: Aren't you ashamed a
    little?
PRINCESS: Of course I am. Aren't you?
CHANCE: More than a little... (44)[14]

What should the Princess be ashamed of? That she wants what she has paid
for? Why should Chance feel ashamed and later claim that this is a moment of
castration? The Princess is doing what Williams's strong women do—claim
their right to sexual satisfaction—but she places it within a material economy.
It is this commodification that unmans Chance. Chance is the male version of
the whore with the heart of gold, a loving romantic at heart, who is redeemed
by voicing patriarchal judgments on his relinquishment of masculine power.
His corruption is caused by his entrapment within a materialistic system. He
is, in Val Xavier's formulation, one of the bought. He tries to gain power
over Alexandra by blackmailing her, but he is no match for such a ruthless
pragmatist: "When monster meets monster, one monster has to give way,
AND IT WILL NEVER BE ME. I'm an older hand at it ... with much more
natural aptitude at it than you have" (43). Chance is also unmanned by his
conventionality, his futile insistence on conventional masculine prerogatives.

    Unlike Alexandra del Lago, Heavenly is an impossibility. Her father will
never let Chance take her away and she is nothing but a "dream of youth,"
broken and rendered sterile by the venereal disease Chance gave her, now
forced to marry the doctor who cut out her diseased womb.

    Alexandra offers Chance a way to get out of town and avoid the
impending very real castration that has been ordered for him. He can remain
in her employ:

PRINCESS: You'd better come down with my luggage.
CHANCE: I'm not part of your luggage.
PRINCESS: What else can you be?
CHANCE: Nothing ... but not part of your luggage. (122)

When his dream of youth is gone, Chance has nothing left but his pride. He
would rather face castration than be Alexandra's toyboy.

    Chance is castrated, not killed, but in Williams's world in which sex is
life, castration is death. His castration is ordered by Boss Finley, the ruthless
politico who "can't cut the mustard." It will be enacted by his sexually profligate
son and his friends. Boss Finley is campaigning for castration of Blacks who
commit miscegenation, and Chance is to have the Black man's punishment
for corrupting and polluting his too-beloved daughter. While castration links
Chance to the racial other and the term "criminal degenerate" links him to

a sexual other, impotence and castration seem to be the way of the world. When Chance tells Alexandra that her forcing him to perform sexually was a form of castration, she counters, "Age does the same thing to a woman" (120). The surgeon's knife does it to Heavenly, but indirectly Chance has castrated her by giving her "the whore's disease."

Sweet Bird of Youth takes place on Easter Sunday, suggesting a redemption the play doesn't allow for. Easter is used ironically here, for there is no escape from time or mortality: "Time—who could beat it, who could defeat it ever? Maybe some saints and heroes, but not Chance Wayne." There is no heaven, only the half-dead Heavenly and the corrupt St. Cloud. The church bells ring at the beginning of the play, but the bell does not toll for the likes of Chance or Alexandra del Lago who live in a world of the body. Anyway, religion is depicted in the play as hypocrisy, the tool of megalomaniacs like Boss Finley.

The play celebrates the endurance of Alexandra del Lago, capable of honesty with herself and others and capable of shining moments of compassion, even love. Yet Alexandra also knows that one is always, essentially, alone in beanstalk country. Alexandra prevails because she is, like her creator, "artist and star!": "Out of the passion and torment of my existence I have created a thing that I can unveil, a sculpture almost heroic, that I can unveil, which is true" (120). Alexandra's acting, recorded on film, can fight time. Only art can, and one can not finish discussing these three plays without considering the importance of art. Sebastian was an artist remembered, unfortunately, for the way he died rather than for his poems of summer. Val was a singer, carrying the legacy of great singers. That legacy remains. Alexandra's triumphs still exist even if her career is almost over. Sex, too, momentarily transcends time, but only momentarily. It is odd that a gigolo wouldn't understand that. But how many American heroes are prized precisely for their lack of understanding?

Perhaps the oddest moment in *Sweet Bird of Youth* is its end in which Chance steps before the audience: "I don't ask for your pity, but just for your understanding—not even that—no. Just for your recognition of me in you, and the enemy, time, in us all." Donald Spoto calls this "the single most jarring interruption of dramatic structure in Williams's work."[15] Williams has seldom been so concerned with giving his leading man the last word, and what a strangely qualified utterance it is. Are we to feel more for the feckless, deluded Chance, the loser, than we feel for Alexandra del Lago, who faces her situation and moves on? Chance only gives up his futile illusions when Alexandra confronts him with the truth about himself and Heavenly. What does he gain by submitting to castration? Is not living with the fact of "the enemy, time," more heroic than giving up because of it? The ending is jarring and weak because, for once, Williams does not understand that the woman, Alexandra, is the core of the play, not Chance. Alexandra's last words to Chance offer the philosophy of adaptability and endurance that are the positive counter to the mutilation of Williams's martyrs: "So come on, we've got to go on" (124). Like many of Williams's heroic women, Alexandra has the strength to face an uncertain, potentially bleak future. Chance, the passive stud, frozen in time, incapable of compromise, can only submit to the completion of his emasculation.

NOTES

1. Gayle Rubin, "The Traffic in Women: Notes Toward a Political Economy of Sex," *Toward an Anthropology of Women*, ed. Rayna Reiter (New York: Monthly Review Press, 1975), 157–210.

2. Eve Kosofsky Sedgwick, *Between Men: English Literature and Male Homosocial Desire* (New York: Columbia University Press, 1985).

3. Tennessee Williams, *Suddenly Last Summer*, *The Theatre of Tennessee Williams*, vol. III (New York: New Directions, 1971), 343–423.

4. For a full discussion of homosexuality in *Cat on a Hot Tin Roof*, see my *Acting Gay: Male Homosexuality in Modern Drama*, revised edn. (New York: Columbia University Press, 1994), 156–62. David Savran also has an excellent, extended discussion of homosexuality in Williams's works in *Communists, Cowboys, and Queers: The Politics of Masculinity in the Work of Arthur Miller and Tennessee Williams* (Minneapolis: University of Minnesota Press, 1992), 76–174.

5. Tennessee Williams, "Desire and the Black Masseur," *Tennessee Williams: Collected Stories* (New York: New Directions, 1985), 205–12.

6. David Savran points out that in Williams's work, "With a remarkable consistency, desire is provoked by differences in race, ethnicity, social class, and age. Almost inevitably, subject and object are configured as antitheses that are congruent with a series of binary oppositions—white/black, wealthy/poor, old/young. Almost inevitably the first in the pair is granted the priority of the desiring subject, while the second is objectified and exoticized, and thereby endowed with the power to arouse sexual desire." *Communists, Cowboys, and Queers*, 125.

7. "While in Italy in 1948, Williams wrote Donald Windham: "[Frederick Prokosch] says that Florence is full of blue-eyed blonds that are very tender hearted and 'not at all mercenary.' We were both getting an appetite for blonds as the Roman gentry are all sort of dusky types." Sebastian's unfeeling sexual exploitation is as much a dramatization of the playwright as is Sebastian's pill-popping and confused sense of private and public personae." "'Something Cloudy, Something Clear': Homophobic Discourse in Tennessee Williams," in Ronald Butters, John M. Clum, and Michael Moon (eds.), *Displacing Homophobia: Studies in Gay Male Literature and Culture*, (Durham, N.C.: Duke University Press, 1989), 157–58.

8. I am aware that Dr. Sugar claims to have a girlfriend he cannot afford to marry, but does this excuse ring true for a doctor even in a state hospital in 1935? He would be better off than much of the Depression-era population who did get married.

9. Tennessee Williams, *Orpheus Descending*, *The Theatre of Tennessee Williams*, vol. III (New York: New Directions, 1971), 217–342. This line also appeared in *Battle of Angels* (1940), Williams's disastrous first "Broadway" play (actually the Broadway production

was scuttled after the Boston tryout), which he rewrote extensively and retitled *Orpheus Descending*. The latter made it to Broadway, but closed after sixty-eight performances. It was made into a movie entitled *The Fugitive Kind* (screenplay by Williams, directed by Sidney Lumet) with Anna Magnani and Marlon Brando. *Battle of Angels* appears in volume 1 of *The Theatre of Tennessee Williams*.

10. I will not recount all the Orphic and Christian parallels that can be mined out of a careful reading of *Orpheus Descending*. For the fullest account, see Rory B. Egan, "Orpheus Christus Mississippiensis: Tennessee Williams's Xavier in Hell" in *Classical and Modern Literature: A Quarterly*, 14 (1993), 61–98.

11. Egan, "Orpheus Christus Mississippiensis," 81. Orpheus is, in the myth, brutally murdered by a band of women, not by men, as in Williams's play.

12. In his recent memoir, *Palimpsest*, Gore Vidal recounts the postwar world of New York's Astor Hotel bar, before what he calls "the ghettoization of 'gay' and 'straight.'" There Alfred Kinsey interviewed male subjects for his revolutionary study of sexual behavior in the human male: "I like to think that it was by observing the easy trafficking at the Astor that he figured out what was obvious to most of us, though as yet undreamed of by American society at large: perfectly 'normal' young men, placed outside the usual round of family and work, will run riot with each other." (New York: Random House, 1995), 102.

13. Drewey Wayne Gunn, "The Troubled Flight of Tennessee Williams's *Sweet Bird*: From Manuscript through Published Texts," *Modern Drama* 24 (1980), 229.

14. Tennessee Williams, *Sweet Bird of Youth*, *The Theatre of Tennessee Williams*, vol. iv (New York: New Directions, 1972), 44.

15. Donald Spoto, *The Kindness of Strangers: The Life of Tennessee Williams* (New York: Ballantine, 1986), 257.

NANCY M. TISCHLER

Romantic Textures in
Tennessee Williams's Plays and Short Stories

I believe in Michelangelo, Velásquez and Rembrandt; in the might of design, the mystery of color, the redemption of all things by beauty everlasting and the message of art that has made these hands blessed. Amen.

This, Tennessee Williams proclaimed to be his own creed as an artist.[1] Like his "Poet" of the short story by that name, Tennessee Williams was a natural romantic whose very existence was one of "benevolent anarchy" ("The Poet," 246). His artistic *creed* (a term of some significance to a man nurtured in theology) signals the primacy of the artist, not God. He was dedicated to: (1) the power of "design" or artistic control over the material world; (2) the "mystery" of color or the non-rational, supernatural gift of beauty, affecting the artist and the audience; (3) the "redemption" of all things by "beauty"— an act of salvation by means of created and experienced splendor; (4) the "message" of art, the need to communicate the artist's vision of reality to the audience; and (5) the "blessedness" of his hands—his conviction that he is the chosen vessel for this important work.

CREDO: "I BELIEVE IN..." WILLIAMS'S ROMANTIC INFLUENCES

Thomas Lanier Williams, also known as Tennessee, was born to be a visionary. He gathered ideas, images, themes, and phrases as he wandered

From *The Cambridge Companion to Tennessee Williams*, edited by Matthew C. Roudané, pp. 147–166 © 1997 Cambridge University Press. Reprinted by permission.

45

through life and wove colorful romantic pictures onto the dark background of his increasing realism to form grand designs and vivid contrasts. He lived his life as a peripatetic poet, one of the everlasting company of fugitives who discover their vocation in their art, transforming experience and giving shape to visions.[2]

Descended from colonial settlers and pioneers, he was quintessentially American, but never a typical pragmatic middle American. He saw himself as the archetypal outsider: a poet in a practical world, a homosexual in a heterosexual society. Living in the "Century of Progress," he preferred candlelight to electricity. A Southerner who lamented the loss of a dignity, elegance, and sense of honor, he was never satisfied with the dreary present and its flat speech. Williams yearned for "long distance," for "cloudy symbols of high romance," or what romantics called the "yonder bank."[3] His characters love a lost, idealized past ("Blue Mountain"), and they live for a dangerous, problematic future ("Terra Incognita"). From beginning to end, Williams's theatrical struggle was also a romantic quest for Parnassus. It was romantic dreamers—quixotic and tattered old warriors, fragile young poets, frightened misfits—whom he celebrated in his poems, stories, novels, and plays. Romanticism was the very fabric of his life and work woven throughout. In his early self-descriptions for Audrey Wood, his longtime agent, he presented a persona deliberately crafted as the romantic loner.[4] This portrait of the peripatetic, penniless writer was then polished and repeated in many articles, interviews, and biographies which followed. (Note especially *Conversations with Tennessee Williams*[5] and *Where I Live*.)

In a statement for the press, developed at the time *The Night of the Iguana* was premiering in New York, he showed that he was aware of his obsession with what he called "the Visionary Company": "This new play, *The Night of the Iguana*, and the one to follow, off-Broadway, which is presently titled *The Milktrain Doesn't Stop Here Anymore*," he explained, "both contain major characters who are poets, and this was not planned, it just happened." He then continues: "In *Suddenly Last Summer* the chief topic of discussion and violent contention was also a poet. So obviously the archetype of the poet has become an obsessive figure, a leit-motif in my recent work for the stage, and possibly was always, since Tom Wingfield in *The Glass Menagerie* was a poet, too, and so was Val Xavier in *Orpheus Descending* essentially a poet, for a singer is a kind of poet, too, just as a poet is a kind of singer."

He then explains that "the idea, the image, of a poet has come to represent to me, as a writer, an element in human-life that put up the strongest resistance to that which is false and impure, in himself and the world..." Such a person is "always a tragic antagonist."

Finally, waxing eloquent about this figure, Williams announces that, "If he is really a poet, by vocation, not affectation, his sword Excalibur or his Holy Grail, is truth as he himself conceives it, and he believes in it as an absolute, as many non-practicing poets in the world also do."[6] Here, most clearly we have the romantic imagery of the chosen vessel for divinely inspired activity.

Williams's letters, his early drafts, his short stories, and his plays often signal the particular artists whose lives captured his attention: D. H. Lawrence, Vachel Lindsay, William Wordsworth, and George Gordon, Lord Byron in the early days; F. Scott Fitzgerald, Mishima Yukio, Jane Bowles, and Jackson Pollock later on; and Hart Crane always.

This whole inclination to observe the world and its people through the eyes of the romantic came as naturally to Williams as writing did. He was related to both Sidney Lanier, the nineteenth-century poet, and to John Sharp Williams, one of the more eloquent of the Southern political orators.[7] To have spent his early youth in the Mississippi Delta, in the home of an Episcopal minister, in the midst of people speaking rich Southern dialects, would be adequate to establish his taste for purple prose and romantic thoughts. It also fixed his identification of youth, Eden innocence, and the bucolic South.

He spent many hours of his childhood in the well-stocked library of his grandfather, a classically educated man. (A portion of this library is currently held in the Tennessee Williams Collection at Washington University in St. Louis.) Among the earliest reading for the young boy were "The Lady of Shalott" and the novels of Sir Walter Scott, the poetry of Coleridge and Poe. Tom Williams's early flowery style derived originally from this saturation in such lyric poets as Sara Teasdale and Edna St. Vincent Millay. In the "Frivolous Version" of a "Preface to My Poems," he noted that he "began writing verse at about the time of puberty," and that his earliest success was an "apostrophe to death" which named a number of the lyric women poets, ending with a tribute to "glorious Millay."[8]

In *Summer and Smoke*, Williams parodies these memories of his adolescent self and his fellow poets of the women's club, portraying the typical genteel Southern poetry club gathering in the manse for lemonade and uplift. The scene reflects Williams's changing preferences among romantic poets. Miss Alma, like her creator, finds the atmosphere of the gathering vaguely oppressive. Her selection of the "dangerous" poet—William Blake—for her topic, foreshadows her sexual rebellion. Without fully realizing that Blake's vision violates her tidy Puritan world, she is drawn to his lyrics because they speak to her own love and frustration. (In another scene, she quotes Oscar Wilde, before she realizes her embarrassing source.) Blake does hold the key to the hidden tiger lurking almost out of sight in the forest of Miss Alma's nature.[9] The short story out of which this play grew, "The Yellow Bird," is even clearer in its rejection of rigid Puritanism. For Williams, it became clear that the art he cherishes is rude, violent, outrageous. He believed he was called to live and think like Cassandra (in *Battle of Angels*), his early social rebel and Val Xavier, his vagrant sensualist.

Tennessee Williams believed that he could never discover his own richest potential until he rejected the anemic romanticism of his repressive, conformist home for the full-bodied romantic life of *Sturm und Drang*. In the months prior to college in 1929, he immersed himself in the biography of "Mad Shelley" and was, as Lyle Leverich tells us, "fascinated that the poet had been wild, passionate and dissolute" (99). His first escape from home came with his enrollment at the University of Missouri at Columbia, where he had a taste of independence. There, as a journalism major, he expanded his understanding of the literary romantics. We know that he read and wrote extensively, finding himself drawn to the nineteenth-century French and Russian writers.

While at Missouri, in 1930, he wrote *Beauty Is the Word* for Professor Ramsay's one-act play contest. Lyle Leverich, in *Tom: The Unknown Tennessee*,[10] notes that the play is significant "not only because its Shelleyan fervor reflects Tom's own enthusiasm for the poet but also because the theme, while not a restatement of Shelley's atheism, was Tom's first attack upon the inhibitions of Puritanism and its persecution of the artist..." In short, he was depicting "the heroism of the freethinker" (113). In a stirring speech, the heroine announces: "Fear is ugliness. God—at least *my* God—is Beauty" (Leverich, 113). Going even beyond Keats's Grecian Urn, by proclaiming that beauty is God, Williams aligned himself with the aesthetes.

The sudden conclusion to his studies at the University of Missouri in 1932, when his father angrily brought him home and put him to work in the shoe factory, reinforced his hatred of St. Louis, factories, and the industrialized world of work. The years 1932 to 1935 were a nightmare for him, the basis for numerous of his later stories and plays about life trapped in a stultifying home situation and a dead-end job. These years fixed permanently in his psyche his recurring themes of claustrophobia and the hunger for "romance." From this torturous time, he forged his image of the Poet climbing out of the factory to the roof, where he can see the sky, the stars, and the distant world. This autobiographical image, which appeared in the early play *Stairs to the Roof*, was to find its richest expression in *The Glass Menagerie*.

Working among intellectual strangers, living at home in the midst of constant hostility also reinforced his sense of loneliness. A decade later, he wrote to Audrey Wood, "Sometimes the solitary struggle of writing is almost too solitary for endurance!"[11] For him, writing was not a pleasant pastime, but an emotional hunger. It was this life of quiet desperation that demanded "redemption" by "beauty everlasting."

It was in 1936, having begun evening classes at Washington University in St. Louis, that he found companions in his quest. At the university, he was an active member of the College Poetry Society, with Clark Mills and William Jay Smith, two poets who were also dedicated to the literary life.

In addition, he found the Mummers, a small theatre group in St. Louis that provided him both company and left-wing orthodoxy typical of the thirties. Working with them, he had some of his earliest—if ephemeral—theatrical successes (*Candles to the* Sun and *The Fugitive Kind*,[12] as well as an anti-war curtainraiser for Irwin Shaw's play *Bury the Dead*, were his main contributions).

At Washington University Williams was also continuing his reading and thinking about the English romantics. There, from the distinguished Professor Otto Heller, he must have learned something of the Germanic philosophic background of the romantic movement, which Coleridge especially had found useful in the development and explication of his ideas.

Though he did frequently quote both Wordsworth and Coleridge, Williams had a pronounced inclination toward the second wave of English romantics. To have preferred not only the poetry, but also the morality of Byron, Keats, and Shelley to the more conservative Wordsworth and Coleridge would have been considered an act of rebellion at the time. (Irving Babbitt, in his famous book on Rousseau, had condemned the younger romantics as "diseased.") Others agreed that their ideas were dangerous, their lives depraved. Byron had boasted publicly (and outrageously) of having slept with two hundred women in two years. Shelley was a wife-swapper who founded a free-love colony.[13] In his twenties and beyond, Williams came to accept the romantics' rejection of "obsolete standards of family life and morality." Such celebrations of the "Cavalier" spirit delighted this rebellious puritan.

The young Tom Williams explored the bohemian world in college (after Washington University, a year at the University of Iowa, where he majored in theatre), and later in New Orleans. In 1939, having finally graduated from college, he left home for good, though he was never entirely free of the cords of love, need, and duty that continually drew him back. The young writer joined the company of fellow bohemians in New Orleans. (Later he spoke affectionately of the cities in America which were home to artists, noting Key West and San Francisco as meccas for writers and painters.[14]) There, trading his old image of the choirboy lyric writer for his new persona as the vagabond poet, Williams changed his nom de plume to "Tennessee."

In these early days, Hart Crane became his mythic hero. In the character and poetry of this modern American romantic he found a perfect mirror for his own experience:[15] the poet on the wing, hungry for the deepest experiences of life, in love with beauty and with poetry, seeking to express the ineffable. Additionally, in the outcast D. H. Lawrence, he found echoes of his own passions. (He visited Lawrence's widow, Frieda, and wrote a play about Lawrence, "I Rise in Flame, Cried the Phoenix," which pictures his unquenchable spirit.) Such latter-day romantics appealed to his faith in his art and his image of the poet as the outsider. They also helped him to define his own experience, give form to his very real passions.

Decades later, having embraced the "Bitch Goddess Success," he found he was increasingly disgusted with himself and his world. He explored authors who had always interested him and who gave voice to his disillusionment: Proust, Baudelaire, and Rimbaud—French neo-romantic symbolists.[16] Plays such as *The Night of the Iguana*, *Suddenly Last Summer*, or *Sweet Bird of Youth* have clear ties to these artists. His defrocked priest, decadent poet, and obsolescent artist are painful reminders of the fierce romantics he had celebrated earlier. Far more decadent than the English romantics, these *fin de siècle* French writers mirrored Williams's own declivity. Rimbaud, a recent critic commented, was noted for: "Furiously hallucinogenic imagery (fueled by hashish and absinthe), bourgeoisie-skewering rudeness, mysticism, proud bisexuality and an adolescent taste for despair."[17] By 1969, Williams himself had sunk into the world of drugs, writing fragments of stories that tended toward fantasy. This trend was foreshadowed as early as the 1948 story of "The Poet," when the vat of mysterious fermented drink fuels the poet's ecstasies and the young followers' orgiastic celebration (246).

Williams's influences became increasingly eclectic. In love with the exotic, he was enamored of Eastern mysticism and Asian dramatic forms. This astonished Williams's fans when they saw *The Milktrain Doesn't Stop Here Anymore*, with Flora dressed in a ceremonial Kabuki costume and the final spotlight on the Angel of Death's mysteriously lighted mobile. The Japanese writer Mishima Yukio was a friend and an especially important influence.[18] He and Williams first met in the sixties, discovered they shared a publisher and tastes in life and art; they considered themselves soul mates. In 1970, Williams traveled to Asia, visiting with Mishima (though not with his traditional family in his home) and saw him shortly before his suicide.[19]

Other neo-romantics, like William Butler Yeats, added to Tennessee Williams's allusions, his worldview, and his imagery. He was an aesthetically adventurous writer who read voraciously and traveled constantly, exploring many regions and ideas. Even those he chose to designate or quote are by no means the only ones who inspired him. To the very end of his life, he was insatiable—reading the latest books, seeing the new plays, experimenting with new styles. Some of his most experimental pieces are yet to be published.

Tennessee Williams's early love of romantic poetry was to leave a deep mark on his plays and stories: poetic speech became his signature. Critics were regularly impressed by the lyricism of his drama.

THESE "BLESSED HANDS": WILLIAMS AS AN INSPIRED WRITER

> The poet distilled his own liquor and had become so accomplished in this art that he could produce a fermented drink from almost any kind of organic matter. He carried it in a flask strapped about his waist, and whenever fatigue overtook him he would stop at some lonely point and raise the flask to his lips. Then the world would change color as a soap bubble penetrated by a ray of light and a great vitality would surge and break as a limitless ocean through him. The usual superfluity of the impressions would fall away so that his senses would combine in a single vast ray of perception which blinded him to lesser phenomena and experience as candles might be eclipsed in a chamber of glass exposed to a cloudless meridian of the sun. ("The Poet," 746)

This visionary poet's experience parallels Wordsworth's "spots of time" in "The Prelude." In this extended autobiographical poem, Wordsworth also described himself as "the Poet." He thought that his writing was "emotion recollected in tranquillity"—an idea Williams frequently quoted and occasionally experienced. As he said, his writing was rarely a result of tranquil recollection. He was far more inclined to the "spontaneous overflow of powerful feeling." In any case, inspiration is essential to the true romantic. Although Williams used real details of his individual experience and dreams, he could not create without this mysterious gift from the muses. This explains Williams's assertion that writing was a *vocation* for him. He had no choice, as his biography clearly demonstrates. During his prolonged apprenticeship in writing, he borrowed, begged, and sponged off friends and family; he signed on for one subsistence-level job after another, rarely holding any for more than a few months—long enough to allow him to survive. Any other work seemed irrelevant in the face of this calling to be a writer. Even writing for the films, in 1943, when he spent six months with MGM, was too artificial and claustrophobic for this free spirit.

Perhaps as a result of spending his first years intimately connected with the Episcopal Church, hearing the language of spiritual leadership, he believed that poetry was a high calling. Over and over, he said that "work" was his favorite four-letter word. It was certainly central to his concept of integrity. He thought no sexual or contractual violation so corrupt as the betrayal of his art or the abandonment of his writing.

Like Coleridge, Tennessee Williams sensed this power of inspiration rushing through him. His references to the wind and his love of wind chimes[20] blend romantic with Pentecostal wind imagery. (Consider "Ode to the West Wind" and "Aeolian Harp" as romantic precedents). When this inspiration faltered, he followed the path of Hart Crane, Coleridge, and de Quincey, using sex, drugs, and alcohol to induce an artificial ecstasy.

Tennessee Williams was a latter-day incarnation of Plato's Poet-as-Inspired-Madman. Biographies and character sketches note the artist writing with a frenzy that astonished visitors. He laughingly said he was not a writer but a compulsive typist. His letters testify to his demonic attack on typewriters, which frequently broke under his constant pounding. Landladies were reluctant to disturb the piles of crumpled paper they found littering the floor where he worked. Scholars find themselves puzzling at the various pages on different papers, unnumbered, often written on different machines.[21] He could work on several pieces at a time, blending in his fertile imagination bits of experience, remembered poetry, phrases he had heard on the street, and images from his reading. Like Coleridge, as described in *The Road to Xanadu* (by John Livingston Lowes), Williams read widely, especially when considering writing about actual people. For example, when working on the life of Lindsay, he read E. L. Masters's life; he spent a long time reading about D. H. Lawrence for a long Lawrence play he finally abandoned. As a result of reading the latest books on Zelda Fitzgerald, which Andreas Brown, the owner of the Gotham Book Mart, had sent him along with other books, knowing of his interest in the Fitzgeralds and Hemingway, Williams was inspired to write *Clothes for a Summer Hotel*. But the magic moment of creativity came not in an intellectual mixing of notes into a coherent thesis, but in the powerful act of chemical fusion that took place in the "deep well" of the unconscious.

Also, in the mode of the true romantic spirit, he never considered a work completely finished. He would attend rehearsals, watch the movement, listen to the sound of the lines delivered on stage, and then revise whole sections, crossing out scenes, revising movement, adding dialogue. Many of his plays exist in variant editions; even when published, they were not complete—largely because they were not satisfactory copies of the Platonic image in his mind. ("The Yellow Bird," then *Summer and Smoke*, evolved into *The Eccentricities of a Nightingale*; *Battle of Angels* metamorphosed into *Orpheus Descending*; *Confessional* grew into *Small Craft Warnings*; and "Three Players of a Summer Game" became *Cat on a Hot Tin Roof*, which had at least two possible third acts.)

The real drive of the romantic is to give form to the individual God-given vision. Like most romantics, Tennessee Williams wrote most powerfully when he worked "inside out." Whether describing his own adventures as a young artist, his mother's pain, his sister's tragedy, or his father's incomprehension, Williams was at his best when his subject was the Dakin/Williams family. He knew that the written words always fell short of the noetic experience; thus his ideal poet avoided freezing his ideas by fixing them on paper, preferring to keep them fluid ("The Poet," 247). Later, he was able to expand this family circle to include theatre people and homeless wanderers, all of whom shared his own values and anguish.

Like the Wandering Jew or the Ancient Mariner, the Williams hero is the lonely stranger who bears a mark setting him apart from other men—a special hunger, an unsatisfied need. Handsome and cursed, he dominates the stage as he does the community. He is the sun to their moons of desire ("One Arm"). A non-conformist, he must speak his outrageous Truth, facing turmoil, expulsion, and death. The Poet (of the short story) is washed by the sea and bleached by the sun until he is finally free of the corrupting flesh.

Tennessee Williams, a child of the Church, born during Passion Week, readily commingled aesthetic and religious mysticism, eroding barriers between art and faith. His imagery of the Poet is frequently laced with references to Christ. Sometimes disciples, the "women," the Pharisees, the Sanhedrin, and the mob elaborate this Williams Christology. Variants on the Crucifixion are common in his work. At one point, when discussing *The Night of the Iguana* with Bob MacGregor, his editor at New Directions, he noted he had "Too many Christ-figures in my work, too cornily presented." He asked that MacGregor remove the extraneous one he had written into Shannon's first entrance description.[22]

Like the brooding Byron, Williams's Poet/Wanderer is a magnet to women. Whether he is the virile farmer in *Seven Descents of Myrtle* or the anguished defrocked preacher in *The Night of the Iguana*, this outcast hero marches to the beat of his own drummer. A creature of flesh, he attracts the lust of others, but needs more than the flesh for his satisfaction. Female characters too—Blanche and Alma—express this tormented dualism, hunger for sexual contact, subsequent self-loathing, and loneliness. They love poetry, cherish an impossible idealism, and despise their own physical needs.

The conflict of the spirit and the flesh is a central agony for the romantic artist: the act of creation is a mystical process of conception, pregnancy, and birth—an aesthetic Incarnation. As the Word was planted by God in the Virgin, so the Idea is the seed planted by Inspiration in the poet—e.g., Sebastian spent nine months nurturing each perfect poem. The eventual birth, after a fierce and painful time of labor, brings forth a creature separate from the bearer. It then takes on a public life of its own, over which the writer/parent has no control. The "incubus in his bosom" ("The Poet," 248) was both natural and invasive, demanding development regardless of the contrary will of the artist.

For Tennessee Williams, the "blessedness" of the artist is also his ironic source of damnation or torment. From the guitar-playing hobo of the Depression-era Delta to the contemporary All American, the Williams hero is unprotected by family, uncomfortable with companions. He inevitably draws hostility. Torn apart by dogs, blowtorched, castrated, or cannibalized, the Williams fugitive is finally chased to earth and destroyed in a catastrophic finale.

THE MYSTERY OF COLOR:
THE ROMANTIC PORTRAYAL OF REALITY

Transforming human experience into art, showing the complexity of human life on stage, was the ultimate challenge for Williams. Whether named Valentine Xavier, Kilroy, Chance Wayne, or Sebastian, the Williams mythic protagonist is a romanticized persona exploring and explaining facets of the artist himself. Williams acknowledged that he never developed a character who did not contain some quality of his own personality elaborated and developed for theatrical purposes.

Basing his dramas on his own anguished life, Tennessee Williams often portrayed the male/female attraction/conflict. The masculine/feminine identity, the need to individuate the growing personality, the love/hate conflicts of the family. Over time, he increasingly moved toward a more subtle symbolic use of multiple facets of human complexity. In *The Night of the Iguana*, for example, the virgin and the widow become spirit and flesh, as well as fully conceived characters. Shannon's good and bad angels demand he choose between two diametrically opposed visions of the future. The ending cannot be happy for him, for either choice demands the rejection of a part of his psyche.

An even more complex vision of the human psyche appears in *Out Cry* with the brother and sister, both of ambivalent gender, who appear to be two sides of a single person, the animus/anima. Williams acknowledges freely his belief in the dual nature of the artist, or at least his kind of romantic artist. Like Alma, Williams believed himself to be a double person, referring frequently to his "doppleganger" or his "blue devils," and to his double vision as "something cloudy, something clear."

In organic writing, the passionate manuscript grows naturally from the passionate life. Williams thereby felt justified in following Millay's caustic advice to burn his candle at both ends. He craved the intensely experienced moment, full of color, variety, and violence. Like Keats, he believed that he must "drink deep" in order to feel the full range of emotions. In himself and in others, Williams cherished the youthful sense of wonder that Keats characterized in "On First Looking into Chapman's Homer." Williams's central characters search for that "surprise" that leaves them "breathless upon a peak in Darien." Without this capacity for breaking out of his own body in the "rapture of vision," life is only another form of death.

In *Small Craft Warnings*, the young man from Iowa—an echo of the youthful Williams on his 1939 trip West—delights in his first view of the Pacific Ocean. The older scriptwriter—a reference to Williams in 1943 during his MGM period—sadly notes that he has lost that quality of amazement. The later works of Williams have the melancholy cast of the romantic who has outlived his childhood to become a sour stoic. The old doctor in *Small Craft Warnings*—painfully underscored by the playwright's brief appearance in the role himself—has lost even the ability to deliver the live child, much less to conceive one. In a sad letter he wrote to his friend and editor, Robert MacGregor from Key West in 1960, he said he was weary of writing but could not stop. "I am like old Aw Boo Ha, the tiger balm king of the Orient who kept building and building his palaces and gardens till they became grotesque because a fortune-teller told him that he would die when he stopped." *Small Craft Warnings, Moise and the World of Reason, Something Cloudy, Something Clear* all contain double or even triple images of the poet, the young man and the old, reflecting what Tennessee Williams called "corruption."

Over the years, as his idealism was tempered with reality, he learned to balance the lyricism with cynical descants, giving up his "early genius" for "the telling of marvelous stories" ("The Poet," 247). He found a mature voice in the subtle textures of human existence, the interplay of personalities, the "net" of words. He loved bold contrasts, startling climaxes, angry confrontations. In his delight with language, he indulged in the juxtaposition of romantic rhetoric with realistic put-down. When Blanche speaks of "Mr. Edgar Allan Poe," Stanley quotes Huey Long, a notorious Louisiana politician of the era. When Amanda refers to her skill in the "art of conversation," Tom laughingly acknowledges that she "sure can talk." Realism intrudes on the dreamer in the Williams drama, as it did in his life.

In a letter to Audrey Wood,[23] he clarified this trend for her and for himself. At the time, he was transforming *Battle of Angels* into *Orpheus Descending*. Apparently, Audrey, always a tough critic for her client/friend, did not have an immediately enthusiastic reaction. He tells her that he too was bothered by the earlier "juvenile poetics, the inflated style" and was seeking to "bring it down to earth," to give the character "a tougher, more realistic treatment." He notes that Cassandra was too "hi-faluting" in the original: "Behold Cassandra, shouting doom at the gates!" He notes that "all that sort of crap ... seemed so lovely to me in 1940. Unfortunately in 1940 I was younger and stronger and—curiously!—more confident writer than I am in the Fall of 1953. Now I am a maturer and more knowledgeable craftsman of the theatre, my experience inside and outside the profession is vastly wider..." But he still insists that some lyrical passages are justified by "heightened emotion." "It's only on rare occasions that our hearts are uncovered and their voices released and that's when poetry comes and the deepest emotion, and expression ... I think they should have this contrast to the coarse common speech. The coarseness is deliberate and serves a creative purpose which is not sensational." (He justified the use of Kilroy in *Camino Real* in similar terms in a letter to Audrey Wood, February, 1946.) He concludes his long defense by insisting that, "Despite the coarse touches in the dialogue, I think the total effect of the play would be one of tragic purity..." This powerful letter reveals that Williams deliberately shifted levels of diction to match the dramatic flow of the play. He was a craftsman as well as a visionary.

The plot patterns of the plays reflect this romantic/realistic duality more effectively than do the stories and the other fiction. "Realistic" drama forced him to conform to recognizable, though exaggerated and compressed, human experience and dialogue. Even his dream visions have touches of reality when shaped for the stage. Short stories and novellas, by contrast, do not constrain the artist in the same way, freeing him to indulge his taste for magic realism. While Alma in *Summer and Smoke* is obliged to sit beneath the fountain's angel and pick up a traveling salesman, the more "magical" Alma in the short story of "The Yellow Bird" can bear a beautiful child who rides off on the back of a dolphin and returns with a cornucopia of treasure.

THE MESSAGE OF ART: COMMUNICATING WILLIAMS'S WORLD-VIEW

"We are all of us sentenced to solitary confinement in our own skins," says Val—and Tennessee. The barriers, walls, curtains in his plays signal the solitude of the individual and the difficulties of communication. Characters retreat to their cells only to meet briefly in bars or restaurants. Like Leibniz's monads, they are isolated, with minimal contact or insight.

The Poet, unable to bear this silence and solitude, is driven to communicate "the presence of something beyond the province of matter" ("The Poet," 251). Williams believed that writers are the messengers of transcendence, informing humanity that humdrum life behind the plow is not the full story. Poets help people to took towards heaven.

For Tennessee Williams, the world was the scene of epic battles—between the Flesh and the Spirit, Good and Evil, God and Satan, Gentle Jesus and Terrifying Jehovah. Unlike the more cynical post-Christian postmoderns, he insisted on the cyclorama as the background for his plays. A sweep of sky and sea, a rainforest; sounds of thunderstorms, lightning, and wind are all signals of God's sovereign power, dwarfing the human activities front and center in our consciousness. This brief moment on the stage of life is not the whole story; our choices here and now define humanity existentially.

In his multilayered creations, nothing is simple: the iguana is not just a small, ugly reptile; it represents mankind in the hands of an angry God. The turtles racing for the sea are not simply evidence of nature's prodigious wastefulness, they are symbols of humanity in the face of an avenging deity. For this child of the Church, each drama is a bit of symbolic action played out under the watchful eye of heaven. The youthful hours Tom Williams spent studying the stained glass windows of St. George's Episcopal Church in Clarksdale, Mississippi, reading the scripture passages, repeating the words of the services were not wasted. Although he rarely went into a church in his later years (even after his conversion to Catholicism in 1969) he did acknowledge that the mass at the local cathedral was more powerful drama than he could ever write. The historic bonds between the Church and the theatre were quite real to him.

Even the most bestial of people in the most superficial relationships feel the need to make connections, discovering moments of grace that are breathtaking. In *The Night of the Iguana*, Shannon and Hannah, who listen to the final lines of Nonno's sonnet have a magic moment of communication. In "The Mutilated," two old women in a seedy hotel room in the Vieux Carré discuss a vision of the Virgin and share a glass of Tokay wine and a Nabisco wafer. Such moments of grace are emanations of transcendence.

This three-storied universe gave Williams's work a remarkable range. In *Summer and Smoke*, he knew he was creating a medieval play with modern twists. In a letter to Audrey Wood he noted that it had a "... sort of Gothic quality—spiritually romantic—which I wanted to create. It is hard for you to use such stuff in a modern play for a modern audience, but I feel it is valid."[24]

Although both heaven and hell were part of his three-storied universe, they were romantic interpretations of the medieval cosmology. Echoing William Blake, Williams spoke of "Innocence" and "Experience" as polar opposites. He also saw that heaven was hell and hell was heaven in the topsy-turvy world of materialistic dreams. Sharing Wordsworth's concept of the innocent child ("Ode on Intimations of Immortality") Tennessee Williams fully believed that he had come into this world "trailing clouds of glory."

Like Wordsworth and Blake, he saw growing up as a process of losing innocence and joy. His poetry and stories are full of images of free children leaping over fences, gamboling in wild nature, drunk with imagination and delight—like those who follow his "Poet." Childhood for him was the halcyon age of Edenic wholeness. He was by nature a follower of Rousseau. No Calvinist, he could not believe that the loss of innocence was a result of sin. Rather it was the fault of society, which refused to allow the child to remain free of fetters. Armies and factories finally claimed the children, pulling them "home," safe from the song of the Poet. Their voices were stilled.

Living in an era bombarded with the ideas of Freud, Williams came to see the discovery of sexuality—the moment the child realized he or she was naked—as the end of innocence. In *The Night of the Iguana*, Shannon explains his own anger at his mother's furious interruption of his childish masturbation. Her assertion that she spoke for God in her unequivocal judgment was sufficient cause for the child to resent both the parent and the deity.

In innocent love scenes like those in *The Rose Tattoo*, *Battle of Angels*, and "A Field of Blue Children," Williams echoes Keats's portrayal of the lovers caught in the moment of anticipation in the frieze on the Grecian Urn or melting into delight in "The Eve of St. Agnes." Following their natural inclinations, untroubled by the nasty-minded puritan culture, the young lovers enjoy fully the prelapsarian spirit of joy in sharing their bodies with one another.

This world and its people are doomed to final destruction. From beginning to end, from *Battle of Angels* to *The Red Devil Battery Sign*, his was an apocalyptic vision.

REDEMPTION BY BEAUTY: ROMANTIC FORM

Like the English romantics, Williams loved lyric poetry. Like them, he adored Shakespeare, but unlike most of the playwrights of the great ages of romanticism, he did not restrict his theatre to poetic closet dramas. It is a tribute to Williams's genius that, in spite of his romanticism, he was able to craft plays that were meant for the stage.

He blended the melodramatic form of the nineteenth century with contemporary realities, counterbalancing the exuberant hyperbole with ironic litotes. Thus Blanche DuBois can wear her feather boa, but Stanley Kowalski, in his undershirt, will sneer at her pretenses at "royalty." A grand old actress, like the Princess Alexandra del Lago, can demand and command, but she knows that she is pathetic rather than tragic, pretentious rather than real. Their exotic names, their large gestures, their taste for rhetoric and overwrought scenes place them solidly in the grand style of the romantics. Yet Williams was enough of a realist to acknowledge their faults, to undercut their theatricalism with irony, but he loved to produce them for our entertainment.

In a beautiful letter to Brooks Atkinson (Key West, 2TLS, "June 7 or 8, 1953"), Williams expressed his gratitude to this faithful old critic for understanding his vision of the theatre. Atkinson, the *New York Times* reviewer, was one of the few who understood what *Camino Real* was really about and expressed his disappointment at its weak reception. Williams insisted that it was written as a "communion with people." "Preserving it on paper isn't enough," he said, "a published play is only the shadow of one and not even a clear shadow. The colors, the music, the grace, the levitation, the quick inter-play of live beings suspended like fitful lightning in a cloud, those things are the play, not words, certainly not words on paper and certainly not any thoughts or ideas of an author, those shabby things snatched off basement counters at Gimbel's." He then goes on to refer to the speech in *The Doctor's Dilemma*, of which he can no longer remember a line. But he does remember that, when he heard it, he thought, "Yes, that's what it is, not words, not thoughts or ideas, but those abstract things such as form and light and color that living things are made of." One of his most lacerating letters in response to a critic was written when Williams thought that Walter Kerr had missed all of the music, color, dance, and theatricality of *Camino Real*. He had missed "the great plastic richness" and the consequent demands on the whole troupe of performers and practitioners. (A copy of the letter, unsigned, undated, and probably unsent, is in the Billy Rose Theatre Collection at Lincoln Center.)

Given Williams's romantic rejection of traditional controls and forced conventions, it is hardly surprising that he would have espoused this dynamic form.[25] From his earliest critical comments, printed as a preface to *The Glass Menagerie*, Williams rejected the realistic theatre with its fourth-wall conventions. His letters are full of passionate pleas to actors, directors, producers not to subvert the poetry of his plays. He had a vision of the theatre as lively painting, poetry in motion; he loved color, dance, and music. Although he mentioned his admiration of Aristotelian form—especially the unities—he felt no compulsion to conform to classic or neoclassical principles of dramaturgy. He preferred to explore his own patterns. Like Pirandello, he was fascinated by the process of perception, the multiple meanings of reality. He enjoyed underscoring the primary role of the artist by showing the dreamer as well as the dream. In *Camino Real*, Don Quixote introduces his vision of the Royal Road that has become the Real Road. Tom Wingfield explains that *The Glass Menagerie* is a "memory" play and that the memory is his.

Perhaps it was an element of his basic comedic view of life that brought this doubleness to his drama. Like Shakespeare with his plays-within-plays, Williams liked to set the narrator outside the drama, thereby allowing an ironic counterpoint to the melodrama of the tale. Tom, like the artist, stands inside the story and outside it simultaneously. Inside, his voice is personal—angry and loving; outside, it is analytic—it is dry and ironic. At the beginning of *The Glass Menagerie*, the Narrator-Tom presses the audience to see the story as a part of the world picture; later he draws attention to himself as a Stage Magician; and finally, he demands our sympathy as he leaves the doomed women to blow from place to place like leaves from Shelley's "Ode to the West Wind." Like other framing devices that Williams used in early plays, the Narrator underscores the play as a play, a presentational device designed to disorient the audience.

Williams's experiments in presentational drama—*Camino Real* as Don Quixote's dream, *Battle of Angels* as a memory play set in a museum, *Out Cry* as the fragment of a clouded memory being reconstructed as it is acted and viewed—were challenges to the popular realistic play with its fourth-wall convention. Williams pressed the artist's "God-like freedom" in the act of creation, able to destroy the illusion at will by calling attention to it as an illusion.[26] This acting-out of the role of the Promethean rebel-as-artist continued to the extent of deconstructing the play as it is being presented. This climaxed in *Out Cry*, where the characters tease out the different levels of illusion and reality as they suffer through their genuine distress.

This fiction of non-control, which is the mark of romantic irony, produces a work riddled with unresolved ambiguities, in which the artist creates a sense of his own inability to master his recalcitrant materials.[27] Thus, we watch Felice-the-actor worrying about the absence of the production crew, Felice-the-character involved in the action of the play, and Felice-the-writer arguing with Clare about the actual events from which the play derived. At the end, the deliberate decision to reenter the world-of-the-play in order to escape the world of the make-believe-theatre is painfully ironic and clearly ridiculous, but somehow right. As Furst notes, without grounding in external reality, we enter the hall of mirrors, "plunged into the persona's paradoxes, ambivalences, ironies, and schizophrenic dualisms..." (33). Williams-the-relativist welcomes this opportunity to force the audience to join him in the curious quest of the romantic, ultimately a quest of the imagination. His imagery of the legless bird is a fitting symbol of the artist who rejects the solid grounding in reality. The flight ends only with death.

The life on stage was for Tennessee Williams an image of the human condition, not simply a chronicle of individual experience. His was a mythic vision, involving people with allusive names, performing ritual actions in the "circle of light." Taking his cue from the Church, he transformed the stage into an altar and the play into a ritual. He allowed no limits on the creator-artist or his claims for his prophetic role. It is no wonder he wrote of that "visionary company." For him, no human was more valuable, on earth or in heaven, than the Artist.

In those last plays, the poetry diminished, the experience of life dimmed, the characters pressed into pitiful choices. But like the Ancient Mariner, the compulsive old playwright continued to fix us with his glittering eye and tell us his compelling tale of the voyage, the violation, the pain, and the aching hunger to expiate his sin. His hands no longer seemed so blessed, his message grew blurred, he saw more of life as ugly, but he never lost faith in the redemptive power of beauty.

As the sweet bird of youth finally flew out of sight, and Williams grew to be an "old alligator," in letters to friends he insisted that he was still a romantic—though now a senile one.[28] One of the saddest pieces of writing in the Harvard Collection is an unfinished letter to the actors in what he called his "last long play for Broadway," asserting that this play was "intransigently romantic." He concluded by saying that, though now an old man, he still responded to the "cry of the players." (1TLS, N.P., N.D.)

NOTES

1. The phrasing is from Shaw's play *The Doctor's Dilemma*, quoted in Tennessee Williams, "Afterword to *Camino Real*," in *Where I Live: Selected Essays* (New York: New Directions, 1978), 69.

2. See, for example, the letter from Tennessee Williams to Audrey Wood, 2TLS, Laguna Beach, CA, June, 1939, in which he identified himself with Vachel Lindsay and provided a lengthy description of a proposed script (Harry Ransom Humanities Research Collection—hereafter HRHRC—University of Texas, Austin).

3. Lillian Furst, *The Contours of European Romanticism* (Lincoln: The University of Nebraska Press, 1979), 3.

4. Tennessee Williams to Audrey Wood, 3TLS, NP [Probably Laguna Beach, CA], May 5, 1939. HRHRC, Austin.

5. Albert J. Devlin, ed., *Conversations with Tennessee Williams* (Jackson, Mississippi: University Press of Mississippi, 1986).

6. This rough draft document entitled "The Visionary Company" is part of the Williams collection at HRHRC, Austin, Texas. I have silently corrected some typographical errors.

7. Lyle Leverich, *Tom: The Unknown Life of Tennessee Williams* (New York: Crown, 1995), 44, describes Senator John Sharp Williams, who was noted for his comic stories as well as his rhetoric.

8 ."Preface to My Poems," in *Where I Live: Selected Essays*, 1 (reprinted from *Five Young American Poets*).

9. See the discussion of Blake and the other romantics in Lawrence S. Lockridge's *The Ethics of Romanticism* (Cambridge University Press, 1989), 22 ff.

10. It is interesting that Lyle Leverich constructs his impressive work in terms of a romantic search, entitling chapters: "Lodestar," "Moonward," "Outer Space," "Wanderings," and "New Harbors." All of these are images of the journey, a standard romantic image.

11. Tennessee Williams to Audrey Wood, 1TLS, Nantucket, July 29, 1946. HRHRC, Austin.

12. This is a different play from the later *Fugitive Kind*, a version of *Battle of Angels*. New Directions plans to publish several of these early plays within the next few years.

13. Alan Ehrenhalt, *The Lost City: Discovering the Forgotten Virtues of Community in the Chicago of the 1950's* (New York: HarperCollins, 1995).

14 .Tennessee Williams, "Home to Key West," in *Where I Live*, 160.

15. See *Hart Crane and the Image of the Voyage*, a work which reveals any number of parallels to Tennessee Williams's life and thought.

16. Tennessee Williams's letters to Margo Jones (in the HRHRC, Austin) in the mid-sixties already mention his regular reading of these authors. Jay Laughlin sometimes shipped him boxes of books that were his own favorites. In return, Williams sent Laughlin materials on Crane, including biographies he thought interesting. (The Laughlin letters are soon to be published at New Directions.)

17. Janet Maslin, in a review of *Total Eclipse*, entitled "Rimbaud: Portrait of the Artist as a Young Boor," in the *New York Times*, November 3, 1995, C–14. Maslin notes that Rimbaud is the source of much contemporary popular culture, including Bob Dylan, Jim Morrison, and Patti Smith.

18. For a full description of Mishima's romanticism, see Susan Jolliffe Napier's *Escape from the Wasteland, Romanticism and Realism in the Fiction of Mishima Yukio and Oe Kenzaburo* (Cambridge, MA: Harvard University Press, 1991).

19. Allean Hale has discovered a "secret" Noh play that Williams wrote as a tribute to Mishima. Williams referred to "The Mutilated" as a "Yes Play" in one typescript version in the Billy Rose Theatre Collection.

20. He thanked Donald Windham for the gift of wind chimes and mentioned them in letters to others as well.

21. See, for example, Lyle Leverich's account of the room in which he lived when he first moved to Key West and lived at the Trade Winds, or Allean Hale's description of the papers she discovered to be his "Secret Manuscript," a Noh Play.

22. See letter from TW to Robert MacGregor, March 27, 1963, in the New Directions Archive.

23. Tennessee Williams to Audrey Wood, 3TLS, from Tangiers, October 14, 1953 HRHRC, Austin.

24. Tennessee Williams to Audrey Wood, 1TLS, from Nantucket, July 29, 1946. HRHRC, Austin.

25. René Welleck, in *Concepts of Criticism*, speaks of the romantics' use of dynamism, organic form, and change. See Furst, 8.

26. Furst, 27.

27. Furst, 31.

28. Tennessee Williams to Oliver Evans, 1TLS, from Rome, July 10, 1971. The Houghton Library at Harvard University.

BIBLIOGRAPHY

Abrams, Mark. *The Mirror and the Lamp*. London: Oxford University Press, 1953.

Barzun, Jacques. *Romanticism and the Modern Ego*. Boston: Little, Brown, 1944.

———. *Classic, Romantic and Modern*. Garden City, New York: Doubleday, 1961.

Bate, Walter Jackson. *From Classic to Romantic*. Cambridge: Cambridge University Press, 1946.

Combs, Robert. *Vision of the Voyage: Hart Crane and the Psychology of Romanticism*. Memphis State University Press, 1978.

Cranston, Maurice. *The Romantic Movement*. Oxford: Blackwell, 1994.

Driver, Tom. *Romantic Quest and Modern Query*. New York: Delacorte Press, 1970.

Furst, Lillian R. *The Contours of European Romanticism*. Lincoln: University of Nebraska Press, 1979.

Lovejoy, Arthur O. *The Great Chain of Being. A Study of the History of an Idea*. New York: Harper & Row, 1936.

Praz, Mario. *The Romantic Agony*. New York: The World Publishing Co. 1933.

BERT CARDULLO

The Blue Rose of St. Louis: Laura, Romanticism, and The Glass Menagerie

Laura Wingfield of *The Glass Menagerie* hardly qualifies as a Romantic superwoman, a majestic ego eager to transcend the "mereness" of mundane human existence. In his narration of the drama at the same time as he plays a part in it, together with his final, self-centered leavetaking from the domestic misery-cum-ménage of his mother and sister, Tom owns that role. But Laura does represent the kind of person for whom the Romantics of the early nineteenth century felt increasing sympathy: the fragile, almost unearthly ego brutalized by life in the industrialized, overpopulated, depersonalized cities of the Western world.

This physically as well as emotionally fragile woman of almost twenty-four escapes from her mid-twentieth century urban predicament in St. Louis, as someone of Romantic temperament would, through art and music through the beauty of her glass menagerie and of the records she plays on her Victrola. Moreover, although she failed to graduate from high school, Laura fondly remembers a choral class she took with Gentleman Jim O'Connor and the three performances of *The Pirates of Penzance* in which he sang the baritone lead. And instead of attending Rubicam's Business College, as her mother had planned, this high-school dropout went daily to "the art museum and the bird houses at the Zoo.... Lately I've been spending most of my afternoons in the Jewel Box, that big glass house where they raise tropical flowers" (33).

From *The Tennessee Williams Annual Review* 1998: pp. 81–92. © 1998 by *The Tennessee Williams Annual Review*.

Like a Romantic, then, Laura has a love for Nature in addition to Art—a nature that is artfully memorialized in her collection of little animals made of glass, and that is painfully absent from the area surrounding the Wingfield apartment, which Williams describes as "one of those vast hive-like conglomerations of cellular living units that flower as warty growths in overcrowded urban centers of lower middle-class population" (21). Indeed, even Laura's name signifies her affinity for the natural together with the transcendent: "Laura" is somewhat ironically derived from the laurel shrub or tree, a wreath of which was conferred as a mark of honor in ancient times upon dramatic poets, military heroes, and athletic victors; and "Wingfield" brings to mind the flight of birds across a meadow and on up into the sky.

Jim's nickname for Laura, "Blue Roses," itself signifies her affinity for the natural—flowers—together with the transcendent—*blue* flowers, which do not occur naturally and thus come to symbolize her yearning for both ideal or mystical beauty and spiritual or romantic love. That beauty is also symbolized by Laura's favorite among the animals in her glass menagerie, the fabled, otherworldly unicorn, as well as by the place where Laura has spent many of her afternoons, the Jewel Box, and what she saw there: tropical flowers, which could be said to come from another world, and which can survive in St. Louis only by being placed in the artificial environment of a hothouse. And that love comes to her, however fleetingly, in the person of her namer, Jim O'Connor, who beatifies Laura by emphasizing what is special, even divine, about her and downplaying her physical disability. He opines:

> A little physical defect is what you have. Hardly noticeable even!
> ... You know what my strong advice to you is? Think of yourself
> as *superior* in some way! ... Why, man alive, Laura! Just look about
> you a little. What do you see? A world full of common people! ...
> Which of them has one-tenth of your good points! Or mine! Or
> anyone else's, as far as that goes—gosh! Everybody excels in some
> one thing. Some in many! (99)

In this speech Jim adopts a Romantic-subjective view of human creation, as opposed to a naturalistic, deterministic, objective one—ironically so, because he himself appears to be one of the common people with his freckle face, flat or scant nose, and mundane job in the same shoe factory where Tom works, and also because, in his aspiration to become a television engineer, he identifies himself with the utilitarian world of mathematics and machines. Nonetheless, Jim echoes here the same sentiment expressed by Amanda when she misunderstands Tom's own rather Romantic notion of instinct and declares that Christian adults want "Superior things! Things of the mind and the spirit! Only animals have to satisfy instincts!" (52). Just as surely, Amanda wanted the same "superior things" when she was a debutante in the Mississippi Delta being courted by the sons of plantation owners, but this Daughter of the American Revolution settled instead for marriage to a "commoner" who worked for the telephone company.

Such a union between a woman of superior if by then effete heritage and a man of lower social status yet vital animalism, or let us say the psychosexual conquest of the former by the latter, is the subject of the book of Tom's that his mother returns against his will to the library, D. H. Lawrence's *Lady Chatterley's Lover*. Amanda dismisses its heady, equal mixture of Freud and Darwin as the filthy output of a diseased mind, but one can surmise that its obscenity is not the only aspect of this novel that troubles her. Her stated idea of a good read is naturally *Gone with the Wind*, Margaret Mitchell's mythic romance of the Old South, the Civil War, and Reconstruction, in which at one point the wellborn Scarlett O'Hara kills a vulgar Yankee intruder who would rape her.

The workaday Jim O'Connor, of course, has no intention of sexually subjugating or psychologically dominating Laura Wingfield. On the contrary, he idealizes rather than reifies her by placing her on a pedestal and equating this young woman with a blue rose. In so identifying Laura, Jim unwittingly recalls that widely recognized Romantic symbol of longing for the infinite, of unrequited yearning for absolute emotional and artistic fulfillment: the blue flower, drawn from the representative novel of early German Romanticism, Novalis' *Heinrich von Ofterdingen* (1802). This prose romance in two books is about the evolution of a young poet of great potential—in this case, a legendary medieval poet and master singer. It chronicles his apprenticeship to his art and search for the archetypal symbol, the blue flower, which had appeared to him in a dream.

For Heinrich, this flower comes to represent not only his artistic longing but also his loving fiancée, who has mysteriously died by the time the second book of the novel begins; this book, never finished by Novalis, was to have shown Heinrich von Ofterdingen's transfiguration into a poet, even as the first book depicted his preparation for the artistic vocation. Similarly, *The Glass Menagerie* is about the evolution (if not the artistic maturation) of the poet Tom—a man in his early twenties who is not by accident given by Jim the nickname of "Shakespeare," one of the heroes of the Romantic movement. *The Glass Menagerie* is also about Tom's effort, through the art of this play, both to find himself and to rediscover or memorialize his beloved sister, a blue flower in human form. The character of Tom, of course, is based in part on Tennessee Williams himself, whose given name was Thomas, even as Laura is modeled after Williams's only sister—Rose.

Laura herself happens to think that "blue is wrong for—roses" (106), but Jim insists that it is right for her because she's pretty "in a very different way from anyone else.... The different people are not like other people, but ... other people are not [so] wonderful. They're one hundred times one thousand. You're one times one! They walk all over the earth. You just stay here. They're common as—weeds, but—you—well, you're—*Blue Roses!*" (105). As her gentleman caller speaks, Laura is aptly bathed in the soft light coming from the new floor lamp her mother has especially purchased for the occasion—a lamp covered by a shade of rose-colored silk that helps to bring out her "fragile, unearthly prettiness" (85)—and she stands before the living-room sofa, suitably framed by its equally new pair of blue pillows. Moreover, Jim's words are reinforced by the image of blue roses projected onto a screen or section of wall between the living- and dining-room areas of the Wingfield apartment.

Laura is indeed different, as Jim maintains, but her difference stems from her physical frailty in addition to her fragile prettiness—both of which are symbolized not only by the figurines of her glass menagerie, but also by the "delicate ivory chair" (29) with which Williams identifies Laura in Scene 2. By physical frailty, I am referring not only to the "childhood illness [that] has left her crippled, one leg slightly shorter than the other, and held in a brace" (5), but also to her frequent faintness, nausea, and colds together with her bout with pleurosis as a teenager. Jim misheard "Blue Roses" when Laura told him, back in high school, that she had had pleurosis, an inflammation of the thin membrane covering the lungs that causes difficult, painful breathing.

His oxymoronic mishearing is similar to Williams's own "incorrect" hearing of "glass menagerie" for "grass menagerie," the enclosure where a collection of *live* wild animals is kept—a "mishearing" underlined by the dramatist's assertion in the "Production Notes" that a single recurring tune [of the play in production] "is ... like circus music ... [which paradoxically should be] the lightest, most delicate music in the world and perhaps the saddest" (9). Jim's mishearing for its part suggests the oxymoronic existence of Laura Wingfield, a young woman of this world who simultaneously, like the lovely but easily broken creatures of her glass menagerie, seems physically unfit for or unadapted to an earthly life. She is too good for this world, the Romantics might say, and for this reason she could be said to be sadly beautiful or bluely roseate, like the soft-violet color of her kimono (29) in Scene 2—the first scene where the screen-image of blue roses appears.

Indeed, Laura's physical as well as emotional frailty betokens an early demise, if not a death-wish on her part—a death that would bestow upon her the ultimate union with Nature so prized by the Romantics and so elusive or unattainable in life. Death imagery may not pervade the surface of *The Glass Menagerie*, but it is at the heart of two poems quoted or invoked by Williams on the screen device included in the authoritative version of the play. The first is "The Ballad of Dead Ladies," by the medieval French poet François Villon, from which the following, recurring line is projected onto the screen as Amanda and Laura appear onstage for the first time in Scene 1 (24), in addition to being projected later in the same scene when Amanda reminisces about the gentlemen callers she once entertained and would now like her daughter to receive (27). The line reads, "Où sont les neiges [d'antan]?", or "Where are the snows of yesteryear?" Villon uses snow here as a symbol of worldly life's evanescence as well as its natural provenance-cum-dissolution, its inevitably lost innocence or tarnished purity"; and Williams ironically connects the humble Laura and her humbled Southern belle of a mother with the great but departed women of Villon's part historical, part legendary ballad, among them Joan of Arc.

Like much of Villon's work, this poem elevates death to the status of a supreme law that ineluctably ends all earthly life yet ushers in the eternity of the Christian afterlife—an afterlife unironically intimated, embraced, or augured in so modern a drama as *The Glass Menagerie* by the title of Scene 5, "Annunciation" (56); by the mid winter-to-late spring time frame of the action; and by verbal references in the play to God the Father, the Virgin Mary, Christian martyrs, resurrection, baptism, paradise, grace, souls, and the erstwhile Catholic practice of eating fish every Friday. There are aural references to resurrection as well in the early-morning church bells at the start of Scene 4 (44), and we find a musical reference to Christ's rising from the dead in the song "The World is Waiting for the Sunrise!" from Scene 5 (57). There is no direct reference to Easter in the play, but certainly such allusions to resurrection as Amanda's calls to her son to "Rise and Shine!" in Scene 4 (46), together with Tom's own blasphemous tale to Laura in the same scene (45) of Malvolio the Magician's escape from a nailed up coffin, suggest that *The Glass Menagerie* takes place around the time of this annual Christian commemoration of Jesus' return to life and ultimate ascension into heaven.

The second poem quoted by Williams is less obviously associated with death, since the playwright uses two lines from it—which, again, appear on the screen between the living and dining rooms of the Wingfield apartment— to anticipate, then announce, the arrival of the Gentleman Caller for dinner in Scene 6. The poem is Emily Dickinson's "The Accent of a Coming Foot," which I quote in full:

> Elysium is as far as to
> The very nearest Room

> If in that Room a Friend await
> Felicity or Doom—
>
> What fortitude the Soul contains,
> That it can so endure
> The accent of a coming Foot—
> The opening of a Door—
>   (1180, Vol. 3, 1963)

Williams cites this poem's penultimate line first, then the final line as Tom brings Jim home to meet his sister (69, 74).

Now we know that all of Dickinson's transcendentalist-inspired work was composed within the characteristically American, late nineteenth-century range of relationships among God, man, and Nature. Furthermore, she was preoccupied in her poetry with the idea of death as the gateway to the next existence, as a special glory that has something in common with the conventional paradises offered in hymns and sermons of her day. Death for Dickinson means leisure, grandeur, recognition; it means being with the few, rare people whom it was not possible to know fully upon earth: she writes, for example, that "Death is potential to that Man / Who dies—and to his friend—" (420, Vol. 2, 1955). Much of life for her is anguish endured in an anteroom to death, which is but a prelude to immortality.

Although Dickinson speaks again and again of transitoriness and isolation in this world, she is not a mystic or a religious poet. Rather, from the whimsical, domestic, even rococo cast of her mind, she flirts with eternity, she is coquettish with God, forgiving Him for his "duplicity" and sometimes going so far as to be brash with Him. God is indeed a puzzling figure in her work, the Creator who perhaps does not know why He has created. He is burglar, banker, father; gentleman, duke, king: a being personified at times as Death, at other times as a sort of lover.

So too is Jim O'Connor of *The Glass Menagerie* a kind of gentleman, just as he was a champion high-school debater and baritone lead, if he will probably never be a captain of industry. For his part, Laura's absconding father (whose presence as a fifth character of sorts hovers over the play through his larger-than-life-size, beatifically smiling photograph above the mantel) can be called a burglar but not a banker, and a lover of other women if no longer of Amanda. Jim certainly never becomes *Laura's* lover, even though she secretly loves him, since he is engaged to be married to another woman; he does, however, adumbrate the death of Laura, her release from this life and return to nature, together with her rebirth in heaven.

In this sense, Jim is indeed, as Tom describes him in his narration, "the long-delayed but always expected something that we live for" (23). The anticipated arrival of someone or something that will provide a form of religious, political, or existential salvation and release to those who await him or it is a familiar subject of modern drama, from Maeterlinck's *The Intruder* to Odets's *Waiting for Lefty* to Beckett's *Waiting for Godot*. Although, ironically, the "expected something" usually does not arrive, the Gentleman Caller does make an appearance in *The Glass Menagerie*—one that is tellingly heralded by Tom's "annunciation" of his upcoming visit (59); by Jim's association with a traditional symbol of Christ, the fish (61); and by Laura's mentioning of his high-school yearbook picture right after she refers to the picture of Jesus' mother in the local art museum (33–34). Yet it is the Gentleman Caller's departure rather than his arrival that provides a final solution to Laura's problems, for in intensifying her desperation and isolation, Jim's permanent disappearance after Scene 7—in combination with the subsequent disappearance of Tom—could be said to hasten her physical and mental deterioration to the point of death.

"The accent of a coming foot" is, of course, Jim's, but it is also that of the Grim Reaper, who awaits Laura, his "friend," in "the very nearest room." Death will spell her *felicitous* doom, however, for it is identified in Dickinson's poem with Elysium, which in classical mythology represents the paradisiacal abode of the virtuous and blessed after they die. It is there that Laura may finally know fully Mr. James Delaney O'Connor, a man who on earth remained for the most part a figment of her imagination. It is on earth as well that Laura's soul may have had the fortitude to endure the accent of Jim's coming foot, his opening of her apartment door, because that accent and that opening would mean not only momentary escape from the prisonhouse of her imagination along with her shyness, but also ultimate, perpetual release from the cellblock of her physically crippled body, the wasteland of her emotionally crippled mind, and the enslavement of urbanized subsistence.

Certainly it is not by accident that Williams gives Laura a June birthday at the same time as he makes Jim's wedding day the second Sunday in June (111). Through her birth, Laura is thus associated with Juno, the ancient Roman queen of heaven; Juno, the goddess of marriage and childbirth; and Juno, the wife of Jupiter, the supreme deity of the ancient Romans, whose weapon was the thunderbolt that can be heard toward the end of Scene 6 (83). Laura may not marry and bear children on earth, but the implication is that in death she will become, or after death she will be resurrected as, the celestial bride of Jesus if not of James-Jupiter.

And surely her death will paradoxically be hastened by the celebration of her birth, for on that day or near that day the man of Laura's dreams,

Gentleman Jim O'Connor, will marry someone else, the unseen and prosaically named "Betty." Since Easter is celebrated at some time in the course of *The Glass Menagerie*'s episodic action, Laura's birthday occurs near Pentecost, or is closer to Pentecost than any other major Christian festival: the seventh Sunday after Easter, the religious holiday marking the descent of the Holy Spirit on the Apostles—and therefore the ideal day to signify or encapsulate the earthly yet transcendent life the chaste Laura Wingfield has led among the lowliest as well as the most noble creatures of God's menagerie.

As further evidence that Williams conceived of Laura as someone experiencing life-in-death or death-in-life, I offer a third poem from which he quotes—this time in the stage directions accompanying the screen title "The accent of a coming foot" in Scene 6. The dramatist writes that "It is about five on a Friday evening of late spring which comes 'scattering poems in the sky'" (69). His direct quotation is slightly inaccurate, but he clearly has in mind "Impressions, IX," by that romantic anarchist of American poetry, E. E. Cummings. I must refer the reader to this work in its entirety, for its dominant images—of life-in-death or death-in-life, ascent and descent, of dawn's early light and the candlelight of dusk, the dreams of sleep or the dreaminess of poetry, of harsh city life and the starry, songful life of the mind—recapitulate those of *The Glass Menagerie*. Here I can only offer the first two stanzas:

> the hours rise up putting off stars and it is
> dawn
> into the street of the sky light walks scattering poems
>
> on earth a candle is
> extinguished   the city
> wakes
> with a song upon her
> mouth having death in her eyes (67)

As I intimated earlier, the lighting of Laura Wingfield—called for most prominently by Williams in the "Production Notes" to the play—is as poetic or expressive as its quotations and signifies just how different or special, if not heavenly, she is in comparison with the Betty O'Connors of this world. Williams writes that "the light upon Laura should be distinct from the others, having a peculiar pristine clarity such as light used in early religious portraits of female saints or madonnas" (9–10). Furthermore, the playwright sometimes makes Laura the visual focus of our attention "in contradistinction to what is the apparent center. For instance, in the ... supper scene ... her silent figure on the sofa should remain the visual center" (9). Beyond this, Williams suggests that the light surrounding Laura, as well as Tom, Amanda, and the Gentleman Caller, show "a certain correspondence to light in religious paintings, ... where the figures are radiant in atmosphere that is relatively dusky" (10). "Relatively dusky"—that is, "blue," as in the "deep blue dusk" from which there issues a "sorrowful murmur" in Scene 6 (83) as a summer-like storm abruptly approaches and Laura becomes too ill to sit down to dinner with Jim O'Connor, her mother, and her brother.

Williams calls for "dim" or "poetic" atmospheric lighting throughout *The Glass Menagerie*, however, not just during the three scenes that occur at twilight or dusk. He writes that such faint illumination is "in keeping with the atmosphere of memory" (9) in this memory play, but it must also be remembered that the time from twilight to dusk—the time of dim or poetic lighting—was the Romantics' favorite because, in its mixture of darkness and light, it is more infinite, more all-embracing, than any other part of the day. In addition, twilight-to-dusk suggested to them a mind that was half awake and half asleep and therefore in sentient retreat from the workaday world, alive to the dreamlike workings of memory. As is Laura's mind toward the end of Scene 5, in the "early dusk of a spring evening" (56), when—in response to her mother's demand that she "make a wish on the [little silver slipper of a] moon" that has just appeared—Laura "looks faintly puzzled as if called out of sleep" (67). Not by chance, the moon appears again in Scene 7, for, in its blending of blackness and brightness, moonlight creates the nighttime equivalent of twilight at sunset.

Twilight can thus be seen as the retiring Laura's favorite time of day, despite the fact that Jim calls it—or its artificial equivalent, candlelight—his favorite after a power outage plunges the Wingfield apartment into what Amanda terms an "everlasting darkness" (87). Jim appropriately comes to his "date" with Laura in Scene 7 "carrying [a] candelabrum, its candles lighted, in one hand and a glass of wine in the other" (88), together with a pack of Life-Saver mints (107). The virtually sacramental wine, in combination with his warmth and charm, gradually "lights her inwardly with altar candles" (97), which is Williams's way of saying that Jim's apparent love has touched Laura's soul by way of her eyes. This naturally is the manner in which romantic or spiritual love, as opposed to animalistic or carnal lust, works, and has been thought to do so since the early Renaissance when the sight of Dante's Beatrice created a hunger for empyreal rather than fleshly beauty: by touching the spirit in emulation of God's love for mankind as well as man's love of God.

When Laura realizes that she has misperceived Jim's intentions or that he has unintentionally misled her, "the holy candles on the altar of [her] face" are accordingly "snuffed out" (108). Indeed, at the end of the play Laura herself blows out the candles that Jim had brought to their encounter, and she does this in recognition not only of her brother Tom's departure from her life, together with that of her father before him, but also of the Gentleman Caller's leave-taking. The implication is that no gentleman caller will ever enter her life again; none will ever be gentle enough among an American people so crassly materialistic to perceive her inner beauty, to appreciate her love for beauty, to understand her unnatural, if not supernatural, place in a world ruled by science and technology instead of heart and soul. That Laura requires such a man—a man, period—to guarantee her happiness, if not her very survival in an unequal contest with the fittest, is a comment less on the manmade oppressiveness of the patriarchal order or the blind selectivity of the biological one, than on her need-cum-desire to anchor the eternal, unearthly feminine in the world of the temporally masculine. In this man's world, waiting for the second global war of the century after having recently weathered the economic war of the Great Depression, and therefore soon to be lit by lightning from mass bombardments, Laura is figuratively condemned to live out her earthly existence in an "everlasting darkness" that has already literally begun to descend on what will become millions of other human beings.

One of them may turn out to be Tom Wingfield himself, for he is a member of the Merchant Marine in the play's present or framing time of 1943–1944. This means, of course, that he was a sailor on the ships that carried weapons and supplies to our armed forces overseas—ships that were prime, and easy, targets for enemy submarines and cruisers. In *The Glass Menagerie's* past action of 1936–1937, as remembered by Tom, he twice discusses his imminent joining of the Merchant Marine, and in each instance the image of a "sailing vessel with Jolly Roger" is projected onto the screen (51,78). Now such a vessel is normally a pirate ship flying the traditional skull-and-crossbones flag, which obviously symbolizes death. Yet, as a merchant seaman, Tom will be furnishing food, clothing, and arms to other men and ships, not stealing such resources from them, as murderous pirates would do. So the image of a sailing craft with the skull-and-crossbones flag seems intended both to mock Tom's fantasy of high adventure on the oceans of the world and to augur his own demise, or descent into darkness at sea, at the hands of a *modern* pirate ship, the privateer.

Tom's death will leave the world in the hands of people like Jim O'Connor, the mock-pirate of the Gilbert and Sullivan comic operetta. Jim's real-life adventures, however, will be limited, as he himself says, to accumulating—or dreaming of accumulating—knowledge, money, and power in that order (100). This is the triad on which democracy is built as far as he's concerned, but it is the foundation of rampant capitalism for most of the rest of us. The Gentleman Caller's cravenly opportunistic dream of material success, or coldly rationalistic strategy for achieving monetary gain, may point the direction in which the American-led, postwar free world must go, but Laura and Tom Wingfield's heroically Romantic dream of spiritual or artistic fulfillment doubtless embodies what that world will lose by going there.

WORKS CITED

Cummings, E. E. *Complete Poems, 1904–1962*. New York: Liveright, 1991.

Dickinson, Emily. *The Poems of Emily Dickinson*. Ed. Thomas H. Johnson. 3 vols. Cambridge, Mass.: Harvard Univ. Press, 1955.

———. *The Poems of Emily Dickinson*. Ed. Thomas H. Johnson. 3 vols. Cambridge, Mass.: Harvard Univ. Press, 1963.

Novalis (Friedrich von Hardenberg). *Heinrich von Ofterdingen*. Trans. Palmer Hilty. New York: Frederick Ungar, 1964.

Villon, François. *Poésies complètes*. Ed. Claude Thiry. Paris: Librairie Générale Française, 1991.

Williams, Tennessee. *The Glass Menagerie*. New York: New Directions, 1966. First published, New York: Random House, 1945.

LINDA DORFF

"I prefer the 'mad' ones": Tennessee Williams's Grotesque-Lyric Exegetical Poems

Shelley's burning was finally very pure!
But the body, the corpse, split open like a grilled pig!
—Tennessee Williams, *Camino Real*

With so few lyrical playwrights in the American theater, it is perhaps too tempting to label Tennessee Williams a romantic, a term that has been loosely employed to characterize his poetic language. Although some critics might agree with Nancy M. Tischler that Williams was a "natural romantic whose very existence was one of 'benevolent anarchy'" ("Romantic" 147), such sentimental characterizations tend to elide the fundamentally problematic nature of Williams's relationship to romanticism and its poetry. Williams's plays dramatize his evolving relation to romanticism in their use of poet-protagonists ranging from the mythic Orpheus (Val Xavier) in *Battle of Angels* (1940) to Arthur Rimbaud in *Will Mr. Merriweather Return from Memphis?* (unpublished , written in 1969). Williams's deeply conflicted attitude toward the romantics becomes obvious by the time of *Camino Real* in 1953, which was at once romantic and anti-romantic. This dissonance is expressed when Lord Byron recalls the romantic cremation of Shelley's corpse on the beach at Viareggio as "finally very *pure!*" (505), only to immediately contradict the notion of spiritual purity with an image of the grotesque "corpse, split open like a grilled pig!" (505). This juxtaposition of the grotesque with the

From *The Southern Quarterly* 38, no. 1 (Fall 1999): pp. 81–93. © 1999 by the University of Southern Mississippi.

beautiful establishes an ironic sensibility that Williams refers to in stage
directions as "serio-comic, grotesque-lyric" (533), anticipating his late
plays in which romantic notions of transcendence are rejected in favor of
a cynical and highly contemporary post-romantic poetics of Rimbaudian
disorder. Whereas the roots of Williams's grotesque-lyric form are complex
and diffuse in his drama, evidence of it appears as early as 1941 in several
poems that are clearly identifiable as exegetical works—that is, poems which
perform an interpretation (exegesis) of another poet's work. These poems
reject the orphic patterns of descent and return found in early romantics
such as Wordsworth, and significantly revision Shelley, Rilke, Rimbaud, and
even his beloved Crane as Williams demarcates his own anti-redemptive,
grotesque-lyric territory.

Williams's exegetical poetry is a natural outgrowth of his cannibalistic
writing process, in which old-text (both his own and others) is recycled into
new-text (his own). In this sort of artistic exegesis, Williams's new-text does
not simply explain or, as Norman J. Fedder has suggested, "assimilate" (13)
the thematic content of an earlier text.[1] Rather, Williams's exegetical writing,
translates a world from the literary language of an earlier writer into his
personal literary language.[2] Gilbert Debusscher seems to suggest a similar
process, noting that rather than directly adopting the ideas of Lawrence into
his own work, Williams "rewrote [Lawrence] in his own terms" ("Creative"
171). Esther Merle Jackson proposes that "Williams' brand of romanticism
is synthetic; it represents an accommodation of artistic and intellectual
traditions inherited from the European past to ideas of form generated by
American life" ("Poetic" 54). Williams's exegetical poems contain more
direct evidences of literary influences than his exegetical dramas,[3] for they
were usually written first. It was sometimes not until years after a poem or
short story was written that Williams would develop elements derived from
them into plays, diffusing traces of influence to the point of invisibility. Most
criticism of Williams's poetry reads it as a gloss to the drama and in this vein
Thomas P. Adler has proposed that Williams's poetry may be read as both an
intertext and a metatext for the plays (64–65). While Adler uses the poems as
a starting point, looking forward intertextually within the formidable corpus
of Williams's work, I propose to look backward, discovering how Williams
used exegetical poems to negotiate his position as a post-romantic writer.

While at many points in his career Williams called himself a romantic,
from the beginning his vision diverged from the high English romanticism
of Wordsworth, for it was marked by a grotesque irony that was more typical
of Germanic or French romanticism. Romantic aesthetic theory, which was
opposed to Enlightenment thought, originated in the writings of Johann
Gottfried Herder during the Sturm und Drang movement of the 1770s in

Germany. It emphasized sensual effects, metaphorical imagery and sought unifying principles for aesthetic works.[4] These ideas were developed by Immanuel Kant, who made a distinction between reason and understanding, in which the truth could only be reached through subjective means.[5] Mikhail Bakhtin notes that the grotesque was important to these early Germanic theorists of romanticism, who believed that they had rediscovered the spirit of Shakespeare and Cervantes (37) in its tragicomic juxtaposition of pathos with bathos, or the beautiful with the monstrous. Victor Hugo further clarified the grotesque for French romanticism in 1827, writing that the grotesque is everywhere: "the ugly exists there beside the beautiful, the deformed next to the graceful, the grotesque on the reverse of the sublime, evil with good, darkness with light" (3:30). This certainly recalls Williams's worlds of "light and shadow" (*Suddenly Last Summer* 358), in which the grotesque becomes nearly beautiful. While ideas from German romanticism influenced the early English romantics,[6] both William Wordsworth and Samuel Taylor Coleridge significantly revised them, emphasizing beauty and all but eliminating notions of the grotesque. In Wordsworth's *Preface to Lyrical Ballads* (1802) he posits his Poet as a man of superior vision who is the "upholder and preserver" (52) of love and beauty. In "On Poesy or Art" (1818), Coleridge views poetry as the medium that unites humans with nature, exemplified by his poem "The Aeolian Harp" (1796), in which an instrument is made to sing by the wind. The early romantics' concern with the role of the imagination in elevating natural objects is heightened in the poems of Percy Bysshe Shelley and Lord Byron, who abandoned the bourgeois existence of Wordsworth for the passionate life of vagabond poets. In the later phase of romanticism, reflected by the work of the French decadent poets Rimbaud and Baudelaire, concepts of vision and nature are radically altered as romanticism becomes preoccupied with the grotesque once again.

Three of Williams's exegetical poems seem to respond specifically to poets and poems which exemplify these shifting constructions of the romantic imagination. The first of these, "Intimations" (1941–42), is an exegetical rejection of odes by Wordsworth, Coleridge, and Shelley that celebrate the ability of poetry to express immortality. Williams's poem radically challenges this basic romantic concept, creating its own meditation on the limitations of poetry. "Part of a Hero" (1956), the second of these response poems by Williams, seems to engage in a debate with poems of Shelley, as if to question the function of the romantic lyric by contrasting it with grotesque imagery. The third of Williams's exegetical poems, "Orpheus Descending" (1951), argues against the orphic poet figures in the work of Hart Crane and Rainer Maria Rilke, for Williams's poet cannot envision rebirth. The nearly anti-romantic—and in particular the anti-redemptive—stances of these poems help to make clearer the extent to which Williams embraced Rimbaud's post-romantic poetics, which were at once grotesque and lyric, visionary and mad. Williams articulates this affinity in an unpublished essay on Rimbaud entitled "These Scattered Idioms" (n.d.), in which he writes "I prefer the 'mad' ones" (3), gesturing at the deliberately fractured aesthetics of his later work, which are far afield from those of Wordsworth.

In his arguments with the romantics, therefore, it is appropriate that Williams engaged with Wordsworth first in his "Intimations" poem. On the surface, Williams's "Intimations" ode seems as if it has nothing to do with Wordsworth's "Ode: Intimations of Immortality from Recollections of Early Childhood" (written 1802–04) and yet, it has everything to do with it. Following a circuitous route, the crisis pattern practiced by Wordsworth and Coleridge traces an orphic cycle of descent into dejection that ends in a rise toward resurrection sparked by a sudden revelation brought about by the contemplation of ordinary things (Abrams, *Natural* 135). Harold Bloom argues that this pattern represents a "dialectic," or a "passionate" argument (*Visionary* 181), that moves from "childlike joy [to a] fall into nature [to a] salvation through nature" (184). The movement toward salvation is constructed as a moment of revelation in which the imagination affects a mystical synthesis with nature. Thus, in "Intimations Ode," Wordsworth's narrator first celebrates the innocent joy of a child's perception of a nature that knows only immortality, and then laments the passing of the "visionary gleam" with a maturity that foresees death. In the end, however, the speaker recognizes in a crisis moment that "truths ... that perish never" are to be found in memories of youth—"that immortal sea / Which brought us thither."

Both Coleridge and Shelley wrote responses to Wordsworth's ode. Coleridge's "Dejection: An Ode" (1802) may be considered an exegetical poem about the "Intimations Ode,"which seems to reject the celebratory tone in the beginning of Wordsworth's Ode, exchanging it for a "smothering weight" of depression. Nevertheless, the poet manages a resurrection from this state as "the shaping spirit of Imagination" is empowered to "rise" and "lift" itself to "rejoice." One of Shelley's last poems, "The Zucca" (1822) is also an exegetical response to the "Intimations Ode"[7] beginning as "infant Winter laughed upon the land" where "no death divide thy immortality." The middle of the poem descends into a lament, and the end is unclear, as the poem is unfinished.

Williams's "Intimations" ode marks a critical departure from English romanticism, for it rejects the Wordsworthian notion of an intimation as a moment that produces a revelation of an inner essence or truth. Whereas Wordsworth's narrator begins his poem by nostalgically recalling a childlike consciousness of immorality "appareled in celestial light," Williams's narrator begins with an alienated outcry from an impossibly wounded voice:

I do not think that I ought to appear in public
below the shoulders.
                    Below the collar bone
I am swathed in bandages already.
I have received no serious wound as yet
but I am expecting several.
A slant of light reminds me of iron lances;
my belly shudders and my loins contract. *(In the Winter* 62)

This bizarre condition recalls an essay by W.H. Auden, in which a wound
is used as a metaphor for the modernist self.[8] Williams's metaphoric wound
"arrives without a cut in the bandage, / mysteriously" (62) as if it had come
from a savage ray of light that seems like an "iron lance." This is a radical
challenge to the idea of nature as the subject of art and source of vision in
early English romanticism. Where Wordsworth and Coleridge celebrated
the eyes of their poet, who could look at ordinary things and envision
the extraordinary, the "dolorous" eyes of Williams's poet seem like "two
hackneyed rhymes, / two pitiful little jingles on epic themes" (62) that are
incapable of translating the unidentified grotesque world that surrounds
him. While Coleridge and Shelley imagined the poet's voice as an Aeolian
harp or lyre Williams's poet is oddly mute, imprisoned behind an "iron
mask of silence" (63). This poet's vision, if there is any to be had, comes
via the pharmacy: "the makeshift pills, like bits of a china rabbit / with on
the bottle the doctor's word *everlasting*" (62). This obvious reference to
Lewis Carroll's Alice recalls the bottle with the note that says "Drink Me,"
which changes her shape. This chemical shape-shifting is antithetical to the
notion of a natural romantic self, and comes closer to Rimbaud's call for the
poet to enter into "all the forms of love, of suffering, of madness" (270) in
order to achieve vision.

When Williams's poet hears "through a rubber tube mortality's roar in
my veins ..." (63), there is no intimation of immortality forthcoming. Rather,
Williams creates a third-person poet figure:

an elderly girl poet
twenty years out of fashion,
bewildered among the debris of romantic boasting,

Bore downstairs her familiar snail's shell, bottle and notebook,
and sat and waited and listened
as a spinster for a caller that still fails to come ... (63)

It is likely that the "elderly girl poet" is Marianne Moore, a "literalist of the imagination" (Moore 577) who was at odds with and perhaps "bewildered" by romanticism. In mentioning her "familiar snail's shell," Williams obliquely alludes to her poems, "To a Snail" and "Poetry" (1919), in which (the latter) argues that poetry should have "imaginary gardens with real toads in them" (578). The elderly girl poet of Williams's poem waits, but her intimation— the gentleman caller—"fails to come." Her death, heralded by "all the heretical host of an out-crying disposition" behind "the iron mask of silence" (63) is an ironic footnote to a poem about intimations that never arrived. In Williams's anti-"Intimations" ode, the grotesquely wounded modernist poet is struck dumb in an anesthetized, modernist inferno that he can glimpse only through his own hellish subjectivity. Jackson has recognized the importance of this subjectivity to Williams's peculiar blending of late romantic ideas with expressionist modes. She writes that:

> Williams, like Nietzsche, is inclined to challenge the pre-established reality of romantic description. He rejects, moreover, many of the fundamental principles which underlie the romantic theory of image-making. Rather, he is concerned with the creation of an art which is superior to and often in contradiction to known reality. Like the expressionists, Williams regards form as abstraction, as a dynamic structure suspended in metaphysical time and space. (*Broken World* 35)

Romanticism and expressionism have at least one thing in common and that is their insistence upon a subjective perspective for the writer, character, and audience/reader. While, as Jackson points out, the romantics contend that they accomplish a type of realism through subjective "perspectives, the formal innovations of twentieth-century modernist expressionists are clearly abstract." Jackson writes that "for Williams, reality itself lies shattered. In the fragmentary world of his new theatre, new images are pieced together from partialities; they are composed from splinters of broken truth" (*Broken World* 36). In his self-consciously constructed, modernist identity, Williams's narrator anticipates the character of Hamm in Samuel Beckett's *Endgame* (1957), who is nearly blind, nearly paralyzed, and unable to create a narrative.

The poem ends with a grotesque-lyric footnote when, from "back of the mask of silence," the narrator remarks, "Blue is such a lovely piece of paper" (63). In its invocation of the English romantics' blue azure sky, this last line sounds like the only credibly Wordsworthian passage in the poem. It functions, however, as a modernist reversal of Coleridge's metaphor in

"The Aeolian Harp" in which that "simplest Lute" (100) is played by the wind. Shelley refashions this metaphor slightly in "Ode to the West Wind" (1819), where, instead of asking the wind to play an instrument, he entreats it to "Make me thy lyre, even as the forest is" (618), as if the poet longs to become at one with his subject-nature. In a decided contrast to the English romantics' attempts to dissolve the boundaries between art/representation and nature, Williams's narrator takes a modernist stance by self-consciously making the blue of the sky into a metapoetic reference[9] about the writer's poem. Williams's "Intimations" is, at last, about the process of writing; it is art about art rather than art masquerading as reality.

In a recent essay on "romantic textures" in Williams's work, Tischler presents a portrait of a Williams who has a "pronounced inclination" (151) toward the second generation of English Romantics, including Shelley, Byron, and Keats. Williams certainly identified with Shelley and Byron's tramp through Europe as vagabond poets, as well as with the passionate lyricism of Shelley. Williams casts a decadent Lord Byron as the primary poet figure of *Camino Real*, who, like the play's other dissolute metacharacters at the end of their road, complains that the "many distractions" (504) of the body have caused him to "sell" his art and lose his power to write. He says, "the metal point's gone from my pen, there's nothing left but the feather" (503). His vision of Shelley's cremation on the beach at Viareggio allows him to recover, for a moment, his visionary status:

> the front of the skull had broken away in the flames, and there—
>
> And there was the brain of Shelley, indistinguishable from a cooking stew!—*boiling bubbling hissing!*—in the *blackening—cracked—pot—*of his skull!
>
> —Trelawney, his friend, Trelawney, threw salt and oil and frankincense in the flames and finally the almost intolerable stench—
>
> —was *gone* and the burning was *pure!*—as a man's burning should be ...
>
> A man's burning *ought* to be pure!—*not* like mine—(a crepe suzette—burned in brandy ...)
>
> *Shelley's* burning was finally very *pure!*
> But the body, the corpse, split open like a grilled pig! (505)

Situated in block eight at the exact center of the play, Byron's vision
of Shelley's burning brain functions as the semiotic core of meaning
in *Camino Real*, radiating the grotesque-lyric image of the burning
purification of the poet's brain throughout the play's desolate landscape.
Williams's disfiguration of Shelley is similar to de Man's theory of Shelley's
disfiguration in his reading of Shelley's late, unfinished poem "The Triumph
of Life" (1822), which dramatizes a "transformation [which] is also said to
be an erasure" (99) from the brain, erasing or effacing knowledge of the
self, and thereby, creating "loss of face," or defacement (100). The erasure
of Shelley's brain through a metaphoric burning purification transforms
Byron, empowering him to make departure "from my present self as I
used to be!" (*Camino Real* 503), venturing into the Terra Incognita—the
wasteland which erases all who enter it—as he cries, "*Make voyages!—
Attempt them!*—there's nothing else ..." (508), as if there is no alternative
but disfiguration.

   Williams was still preoccupied with Shelley's death three years after
Camino Real, which he refers to in his exegetical poem "Part of a Hero."
Here the grotesque-lyric tone has softened into an ironic mourning. While
Williams does not identify the poem's subject as Shelley, the tone and
imagery are markedly similar to those in Shelley's long elegy on the death
of Keats, "Adonais" (1821). In the poem's beginning, Williams's narrator
observes a Shelley-like figure collecting sticks and building fires, as if he were
metaphorically watching Shelley write his fiery tribute to Keats. Williams's
narrator begins with the ironic observation that

> I don't suppose that he will be able to build these fires much
> longer as part of himself must burn like a match struck to light
> them. (58)

These lines are strikingly similar to Shelley's observation that Keats's "spirit's
self has ceased to burn, / With sparkless ashes load an unlamented urn"
(Stanza 40, 495). Williams's narration chides Shelley's near-religious fervor
in building his pyre to Keats, calling it a "silly pile of debris" (58) that he
probably burns to warm "something he once took for something of God in his
heart" (58). Distantly observing that "each fire may be fatal to him, becoming
his auto-da-fé" (58), he remarks that "I don't suppose / there will be much
left to dispose of, / a handful of powder, bluish and very dark" (58–59). He is
distinctly cooler than Shelley's "Dust to the dust! but the pure spirit shall flow
/ Back to the burning fountain whence it came" (494). Williams's narrator
cannot resist being touched by Shelley's lyricism, however, and he gives in to
it toward the poem's end:

Still, as he goes, as the sable-plumed wind removes him
with that mechanical mourning sound of air's motion,
I will remark to myself, He has gone beyond us.
I may even feel a touch of his exultation. (59)

In referring metapoetically to the "sable-plumed wind that removes him," Williams is speaking of his own exegetical pen, in which the Aeolian harp is not imitated, but rather, makes an ironic, grotesquely modern "mechanical mourning sound." Still, he says, Shelley "did own one essential part of a hero, / the idea of life as a nothing-withholding submission of self to flame" (59). This last line of the poem comes close to being Williams's artistic credo, and it is in moments like this that he refuses to reject romantic ideals, but passionately rewrites his own versions.

The third exegetical poem discussed here, "Orpheus Descending," also reflects Williams's revisioning of romanticism, this time through Orpheus, the ideal romantic poet. The figure of Orpheus became popular in romantic literature because the myth's death-to-rebirth structure repeated the trajectory of romantic aesthetics. The romantic crisis poem, for example, could plunge into dejection as Orpheus descended to hell, but must rise at the end, for this structure was based on the Augustinian crisis-pattern that regards life as "ascending stages of self-formation" (Abrams, *Natural* 136). St. Augustine's Christian ideology of resurrection derives, in part, from its Greek religious ancestors, which include orphism. Therefore, Orpheus, like Christ, became a favored image of rebirth for the first- and second-generation English romantics.

In *Emerson and the Orphic Poet in America*, R. A. Yoder articulates a split in the American orphic tradition, which occurs between those later poets who follow Emerson and those who follow Whitman. Followers of the Emersonian line, such as Wallace Stevens, might be thought of as Apollonian, continuing the tradition of poetry shaped by an encounter between self and nature, focusing "the orphic aspirations of the poet on ordinary human needs" (Yoder 192). But the Whitmanian line, to which Crane and Williams belong, focuses more widely on the "myth of the whole cosmic man" (Yoder 192), seeking to outline larger, spatial patterns of order and perhaps to re-figure the poet's relation to a modern version of nature in a "proto-epic" (Yoder 191). The Whitmanian tradition could be thought of as the Dionysian branch of American orphic poets, who construct new poetic forms, dismembering the old ones and seeking "Orpheus and the poetic work in artifact" (Yoder 191) rather than in nature. Williams clearly recognized his affinity for the Dionysian element from the beginning, which he acknowledged in a 1951 essay, stating: "It is dissatisfaction with empiric evidence that makes the poet and mystic, for it is the lyric [romantic] as well as the Bacchantic [grotesque] impulse" ("Meaning" 55).

Williams was most drawn to poets who either directly or indirectly enact an orphic scattering (*sparagmós*) in their poetry. In these poets—Crane, Rilke, and Rimbaud—the emphasis is on a disorder and dismemberment rather than on resurrection. Many of Williams's early plays offered some sort of redemptive ending, but with *Suddenly Last Summer* in 1958, he no longer allowed his plays to ascend at the end, which is part of the reason critics became so dissatisfied with them. Williams's artistic innovations had always been more radical in poetry and fiction than he was on the public stage, and as early as the 1940s, he began to eliminate the ascent of resurrection and its promise of salvation in his exegetical poems to Crane and Rilke.

From the time Williams discovered Hart Crane's work in 1936, just four years after Crane's suicide leap into the Caribbean, he claimed Crane as his literary ancestor and began to negotiate his position in relation to Crane. Declaring Crane to be the greatest American poet since Whitman, Williams said that he wanted to bring "poetry of [Crane's] stature in[to] the theatre" ("Role of Poetry" 20). Although Williams acknowledged the influence of dozens of writers throughout his career,[10] he identified most strongly with Crane, frequently cataloging parallels between their lives: both grew up in repressive, middle-class families with powerful mothers, both were homosexual, both experienced desire as a consuming, destructive force, both had bouts of madness and suffered from alcoholism, and both were committed to their art above all else. Williams's intense interest in Crane, however, was not focused as much on his life as it was on his work. Evidence pointing to the presence of Cranian influence in Williams's work is readily apparent in an obvious, scattered trail of epigraphs and titles borrowed from Crane's poetry,[11] but the core of influence is submerged much deeper than these vestigial traces might at first suggest. In a meditation on the theory of postmodern literary biography, Nicholas Pagan notes that "like Orpheus, Hart Crane can only exist for Williams as part of a text" (75–76), and, perhaps logically, Williams used Crane's poetic imagery much as he used the myth of Orpheus—to structure his dramatic texts. By the time Cranian influence reaches a full length play such as *Suddenly Last Summer*, however, it has become deeply buried in the text. Cranian structural influence becomes clearer when encountered in the exegetical poems that respond to Crane (and there are several in the 1956 collection *In the Winter of Cities*[12]), particularly "Orpheus Descending."

The first three stanzas of "Orpheus Descending" envision the bizarre "under kingdom" where no light exists and people are so weighted down with gold and heavy jewels that they cannot breathe and are "crushed." This is clearly an underwater kingdom of the dead which echoes Shakespearean[13] and Cranian images of death at the bottom of the sea. Williams exegetically rewrites Cranian dismemberment tropologies of the ocean in which Crane figured the sea as a site of birth (the mother Ananke) and dismembering death: "like ocean athwart lanes of death and birth" ("Ave Maria"). In "Voyages III" Crane imagines a sexual transcendence as:

> Star kissing star through wave on wave unto
> Your body rocking!
>   and where death, if shed,
> Presumes no carnage, but this single change,—
> Upon the steep floor flung from dawn to dawn
> The silken skilled transmemberment of song;
>
> Permit me voyage, love, into your hands ... (36)

In this passage, Crane rewrites Walt Whitman's image of rocking waves that whisper "death" in "Out of the Cradle Endlessly Rocking"[14] as an image of homosexual dismemberment. Sexual rocking of the waves flings the body asunder, dismembering it until the "single change" joins the body's members in a "silken transmemberment" of the poet's song, completing the orphic cycle with the metaphoric ascent of transcendence.

In his poem "Orpheus Descending," however, Williams's underwater Hades does not seem to permit any movement that would make a transmemberment possible. The narrator, addressing Orpheus, questions, "How could a girl with a wounded foot move through it?," indicating that Eurydice could not possibly follow him out of the underworld. When he asks, "How could a shell with a quiver of strings break through it?," he suggests that Orpheus's lyre, which could tame savage beasts, cannot break through to the dead. Here, Williams exegetically revises Crane, whose epic poem "The Bridge" (1930) celebrated the Brooklyn Bridge as "harp and altar of the fury fused," its "choiring strings" (44) played by the traffic crossing it rather than by the wind. Crane turns the bridge into an Aeolian harp of the industrial age, or, as Allen Grossman has suggested, an "orphic machine" (233). The poem celebrates a return, or resurrection, in an ascent "upward" in its final section, "Atlantis," that is heralded by the bridge's "orphic strings" (108). Here, the legend of Orpheus, the "floating singer late!" is fixed in the "everpresence" (107) of the stars in the "azure swing" (108) of the romantic sky.

In "Lachrymae Christi" Crane affects another transcendent ending, in which he fuses the image of a crucified Christ onto an image of a dismembered Dionysus:

> And as the nights
> Strike from Thee perfect spheres,
> Lift up in lilac-emerald breath the grail
> Of earth again—
>   Thy face
> From charred and riven stakes, O
> Dionysus, Thy
> Unmangled target smile. (20)

Transcendence in this poem occurs, as Thomas E. Yingling has pointed out, not in the Christian idea of resurrection, but in the joy surrounding the ritual of Dionysian dismemberment.

Unlike Crane's Orpheus, the dismembered body of Williams's orphic poet does not achieve any form of romantic transcendence. Rather, it remains dismembered, a scattered body of parts that will not be united as a whole. The last stanzas of "Orpheus Descending" exegetically revise Crane's ending to "Lachrymae Christi":

> And you must learn, even you, what we have learned,
> the passion there is for declivity in this world,
> the impulse to fall that follows a rising fountain.
>
> Now, Orpheus, crawl, O shamefaced fugitive, crawl
> back under the crumbling broken wall of yourself,
> for you are not stars, sky-set in the shape of a lyre,
> but the dust of those who have been dismembered by Furies! (28)

Written in 1951, two years before *Camino Real*, the poem anticipates Lord Byron's lament that *"there is a passion for declivity in this world!"* (508). In Williams's work, descent, or declivity, is the path most taken, for his fugitive kind are not romantically reborn, but scattered grotesquely to the dismembering winds.[15] Instead of being transmembered into stars with Crane's Orpheus, Williams's poet is not a phoenix, but remains a pile of ashes.

Although Crane is Williams's most pervasive influence from early to late work, Williams is most in agreement with Rimbaud's articulation of poetic vision as a calculated "disordering of the senses" ("dérèlement de tous les sens"), in which the body is given over to

> all the forms of love, of suffering, of madness; he himself experiments, he exhausts within himself every poison, in order to retain only its quintessence. Insufferable torture wherein he

becomes supremely the great diseased one, the great criminal, the great accursed—and the supreme Savant!—For he reaches the unknown! ... He reaches the unknown, and even though, made mad, he should end by losing the understanding of his visions, he has at any rate seen them! (270–71)

Rimbaud figures the poet's entry into vision through love, suffering, madness, and intoxication, but it is not the choice of "poison," nor the resulting madness which matters, for all of these are merely points of passage on the poet's journey toward vision. It is the disordered vision itself—"the unknown!"—that counts. While Williams's early plays are concerned which charting the trajectory of the subject's descent into a disfigured, visionary state, the late plays embrace Rimbaud's privileging of vision over journey. The late visionaries have already become Rimbaud's poet: the "great diseased one, the great criminal, the great accursed—and the supreme Savant!" and their grotesque visions of "the unknown" become the content and form of Williams's late dramaturgy, which, while it still employs some modes of the expressionist theater, has moved into unknown, experimental territory.

Williams's aesthetic shift in the direction of the late plays began to occur in the mid-1950s, at the time he happened to write another exegetical poem—one that celebrates Rimbaud. In "Those Who Ignore the Appropriate Time of Their Going" (1955) Williams's imagery, such as "drunken bed partners" (39) intertextually refers to Rimbaud's "The Drunken Boat" (1871). Here, Williams's bed replaces Rimbaud's boat, substituting sexuality as the vehicle for a poet's entrance into the unknown. The poem, however, seems to engage more definitively with Rimbaud's theoretical writings about poets and poetry as Williams's narrator lauds the title characters as "the most valiant explorers, / going into a country that no one is meant to go into" (37). In an unpublished meditation on Rimbaud's "planned program of self-destruction [that] was necessary to become a visionary," Williams wrote that "I prefer the 'mad' ones because I think they see the world more truly and clearly" ("These Scattered Idioms" 1, 3).

In his preference for the "mad" romantics, Williams does not simply adopt Rimbaud's aesthetics of disorder, but recasts them as an element in his own grotesque-lyric poetics, which dominate the stages of his late plays. Indeed, a rudimentary understanding of Williams's exegetical poems may provide insight not only into Williams's problematic relationship to the romantics, but into his entire body of work and his writing process itself. These poems reveal that his writing process did not simply engage in an uncritical rehashing of vaguely romantic ideas, but that it enacted dialogues with specific romantic poems about the nature and function of poetry. Similar exegetical responses exist in much of Williams's drama at deeper, subtler levels, but because of the popular characterization of Williams as a naive southern regionalist, most critical examinations of his drama have not looked deeper than autobiography in their interpretations of his content and form. As his exegetical poems suggest, however, Williams was a highly literate modernist whose texts are as deeply layered as those of Joyce or Proust, presenting a challenge to critics in the coming century.

NOTES

Grateful acknowledgment is given for permission to quote from unpublished material by Tennessee Williams ("These Scattered Idioms") to The University of the South and to the Tennessee Williams collection, Rare Book and Manuscript Library, Columbia University. Copyright © 1999 by The University of the South. Printed by permission of the University of the South, Sewanee, Tennessee.

1. For criticism on Williams's influences, see Gilbert Debusscher, "European and American Influences on the Dramas of Tennessee Williams," 167–88, "French Stowaways on an American Milktrain: Williams, Cocteau, and Peyrefitte," 399–408, and "'Minting Their Separate Wills': Tennessee Williams and Hart Crane," 113–30; Norman J. Fedder, *The Influence of D.H. Lawrence on Tennessee Williams*; Drewey Wayne Gunn, "More Than Just a Little Chekhovian: *The Seagull* as a Source for the Characters in *The Glass Menagerie*," *Modern Drama* 33:3 (1990) 313–21; John Allen Quintus, "The Loss of Things Dear: Chekhov and Williams in Perspective," *English Language Notes* 18 (Mar. 1981) 201–06; Nancy M. Tischler, "Romantic Textures in Tennessee Williams' Plays and Short Stories," 147–66, and "Tennessee Williams: Vagabond Poet," *The Tennessee Williams Annual Review* (1998) 73–79. For a recent study of influence that does not rely on biographic methods and goes beyond commentary on epigraphs, see Robert F. Gross, "Consuming Hart: Sublimity and Gay Poetics in *Suddenly Last Summer*," *Theatre Journal* 47:2 (1995) 229–51.

2. This is different from Harold Bloom's theory that poetic influence proceeds as a misreading of a precursor by a later poet, an "act of creative correction that is actually and necessarily a misinterpretation" (*Anxiety* 30), in that I am not suggesting that Williams's writing is a psychological endeavor to correct a father figure. I believe, with Robert F. Gross (243) and Thomas E. Yingling (22), that Harold Bloom's theory of influence, which is a reenactment of Freud's family romance and its oedipal agons, is a heterosexual paradigm that is not easily adaptable to gay writers.

3. Williams wrote several exegetical dramas focusing on the deaths of poet figures, including *I Rise in Flame Cried the Phoenix* (1941) about D.H. Lawrence, *Clothes for a Summer Hotel* (1980) about Scott and Zelda Fitzgerald, and *Steps Must Be Gentle* (written ca. 1947) about Hart Crane.

4. See Johann Gottfried Herder, *Sämmtliche Werke* (Stuttgart, 1827–30) 5: 220.

5. See Immanuel Kant, *Critique of Pure Reason*, 1781, trans. F. Max Muller (Garden City: Anchor, 1966).

6. Samuel Coleridge studied Kant, Fichte, and Schelling and used the distinction between reason and understanding in his own distinction between the imagination—the "esemplastic" power that unifies things—and "fancy," which only juxtaposes "fixities and definites" (Abrams, *Mirror* 161–62).

7. M. H. Abrams notes that "The Zucca" is Shelley's "unfinished version of the Intimations Ode" (*Natural* 390).

8. See W. H. Auden, "Letter to a Wound," 1934, *Twentieth Century Culture: The Breaking Apart*, ed. Robert Phelps (New York: George Braziller, 1965) 69–72.

9. Willie does the same thing in *This Property Is Condemned* (1941) written in the same year as "Intimations," when she says that the sky is as "white as a clean piece of paper" (256).

10. In addition to Crane, those who most likely influenced Williams are: Dante, Yeats, Lawrence, Chekhov, Strindberg, Rilke, Shelley, Byron, Rimbaud, Baudelaire, Lorca, Mishima, Eliot, Pirandello, Pinter, Beckett, Joyce, Pound, Proust, Blake, Wilde, the Fitzgeralds, Jane Bowles, Carson McCullers, Faulkner, and Flannery O'Connor, Lindsay, Whitman and Melville, among others.

11. Gilbert Debusscher has noted that Williams's epigraphs appear to function "as mottos or titles ... as indications of the material's deeper meaning as conceived, with critical perspective, by the playwright himself" ("Creative" 174). Critics usually employ Williams's epigraphs as a springboard into thematic criticism that has little to do with matters of influence.

12. In addition to "Orpheus Descending," poems in *In the Winter of Cities* that seem to perform an exegesis of Crane (on some level) include "The Siege," "The Angels of Fructification," "Photograph and Pearls," "The Summer Belvedere," "Descent," "The Legend," "The Death Embrace," "The Christus of Guadalahara," "This Island Is Memorable to Us," "San Sebastiano de Sodoma," "The Last Wine," and "A Separate Poem."

13. In Shakespeare's *Richard III*, Clarence foresees his own death in a vision of drowned men:

Methoughts I saw a thousand fearful wracks;
A thousand men that fishes gnaw'd upon;
Wedges of gold, great anchors; heaps of pearl,
Inestimable stones, unvalued jewels,
All scatt'red in the bottom of the sea:
Some lay in dead men's skulls, and in the holes
Where eyes did once inhabit. (Act 1, sc. 4, l. 24–30)

14. Hart Crane wrote exegetical poems to Shakespeare, Dickinson, Poe and Melville. Allen Grossman theorizes that in these poems Crane positions himself as the "outside describer, the Daedalian survivor of enterprises like his own" (226).

15. In Crane, the wind is always a trope for dismemberment, as observed by Cranian scholars Thomas E. Yingling and Lee Edelman. Williams uses wind in stage directions or in poetry in much the same dismembering manner, in sharp contrast to Nancy M. Tischler's contention that Williams's "references to wind and his love of wind chimes blend romantic with Pentecostal wind imagery" ("Romantic" 154).

WORKS CITED

Abrams, M. H. *The Mirror and the Lamp: Romantic Theory and the Critical Tradition* Oxford: Oxford UP, 1953.

———. *Natural Supernaturalism: Tradition and Revolution in Romantic Literature*. New York: Norton, 1971.

Adler, Thomas P. "Tennessee Williams' Poetry: Intertext and Metatext." *Tennessee Williams Annual Review* (1998): 63–72.

Bakhtin, Mikhail. *Rabelais and His World*. Trans. Helen Iswolsky. Bloomington: Indiana UP, 1984.

Bloom, Harold. *The Anxiety of Influence*. New York: Oxford UP, 1973.

———. Introduction. *Tennessee Williams. Modern Critical Views*. Ed. Harold Bloom. New York: Chelsea House, 1987. 1–8.

———. *The Visionary Company: A Reading of English Romantic Poetry*. New York: Anchor, 1963.

Coleridge, Samuel Taylor. *The Poems of Samuel Taylor Coleridge*. Ed. Ernest Hartley Coleridge. London: Oxford UP 1931.

Crane, Hart. *Complete Poems of Hart Crane*. 1933. Ed. Marc Simon. New York: Liveright, 1993.

Debusscher, Gilbert. "Creative Rewriting: European and American Influences on the Dramas of Tennessee Williams." *The Cambridge Companion to Tennessee Williams*. Ed. Matthew C. Roudane. Cambridge: Cambridge UP, 1997. 167–88.

———. "French Stowaways on an American Milktrain: Williams, Cocteau, and Peyrefitte." *Modern Drama* 25:3 (1982): 399–408.

———. "'Minting Their Separate Wills': Tennessee Williams and Hart Crane." *Modern Drama* 26:4 (1983). Rpt. in Bloom. 113–30.

de man, Paul. *The Rhetoric of Romanticism*. New York: Columbia UP 1984.

Fedder, Norman J. *The Influence of D.H. Lawrence on Tennessee Williams*. London: Mouton, 1966.

Grossman, Allen. "Hart Crane and Poetry: A Consideration of Crane's Intense poetics with Reference to 'The Return.'" *Critical Essays on Hart Crane*. Ed. David Clark. Boston Hall, 1982.

Hugo, Victor. Preface to Cromwell. 1827. *Oeuvres complètes*. 18 vols. Paris: 1967–70.

Jackson, Esther Merle. *The Broken World of Tennessee Williams*. Madison: U of Wisconsin P, 1965.

———. "Tennessee Williams: Poetic Consciousness in Crisis." Tharpe. 53–72.

Moore, Marianne. "Poetry." *The College Anthology of British and American Verse*. Ed. A. Kent Hieatt. Boston: Allyn and Bacon, 1964. 577–78.

Rimbaud, Arthur. Letter to Paul Demeny. 15 May 1871. *Oeuvres Complètes*. Ed. Rolland de Reneville and Jules Mouquet. Paris: Pleiade, 1963.

Shelley, Percy Bysshe. *The Complete Poems of Percy Bysshe Shelley*. Notes by Mary Shelley. 1839. New York: Modern Library, 1994.

Tharpe, Jac, ed. *Tennessee Williams: A Tribute*. Jackson: UP of Mississippi, 1977.

Tischler, Nancy M. "Romantic Textures in Tennessee Williams' Plays and Short Stories." *The Cambridge Companion to Tennessee Williams*. Ed. Matthew C. Roudane. Cambridge: Cambridge UP, 1997. 147–66.

Williams, Tennessee. *Camino Real*. 1953. *The Theatre of Tennessee Williams*. Vol. 2. New York: New Directions, 1971. 417–591.

———. *In the Winter of Cities*. 1964. New York: New Directions, 1977.

———. "The Meaning of The Rose Tattoo." 1951. *Where I Live*. 55–57.

———. "Preface to My Poems." 1944. *Where I Live*. 1–6.

———. "The Role of Poetry in the Modern Theatre." 1945. *Conversations with Tennessee Williams*. Ed. Albert J. Devlin. Jackson: UP of Mississippi, 1986. 20–24.

————. *Suddenly Last Summer*. 1958. *The Theatre of Tennessee Williams*. Vol. 5. New York: New Directions, 1971.

————. "Tennessee Williams Survives." 1970. *Conversations with Tennessee Williams*. Ed. Albert J. Devlin. Jackson: UP of Mississippi, 1986. 161–83.

————. "These Scattered Idioms." Ts., n.d. Tennessee Williams Papers. Columbia U, New York.

————. "The Timeless World of a Play." 1951. *Where I Live*. 49–54.

————. *This Property Is Condemned*. 1941. *27 Wagons Full of Cotton*. 1945. *The Theatre of Tennessee Williams*. Vol. 6. New York: New Directions, 1981. 245–61.

————. *Where I Live: Selected Essays*. Ed. Christine R. Day and Bob Woods. New York: New Directions, 1978.

Wordsworth, William. "Ode: Intimations of Immortality from Recollections of Early Childhood." *The College Anthology of British and American Verse*. Ed. A. Kent Hieatt. Boston: Allyn and Bacon, 1964. 296–301.

————. *Preface to Lyrical Ballads*. 1802. *Literary Criticism of William Wordsworth*. Ed. Paul M. Zall. Lincoln: U of Nebraska P, 1966.

Yingling, Thomas E. *Hart Crane and the Homosexual Text: New Thresholds, New Anatomies*. Chicago: U of Chicago P, 1990.

Yoder, R. A. *Emerson and the Orphic Poet in America*. Berkeley: U of California P, 1978.

D. DEAN SHACKELFORD

"The Transmutation of Experience":[1] The Aesthetics and Themes of Tennessee Williams's Nonfiction

Readers have often used the nonfiction essays of Tennessee Williams to interpret his plays, fiction, and poetry, and to assess his work as a whole. Although there have been frequent references to Tennessee Williams's personal essays, prefaces to his own plays, and reviews of others' creative work, little if any critical attention has been given to what these nonfiction pieces contribute to our understanding of Williams the individual, the artist, the intellectual, and the critic. Williams the personal essayist, social critic, and literary theorist does, however, deserve serious scholarly attention.

Close examination of the many short pieces[2] Williams wrote for periodicals and as introductions and prefaces to the creative work of his own and his friends and colleagues reveals not only an effective and worthy prose style but also a perceptive sense of the world after World War II and the creative potential and practice of fellow artists. In "Critic Says 'Evasion,' Writer Says 'Mystery,'" which originally appeared in the *New York Herald Tribune* of 17 April 1955, in response to Walter Kerr's critique of *Cat on a Hot Tin Roof*, and is reprinted in *Where I Live*, Williams also anticipates contemporary theories of the reader and the multiplicity of meanings in a text by suggesting that the "truth about human character in a play, as in life, varies with the variance of experience and viewpoint of those that view it" (70). While he is referring to criticisms that he is being ambiguous about Brick's

From *The Southern Quarterly* 38, no. 1 (Fall 1999): pp. 104–116. © 1999 by the University of Southern Mississippi.

sexual identity, this passage is only one example of how his nonfiction works illustrate his sophisticated style as well as anticipate and open the possibility for contemporary post-structuralist approaches to reading literature.

Williams's nonfiction includes personal essays and reflections, prefaces to his own works, and reviews and criticism of the creative work of others, mostly friends. These subgenres are by no means mutually exclusive, for Williams's prose is often loosely structured, organic, and informal, and he combines these three categories oftentimes in one essay or review. Therefore, for purposes of discussion, the present study of Williams's nonfiction will address the primary themes evident in the personal essays and some theoretical components of his commentaries about his own and others' work. Before examining significant themes in and examples of the nonfiction, one should, however, be familiar with pertinent biographical details related to these ignored works.

According to Lyle Leverich's *Tom: The Unknown Tennessee Williams*, after twelve-year-old Tom was asked to read a commentary on Tennyson's "Lady of Shalott" in front of class and he received a positive response, he decided to become a writer (64); moreover, his first publication, "Isolated," was an essay. It appeared in the student newspaper, *The Junior Life*, in November 1924, while he was a student at Blewett High School. He was first published professionally in *Smart Set* and *Weird Tales*, a pulp magazine, in 1928 (Leverich 82). During his high school years he won several literary contests, but only when he entered college in St. Louis at Washington University did he begin the serious study of literature and the Western critical heritage.

After graduating from University City High School in St. Louis in June 1929, Williams enrolled as an undergraduate journalism major at the University of Missouri in Columbia. At that time he studied the poetry and biography of Percy Bysshe Shelley and became a member of the Missouri Chapter of the College Poetry Society (Leverich 125). His critical and biographical reading, and his journalism classes, likely helped him develop stylistic clarity and precision in prose. After a stint at the St. Louis International Shoe Company, he enrolled at Washington University, beginning in September 1935. There he studied literature more formally and began to develop a critical sensibility which can be observed through studying his own prefaces and other literary criticism.

During these college years, he read many canonical writers as well as contemporary playwrights. He examined the plays of Eugene O'Neill for a course in which he wrote a critical essay entitled "Some Representative Plays of O'Neill and a Discussion of His Art," whose style the professor labeled "a bit too truculent" (Leverich 183). He also studied English literature under Dr. Otto Heller, a well-known scholar of Henrik Ibsen, and wrote a term paper entitled "Birth of an Art (Anton Chekhov and the New Theatre) by T. L. Williams" (Leverich 217). However, he ended his career at Washington University partly because he did not enjoy his classes under Heller: "Although Tom's notebooks attest to the fact that he was well read ... he became increasingly annoyed by the professor's intellectual posturings" (Leverich 183).

His reaction to Heller was the beginning of a long animosity with the critical and, to some extent, academic world which, in his estimation, failed to understand his artistry and appreciate his plays, especially his most experimental and late ones. He would become a college graduate only after attending the Writers' Workshop at the University of Iowa and experience what Leverich calls "a drama department that espoused his philosophy of a theatre in action" (226).

These shaping influences enabled Williams to develop as a prose stylist and critic of his own and others' works. When he began to establish himself as a playwright, he had already written prose for his public school and college classes, and had been actively involved in reading, assessing, and writing poetry and prose. His personal essays and literary criticism demonstrate not only his knowledge of classical and modern literature, including drama, but also his distrust of "intellectual posturings." Since the biographical context for examining Williams as a prose writer has been established , a closer look at some representative illustrations of the style and subject matter of Williams's nonfiction will be undertaken at this point.

Several recurring themes are evident in his personal essays. These include endurance and struggle; the problem of the artist in American society; the struggle over class, materialism, and the American dream; and the devaluation of the individual. Within these contexts, a number of essays contain a social critique of McCarthyism itself or the tendency toward such an extreme in American society.

To Williams endurance and struggle build stronger character. In one of his best essays, "On a Streetcar Named Success," a piece which originally appeared in the *New York Times* on 30 November 1947, just before the premiere of *A Streetcar Named Desire*, he reflects this own experience as a successful new writer first receiving supportive critical attention. While discussing his past experience, he implies that the hard work may have been more beneficial than the actual reality of success: "The sort of life which I had had previous to this popular success was one that required endurance, a life of clawing and scratching along a sheer surface and holding on tight with raw fingers to every inch of rock higher than the one caught hold of before, but it was a good life because it was the sort of life for which the human organism is created" (*Where I Live* 16). Success is "a catastrophe" because to Williams a life without struggle ceases to be a life with meaning, as this passage suggests: "But once you fully apprehend the vacuity of a life without struggle you are equipped with the basic means of salvation" (21). This essay shows that not only does Williams see endurance as the triumph of humanity, a theme which he repeats in his plays time and again, but he also sees himself in his characters.

Part of the problem with success for the artist in American society, according to Williams, is a curious ambivalence toward his place in a culture which has marginalized him. In another significant personal essay, "A Writer's Quest for Parnassus," he addresses this ambivalence. Drawing upon assumptions about the ideal locale for the American expatriate, he points out that for him, both personally and artistically, Rome inspires much more creative writing and personal freedom than America or Paris, the site of the "Lost Generation" after World War I. Throughout the essay Williams suggests that Rome is the ideal place for the writer. He states of the Romans: "Their history has made them wiser than Americans. It has also made them more tolerant, more patient, and considerably more human as well as a great deal sadder" (34). Referring to the mythical Parnassus in his title, Williams also admonishes America for her lack of appreciation for sensitivity and romance—implying the harshness of everyday life in this country which is so antithetical to the pursuit of art.

Art thus becomes secondary to pursuit of the American dream, a material quest for success which often destroys the human (and the artist's) spirit. In the pre-*Streetcar* essay referred to earlier, Williams also refers to the Cinderella story as "our favorite national myth" ("On a Streetcar" 15), implicitly criticizing capitalism and its potential for exploitation: "Nobody should have to clean up anybody else's mess in this world. It is terribly bad for both parties, but probably worse for the one receiving the service" ("On a Streetcar" 20). The only endeavor worth pursuing is done so at the price of struggle, suggesting that capitalism becomes problematic as an end in itself—especially when one feels too comfortable.

At the heart of these social critiques is an implicit attack on McCarthyism and its devaluation of the individual. Significantly, Williams identifies the social roots of McCarthyism, a distrust of difference and people of other cultures and beliefs: "If these comments make me seem the opposite of a chauvinist, it is because of my honest feeling, after three years of foreign travel, that human brotherhood that stops at borders is not only delusive and foolish but enormously evil" ("A Writer's Quest" 34). His critical attitude concerning political McCarthyism is most fully revealed in another section of "A Writer's Quest": "British and American writers are more inclined to travel than others. I think the British travel to get out of the rain, but the

American artist travels for a more particular reason, and for one that I hesitate to mention lest I be summoned before some investigating committee in Congress" (29). In this passage and elsewhere, Williams implicitly criticizes American society as being cold and intolerant of the individual, an attitude he surreptitiously explores through Brick's mysterious past in *Cat on a Hot Tin Roof*, produced originally in 1955 during the McCarthy era, as David Savran's book *Communists, Cowboys, and Queers* points out.[3]

In general the central themes of his personal essays are developed through a clarity of voice and vision. His essays clearly exemplify a style which is leisurely and inviting for the audience, as Alec Baldwin's readings from Williams's prose at the 1997 Tennessee Williams Literary Festival clearly demonstrated.[4] His prose style is almost always characterized as terse, witty, concrete, poetic, intelligent, and precise while, like his plays, simultaneously lyrical, even rhapsodic.

For example, in his essay entitled "Tennessee Williams: The Wolf and I," Williams narrates the entertaining but painful story of his bad experience with Wolf, his new dog. After being bitten in a hotel room, Williams is treated by an inept physician. Characterized by self-mockery, what some people today might label a "camp sensibility,"[5] this essay is anecdotal and more entertainment than serious artistry, but it shows that even during a difficult period in Williams's personal life, he was able to laugh at himself. His prose style is exemplified well through the essay's use of wit, as this passage reveals: "The doctor looked at my ankles and said, 'Oh, the Wolf has bitten you to the bone of each ankle,' which was an astute and accurate observation" (5). Later on, he describes the process of being taken to the hospital by two men in white jackets: "I had never been on a stretcher before nor had I ever before gone downstairs in the freight elevator of a large hotel. The novelty of both experiences did nothing to reassure me ..." (5). As a whole, the essay "Wolf and I" reflects the kind of self-mockery, campiness, and humor often associated with Williams's plays. In addition; the style reflects the same tendency toward clarity, terseness, and metaphor seen elsewhere.

Another characteristic feature of Williams's nonfiction is the use of frequent references and allusions to the works of the people whom he most admired. His primary dramatic forbear, he often liked to say, was Anton Chekhov. In addition, Williams deeply admired the poetry and drama of Federico Garcia Lorca, a fellow homosexual. His fellow southern writers, William Faulkner, Carson McCullers, Donald Windham, and Truman Capote, and his other friends and associates, including Paul and Jane Bowles, and Clark Mills (whom he had known in St. Louis while enrolled at Washington University), are also frequently referred to in Williams's nonfiction and letters—often directly by name (Leverich 155). As these examples suggest, perhaps the most characteristic feature evident in his nonfiction works is personal reflection on his own and others' work. In fact, the difficulty of examining Williams's nonfiction is that, like much contemporary literature, it resists neat categorization and thus anticipates the blurring of genre and form so often discussed in connection with postmodernism.

Rather than look at the prefaces to and commentaries about his own work in separate categories, therefore, the best way to approach these critical and theoretical works is through examining the concepts upon which Williams draws and those from which he departs. A significant purpose of the present examination of Williams's nonfiction is to establish how he anticipates many contemporary debates about the nature of literature, theory, and interpretation. Thus, an exploration of individual essays is less instructive than a look at some literary and theoretical constructs with which Williams is working in his nonfiction and his criticism.

A student of western literature and the Eurocentric dramatic heritage, Williams, in his critical works, drew upon two primary theories of art. The first, derived largely from Aristotle's conception of tragedy but generally practiced in the history of western literature from the ancients to the twentieth century, was representation, a concept which contemporary literary theorists have begun to problematize more and more. Conventional readings of Aristotle place emphasis on mimesis, or art as a mirror or imitation of life because in *The Poetics* Aristotle describes tragedy in this manner.

> Tragedy, then, is an imitation of an action that is serious, complete, and of a certain magnitude; in language embellished with each kind of artistic ornament, the several kinds being found in separate parts of the play; in the form of action, not narrative; through pity and fear affecting the proper purgation of these emotions. (36)

In "The Timeless World of a Play," Williams reiterates Aristotle's notion of drama as a mirror or reflection of reality: "So successfully have we disguised from ourselves the intensity of our own feelings, the sensibility of our own hearts, that plays in the tragic tradition have begun to seem untrue" (263). Implicitly, then, he is agreeing with Aristotle's view that art is a mirror of reality. Similarly, when describing his commitment to the still problematic play *Orpheus Descending*, Williams states, in "The Past, the Present, and the Perhaps," that "beneath that now familiar surface it is a play about unanswered questions that haunt the hearts of people and the difference between continuing to ask them, a difference represented by the four major protagonists of the play ..." (220). Williams clearly shows that he is after representation and, at the same time, suggests, like Aristotle, that tragedy can only imitate or mirror life—not literally convey it (note the phrase "familiar surface"). To get at the truths through which his dramas penetrate, one, therefore, has to look beneath the surface. Looking at Williams's prefaces to his works suggests that he accepts Aristotelian conceptions of tragedy and representation but is aware of the problems brought about by a purely mimetic theory of art.

A second, conventional approach to art which is evident in Williams's nonfiction is romantic and expressivistic. When discussing *Cat on a Hot Tin Roof* in "Person-to-Person," he admits, "Of course it is a pity that so much of all creative work is so closely related to the personality of the one who does it" (3). This comment reflects not only the Aristotelian conception of mimesis but also echoes the Platonic notion of the world beyond the real to the imagined or idealized. To expand upon this view, Williams uses the term "organic" more than any other in his nonfiction to describe his conception of art and the artist.

In his essays on the controversial *Camino Real* particularly, Williams embraces the organic theory of art and heavily criticizes audiences for their response to the play. Deconstructing Aristotelian notions of mimesis, Williams, in the foreword to *Camino Real*, calls it "the construction of another world, a separate existence" and claims "it is nothing more nor less than my conception of the time and world that I live in ..." (419). This organic theory—that is, the idea that art is an outgrowth of the poetic imagination—places Williams in the tradition of the literary criticism of Coleridge in *Biographia Literaria*. Coleridge suggests that the poet of imagination is able to use the tradition to create his own aesthetic experience, distinguishing between the imagination and the fancy. "Fancy" implies a kind of artistic control and "mechanical" mastering of the techniques of art.[6]

When describing a book of poetry written by his friend, Oliver Evans, Williams also refers to the organic theory of art. His foreword to *Young Man with a Screwdriver*, for example, emphasizes their friendship and places his work within "the oldest and purest tradition" of writing spontaneous, immediate poetry (2)—again, organic and romantic theory. He also praises Evans's "latitude and variety both in subject and quality" (2) and refers to him as "singer" (3)—all romantic images of the artist.

Other reviews reflect this conventional approach to textuality as well. When introducing the poetry collection of Gilbert Maxwell, entitled *Go Looking: Poems 1933–1953*, Williams compares his situation in assessing his friend's work with that of Eugene O'Neill in trying to write a foreword to Hart Crane's first book. Though such effusiveness is characteristic of Williams's tendency toward romantic emotionalism, Maxwell is far from being Hart Crane, and I am sure Williams, who admired and identified with Crane more

than any other poet, knew this was hyperbole as well. Maxwell is, however, a
lyric poet who would appeal to a playwright who sees personal lyricism as his
most characteristic element.

The critical tension between art as a representation of external reality—
society—and art as a reflection of the subjectivity of the writer in western
literature and criticism is evident not only in Williams's nonfiction but also
through contemporary gay approaches to Williams's works. Furthermore, his
essays anticipate current debate over the role of authorship and work. With
regard to the death of author arguments of contemporary theorists such as
Michel Foucault and Roland Barthes,[7] Williams would be both in agreement
and disagreement for varying reasons.

He could never envision art without the presence of the artist—
making him clearly a necromantic, humanistic, and poetic artist despite his
frequently naturalistic, brutally realistic portrayals of violence and sexuality.
Yet his attitudes are not always consistent even about the autobiographical
dimensions of his works. As anyone who has read the numerous interviews
regarding the role of homosexuality in his plays can recall, he often denies
and underestimates the role of his own gay subjectivity in his creative work.[8]
Perhaps the best way to see Williams's ambivalence about his gay subjectivity
is to suggest that, like Foucault, he tries to decenter the text and erase, at
least in print, the idea that his works are about homosexuality—rejecting
essentialist notions about textuality, the construction of the self, and the
author's presence.

Such a practice also enables Williams to effect his organic theory
of writing as well as to practice now recognized truisms of contemporary
literary criticism: the inseparability of the text from the reader and the
subjectivity at the heart of all interpretation. When he writes about Brick
in *Cat on a Hot Tin Roof*, probably his gayest play before he came out in
an interview on television with David Frost in 1970, he strongly resists
reductionist readings of his alcoholic character—a notion which perhaps
indicates his desire for multiple interpretations of the play and anticipates
deconstructionist approaches to literature arguing for the multiplicity of
meaning. In describing Brick's character, for example, he says, in what
amounts to a short essay and analysis in the printed version of the play:
"Some mystery should be left in the revelation of character in a play, just
as a great deal of mystery is always left in the revelation of character in life,
even in one's own character to himself. This does not absolve the playwright
of his duty to observe and probe as clearly and deeply as he legitimately
can ..." (115). The resistance to one reading of Brick's character anticipates
deconstructionist arguments against essentialism. While Williams would
be probably uncomfortable with the increasing complexity in debate

surrounding textuality, he would, at the same time presumably, be open to many possible readings of Brick's character.

Thus, like many contemporary literary theorists, Williams problematizes subjectivity as a critical construct and opens up the possibility for Lacanian and other post-structuralist readings of literature. For example, in "If the Writing Is Honest," in which he reviews Inge's play *The Dark at the Top of the Stairs*, he distinguishes between representation theory—that is, art as a reflection of truth—and romantic conceptions of the artist. Sounding Platonic, Williams suggests that writing "isn't so much ... [the artist's] mirror as it is the distillation, the essence, of what is strongest and purest in his nature, whether that be gentleness or anger, serenity or torment, light or dark" (100). Such words also bring to mind Jungian mythical criticism and Lacan's references to the mirror stage of a child's development.

Even some of the language in the essay opens up the text to Lacanian readings, as the following anecdote referring to the shadow and light would seem to suggest:

> After I had gone back to Chicago to finish out the break-in run of *Menagerie*, Bill came up one weekend to see the play. I didn't know until then that Bill wanted to be a playwright. After the show, we walked back to my hotel ... and on the way he suddenly confided to me, with characteristic simplicity and directness, that being a successful playwright was what he most wanted in the world for himself. This confession struck me, at the time, as being just a politeness, an effort to dispel the unreasonable gloom that had come over me at a time when I should have been most elated, an ominous letdown of spirit that followed me like my shadow wherever I went.... I think that Bill Inge had already made up his mind to invoke this same shadow and to suffuse it with light: and that, of course, is exactly what he has done. (103–04)

Williams uses a mythical approach to textuality as well as opens up the possibility for psychoanalytic explorations of art. Furthermore, Inge's shadow could be interpreted as an image of the self and an exploration of the problematized subject, which Lacan sees as a construction of language and art.[9] Williams's slippery subjective voice and Inge as a construction of this voice open up further possibilities for post-structuralist readings.

Moreover, Williams anticipates current literary debates concerning privileging one form or genre of literature over another. In other words, he is already raising questions about conventional formalism and canonicity. This is particularly evident when one examines his reviews of the novels of Carson

McCullers, a personal friend. *Reflections in a Golden Eye*, certainly not the best of Carson McCullers's novels, was the subject for one of Williams's most effective works of nonfiction, the introduction to the novel's first edition of 1950.

The essay implicitly attacks traditional critics for their lack of appreciation for McCullers's second novel. Once categorized as a member of the southern gothic school, McCullers, he argues, is unable to move beyond this limited and essentialist notion of her fiction. Pointing out the tenderness of *The Heart as a Lonely Hunter* as a buttress against criticism for her use of the grotesque in *Reflections*, Williams believed the harsh assessment of the latter novel resulted in critical attitudes that McCullers had not lived up to the potential shown in her first novel and reflected a darker vision. Calling McCullers the "greatest living writer" (136) in his essay "Biography of Carson McCullers," Williams praises *Clock without Hands*—McCullers's biggest critical disaster (and, to my mind, too imitative of Faulkner). Such comments suggest Williams is aware of the tendency to canonize—thus privilege—her first novel and read the remainder of her work as lesser fictions. The essay also raises questions about representation in McCullers's works and criticizes non-southerners for their misreadings of southern literature in a manner reminiscent of Flannery O'Connor in *Mystery and Manners*.

Another post-structuralist dimension to Williams's literary criticism is a tendency to accept certain assumptions of formalism and modernism and to reject others. In the same essay, he argues that McCullers's second novel demonstrates a mastery of design—a term reminiscent of formalism—and succeeds more perfectly in establishing its own reality, in creating a world of its own, a quality which he considers characteristic of a great artist (46–47)—commentary which again reflects his awareness of formalism and his application of the assumptions of his organic theory. On the other hand, he states that *The Member of the Wedding* is a better novel, saying that it combined the heartbreaking tenderness of the first with the sculptural quality of the second (47). Although privileging one McCullers novel over another, this commentary implies that art is an organic whole while at the same time deconstructs the problem of form in the second novel by suggesting that content may be separate from form in incongruous ways. He goes further: "*Reflections in a Golden Eye* is one of the purest and most powerful of those works which are conceived in that Sense of the Awful which is the desperate black root of all significant modern art" (46).

Williams would also be comfortable with the assumptions of Cultural Studies[10] and New Historicism concerning the relation of art to time and place. In a review of Paul Bowles's novel *The Sheltering Sky*, Williams acknowledges that he lives in a different world than writers of the past and places Bowles within the context of post–World War II existentialism. Describing Bowles in almost postmodern terms which suggest the breakdown of conventional literary form, William, using a poetic style characteristic of all his nonfiction and his plays as well, states concerning *The Sheltering Sky*:

> There is a curiously double level to this novel. The surface is enthralling as narrative. It is impressive as writing. But above that surface is the aura I spoke of, intangible and powerful, bringing to mind one of those clouds that you have seen in summer close to the horizon and dark in color and now and then silently pulsing with interior flashes of fire. ("Allegory" 7)

Using impressionistic language, Williams assesses the allegorical dimensions of Bowles's vision and the dangerous moral nihilism into which humanity is going at present (38). Williams's reading of Bowles connects with traditional historicism while opening up the possibility for examining tensions within popular culture and American society after World War II in a way similar to Foucault's arguments against the human subject as apart from the construction of time and place.

In "The Human Psyche—Alone," a review of another work by Paul Bowles, Williams repeats his earlier reference to the existentialist dimensions of Bowles's fiction. Here he addresses the same questions which he does in the prefaces to his own plays and nonfiction: human alienation, the artist in society, and hardness of perception (39), the latter phrase of which I take to mean Bowles's portrayal of the realities of life as he sees them (compare Williams's brutality and violence in his own plays). Bowles is described as predominately a philosophical writer concerned with human alienation in *The Delicate Prey and Other Stories*. At the same time Williams emphasizes personal lyricism and critiques literature celebrating American culture in a positive way and denying the darkness within the human psyche. This review also includes Lacanian elements problematizing the subject, as this passage reveals: "Nowhere in any writing that I can think of has the separateness of the one human psyche been depicted more vividly and shockingly" (37).

By pointing out Bowles's deconstruction of the self, Williams anticipates Jacques Derrida's notion of the multiplicity of meaning and the destruction of binaries as well.[11] Like Julia Kristeva's arguments in "Semiotics: A Critique of Science and/or a Critique of Science," Williams recognizes Bowles's complex interrogation of the self as a signifying agent and the fiction writer's approach to the fragmented human condition. His subjective response to Bowles reflects both his friendship and his perhaps unconscious awareness that meaning is at least partly constructed by the self and society. He sees in Bowles a shift in western literature and anticipates contemporary theoretical approaches such as reader-response theory and deconstructionism—providing for a multiplicity of meanings for Bowles's novel by pointing out its ambiguities and emphasizing the novel's irresolutions of the modern dilemma.

Throughout all his literary criticism, Williams blurs the social and critical constructions of author and subject, self and other, and art and life. His awareness that these binaries are almost inseparable from one another shows his affiliation with postmodern debates concerning the object and the subject and contemporary literary explorations of the "funhouse"—the artist's withdrawal into a world of imagination. In other essays Williams also anticipates postmodern questions about the role of art and social construction, leading to further debates about feminism, queer theory, and cultural studies in his critical and creative work.

In a piece entitled "Let Me Hang It All Out," Tennessee Williams describes his attempts at writing personal and critical essays as awkward adventures in the field of nonfictional prose. Despite such self-criticism, Williams the playwright is an effective, entertaining, and often perceptive prose writer. As a personal essayist, he moves from the personal to the critical to the social in one fell swoop. As a theorist of drama and critic of his own work, he is particularly significant. He understands his place in the western dramatic and literary traditions, and he recognizes the value of and importance of literature and nonfiction prose to American society and culture. When Williams reviews the fiction, poetry, and drama of fellow writers, he praises the work, saving severe criticism for the mean-spirited critics who, in his estimation, had failed to appreciate his experimental late plays and the works of his friends. Much of what is reflected in Williams nonfiction is a sensitive soul who understands the inseparability of art and the artist, subject and object, self and other—and an individual who will not be deliberately cruel (at least in print) toward his close friends and colleagues. As such a brief survey of his prose work suggests, there is much more to be said concerning this unexplored territory in Williams studies.

NOTES

1. The title of this essay comes from Williams's "A Summer of Discovery," which was originally published in the *New York Herald Tribune* and reprinted in *Where I Live: Selected Essays*. There he describes the process of writing as "the most necessary impulse or drive toward ... [the writer's] work, which is the transmutation of experience into some significant piece of creation ..." (140).

2. Williams wrote many prefaces and introductions to his own works as well as reviews and introductions to the works of others. George W. Crandell's *Tennessee Williams: A Descriptive Bibliography* references more than fifty such pieces. The majority have been reprinted in *Where I Live*.

3. This play has frequently been read as a commentary on McCarthyism. Brick's fear of the possible repercussions about his relationship with Skipper is sometimes read as a reflection of the playwright's fear of disclosure, a point which Savran mentions. Philip C. Kolin's new book, *Tennessee Williams: A Guide to Research and Performance*, cites other readings of the play, including Clum's "'Something Cloudy, Something Clear'," Dukore's "The Cat Has Nine Lives," and Shackelford's "The Truth That Must Be Told: Gay Subjectivity, Homophobia, and Social History in *Cat on a Hot Tin Roof*."

4. At the 1997 Tennessee Williams/New Orleans Literary Festival in March 1997, Baldwin was the invited celebrity speaker. During one segment of the festival, he read selected essays by Williams and commented on the personal immediacy and comical dimensions within them.

5. While the term camp is subjective and contextual, I am using it to suggest the gay sense of self-mockery and "double consciousness" (a term borrowed from W. E. B. DuBois) of comic irony evident through a detached view of self through one's own and others' eyes simultaneously. David Bergman's *Camp Grounds: Style and Homosexuality* and Judith Butler's *Gender Trouble* are two important resources on the complexity of camp in the gay sensibility.

6. In *Biographia Literaria* Coleridge identifies the primary imagination as "the living power and prime agent of all human perception" and fancy, or the secondary imagination, "as an echo of the former ... differing only in degree, and in the mode of its operation" (387).

7. Foucault problematizes the constructs of authorship and work in "What Is an Authors" saying, "The author is ... the ideological figure by which one marks the manner in which we fear the proliferation of meaning" (353). Following Foucault's logic, Barthes argues for the "death of the Author" and the "birth of the reader" (226) as a result.

8. In numerous interviews reprinted in Albert Devlin's *Conversations with Tennessee Williams* and elsewhere, he tries to deny that homosexuality is a central issue in his works.

9. See, for example, Lacan's essay "Desire and the Interpretation of Desire in *Hamlet*" and "The Mirror Stage as Formative of the Function of the I as Revealed in Psychoanalytic Experience."

10. For a good introduction and definition of the broad category "Cultural Studies," see "Notes towards a Definition of Cultural Studies" by Robert Con Davis and Ronald Schleifer.

11. This can be seen of course in many works by Jacques Derrida, including *Of Grammatology and Writing and Difference*. A good resource would be Peggy Kamuf's *A Derrida Reader*.

WORKS CITED

Aristotle. *Poetics. Dramatic Theory and Criticism: Greeks to Grotowski*. Ed. Bernard F. Dukore. New York: Holt, 1974. 31–55.

Barthes, Roland. "The Death of the Author." *Falling into Theory: Conflicting Views of Reading Literature*. Ed. David H. Richter. New York: Bedford Books, 1994. 222–26.

Bergman, David, ed. *Camp Grounds: Style and Homosexuality*. Amherst: U of Massachusetts P, 1993.

Butler, Judith. *Gender Trouble: Feminism and the Subversion of Identity*. New York: Routledge, 1990.

Clum, John M. "'Something Cloudy, Something Clear': Homophobic Discourse in Tennessee Williams." *South Atlantic Quarterly* 88 (1989): 161–79.

Coleridge, Samuel Taylor. "From *Biographia Literaria*." *The Norton Anthology of English Literature*. Vol. 1. Ed. M.H. Abrams. New York: Norton, 1993. 378–95.

Crandell, George W. *Tennessee Williams: A Descriptive Bibliography*. Pittsburgh: U of Pittsburgh P, 1995.

Davis, Robert Con, and Ronald Schleifer. "Notes towards a Definition of Cultural Studies." *Contemporary Literary Criticism: Literary and Cultural Studies*. Eds. Robert Con Davis and Ronald Schleifer. White Plains, NY: Longman, 1994. 668–80.

Derrida, Jacques. *Of Grammatology*. Trans. Gayatri Chakravorty Spivak. Baltimore: Johns Hopkins UP, 1976.

———. *Writing and Difference*. Trans. Alan Bass. Chicago: U of Chicago P, 1978.

Devlin, Albert J., ed. *Conversations with Tennessee Williams*. Jackson: UP of Mississippi, 1986.

Dukore, Bernard F. "The Cat Has Nine Lives." *Tulane Drama Review* 8.1 (1963): 95–100.

Kolin, Philip C., ed. *Tennessee Williams: A Guide to Research and Performance*. Westport, CT: Greenwood, 1998.

Foucault, Michel. "What Is an Author?" Davis and Schleifer. 365–76.

Kristeva, Julia. "Semiotics: A Critical Science and/or a Critique of Science." Davis and Schleifer. 274–82.

Lacan, Jacques. "Desire and the Interpretation of Desire in *Hamlet*." *The Seminar, Book VII: The Ethics of Psychoanalysis, 1959–1960*. Trans. Dennis Porter. New York: Norton, 1992.

———. "The Mirror Stage as Formative of the Function of the I as Revealed in Psychoanalytic Experience." Davis and Schleifer. 383–86.

Leverich, Lyle. *Tom: The Unknown Tennessee Williams*. New York: Crown, 1995.

Murphy, Brenda. *Tennessee Williams and Elia Kazan: A Collaboration in the Theatre*. Cambridge: Cambridge UP, 1992.

O'Connor, Flannery. *Mystery and Manners: Occasional Prose*. Ed. Sally Fitzgerald. New York: Farrar, 1969.

Savran, David. *Communists, Cowboys, and Queers: The Politics of Masculinity in the Work of Arthur Miller and Tennessee Williams*. Minneapolis: U of Minnesota P, 1992.

Shackelford, Dean. "The Truth That Must Be Told: Gay Subjectivity, Homophobia, and Social History in *Cat on a Hot Tin Roof*." *Tennessee Williams Annual Review* 1 (1998): 103–18.

Williams, Tennessee. "An Allegory of Man and His Sahara." *New York Times Book Review* 4 Dec. 1949: Sec. 7.

———. "Biography of Carson McCullers." *Where I Live*. 133–36.

———. *Cat on a Hot Tin Roof*. *The Theatre of Tennessee Williams*. Vol. 2. 9–215.

———. "Critic Says 'Evasion,' Writer Says 'Mystery.'" *Where I Live*. 70–74.

———. Foreword/Afterword. *Camino Real*. *The Theatre of Tennessee Williams*. Vol. 2. New York: New Directions, 1990. 419–424.

———. Foreword. *Young Man with a Screwdriver*. By Oliver Evans. U of Nebraska P, 1950. 1–3.

———. "The Human Psyche—Alone." *Where I Live*. 35–39.

———. "If the Writing Is Honest." *Where I Live*. 100–04.

———. Introduction. *Reflections in a Golden Eye*. By Carson McCullers. *Where I Live*. 40–48.

———. "Let Me Hang It All Out." *New York Times* 4 Mar. 1973: Sec. 2.

———. "On a Streetcar Named Success." *Where I Live*. 15–22.

———. "The Past, the Present, and the Perhaps." *The Theatre of Tennessee Williams*. Vol. 3. 219–24.

———. "Person-to-Person." *Where I Live*: 75–80.

———. "Some Words Before." *Go Looking: Poems 1933–1933*. By Gilbert Maxwell. Boston: Bruce Humphries, 1954.5–6.

———. "A Summer of Discovery." *Where I Live*. 137–47.

———. "The Timeless World of a Play." *Where I Live*. 49–54.

———. "Tennessee Williams: The Wolf and I ..." *New York Times* 20 Feb. 1966: Sec. 2.

———. *The Theatre of Tennessee Williams*. New York: New Directions, 1990.

———. "The Timeless World of a Play." *The Theatre of Tennessee Williams*. Vol. 2. 259–64.

———. *Where I Live: Selected Essays*. Eds. Christine R. Day and Bob Woods. New York: New Directions, 1979.

———. "A Writer's Quest for a Parnassus." *Where I Live*. 28–34.

Bibliography of the Nonfiction of Tennessee Williams

"The Agent as Catalyst." *Esquire* (Dec. 1962): 216–18+.

"An Allegory of Man and His Sahara." *New York Times Book Review* 4 Dec. 1949: Sec. 7.

"Author and Director: A Delicate Situation." *Where I Live*. 93–99.

"Biography of Carson McCullers." *Where I Live*. 133–36.

"*Candida*: A College Essay." *Shaw Review* 20.2 (1977): 60–62.

"The Catastrophe of Success." *Story* (Summer 1948): 67–72.

"Critic Says 'Evasion,' Writer Says 'Mystery.'" *Where I Live*. 70–74.

"Facts About Me." *Where I Live*. 58–62.

"Five Fiery Ladies." *Where I Live*. 127–32.

Foreword/Afterword. *Camino Real*. *The Theatre of Tennessee Williams*. Vol. 2. 419–24.

Foreword. *Constructing a Play*. By Marian Gallaway. New York: Prentice, 1950. vii–xi.

Foreword. *Feminine Wiles*. By Jane Bowles. Santa Barbara, CA: Black Sparrow P, 1976.

Foreword. *Sweet Bird of Youth*. *The Theatre of Tennessee Williams*. Vol. 4. 3–7.

Foreword. *Young Man with a Screwdriver*. By Oliver Evans. U of Nebraska P, 1950. 1–3.

"Homage to Key West." *Where I Live*. 160–64.

"The Human Psyche—Alone." *Where I Live*. 35–39.

"I Am Widely Regarded as the Ghost of a Writer." *New York Times* 8 May 1977: Sec. 2.

"If the Writing Is Honest." *Where I Live*. 100–04.

"I Have Rewritten a Play for Artistic Purity." *New York Times* 21 Nov. 1976: Sec. 2.

Introduction. *The Dark at the Top of the Stairs*. By William Inge. New York: Random, 1958. vii–[ix].

Introduction. *The Lonely Hunter*. By Virginia Spencer Carr. Garden City, NY: Doubleday, 1975.

"Introduction to Carson McCullers's *Reflections in a Golden Eye*." *Where I Live*. 40–48.

Introduction. *The World of Tennessee Williams*. By Richard Leavitt. New York: Putnam's, 1978. ix–x.

"Let Me Hang It All Out." *New York Times* 4 Mar. 1973: Sec. 2.

"The Man in the Overstuffed Chair." *Antaeus* (Spring/Summer 1982): 281–91.

"The Meaning of *The Rose Tattoo*." *Where I Live*. 55–57.

"The Misunderstandings and Fears of an Artist's Revolt." *Where I Live*. 169–71.

"Notes after the Second Invited Audience: (And a Troubled Sleep)." [Afterword to *Small Craft Warnings*]. *The Theatre of Tennessee Williams*. Vol. 5. 288–92.

"On a Streetcar Named Success." *Where I Live*. 15–22.

"The Past, the Present, and the Perhaps." *The Theatre of Tennessee Williams*. Vol. 3. 219–224.

"Person-to-Person." *Where I Live*. 75–80.

"Playwright's Preface." *Vancouver Playhouse Program Magazine* (Oct. 1980): 17.

"The Pleasures of the Table." *Where I Live*. 165–68.

"Preface: The Man in the Overstuffed Chair." *Tennessee Williams: Collected Stories*. New York: New Directions, 1985. vii–xvii.

"Preface to My Poems." *Where I Live*. 1–6.

"Prelude to a Comedy." *Where I Live*. 121–26.

"Questions without Answers." *Where I Live*. 15–22.

"Reflections on a Revival of a Controversial Fantasy." *Where I Live*. 111–13.

"The Rose Tattoo in Key West." *Harper's Bazaar* (Feb. 1955): 124.

"Something Wild..." *Where I Live*. 7–14.

"Some Words Before." *Go Looking: Poems, 1933–1953*. By Gilbert Maxwell. Boston: Bruce Humphries, 1954. 5–6.

"A Summer of Discovery." *Where I Live*. 137–47.

"Tennessee Williams Presents His POV." *Where I Live*. 114–20.

"Tennessee Williams: The Wolf and I ..." *New York Times* 20 Feb. 1996: Sec. 2.

"The Timeless World of a Play." *The Theatre of Tennessee Williams*. Vol. 2. 259–64.

"Too Personal?" *Where I Live*. 155–59.

"To William Inge: An Homage." *New York Times* 1 July 1973: Sec. 2.

"T. Williams' View of T. Bankhead." *Where I Live*. 148–54.

"We Are Dissenters Now." *Harper's Bazaar* (Jan. 1972): 40–41.

"W. H. Auden: A Few Reminiscences." *Harvard Advocate* 108.2–3 (1975): 59.

"Where My Head Is Now and Other Questions." *Performing Arts* [Los Angeles] (Apr. 1973): 26–27.

"The World I Live In." *Where I Live*. 88–92.

"A Writer's Quest for a Parnassus." *Where I Live*. 28–34.

VERNA FOSTER

Desire, Death, and Laughter: Tragicomic Dramaturgy in A Streetcar Named Desire[1]

Tennessee Williams, like Ibsen, Chekhov, and O'Casey before him, understood that in modern drama tragic experience can be expressed only through tragicomedy.[2] In an interview in 1974 he remarked, "One can't write a tragedy today without putting humor into it. There has to be humor in it now; it's so hard for people to take tragedy seriously because people are so wary now" (Devlin 273). While working on *A Streetcar Named Desire* in 1945, he commented in a letter to his agent, Audrey Wood, that he was "writing it with as much lyrical and comedy relief as possible while preserving the essentially tragic atmosphere" (Qtd. in Burks 21). The comedy in *Streetcar*, however, does not simply provide relief from the play's tragic strain; rather the tragic and the comic function symbiotically, the comic modifies, and by subverting, also protects what is tragic from becoming either melodramatic or laughable and, indeed, renders the tragic more bitter. Lyle Leverich reports in his biography of the dramatist that while watching his own plays in the theatre, Williams would often choose moments of pathos or suffering to laugh out loud with his "mad cackle," which he has said was "only a substitute for weeping."[3] If a "mad cackle" is the equivalent of "weeping," then, as Shaw remarked of Ibsen in *The Wild Duck*, Williams presents tragicomedy as "a much deeper and grimmer entertainment" than tragedy (32).

From *American Drama* 9, no. 1 (Fall 1999): pp. 51–68. © 2000 by American Drama Institute.

Although many critics, especially in the earlier years of the play's reception, have read *A Streetcar Named Desire* as a tragedy, such a reading not only raises problems about Blanche as a tragic protagonist, but also fails to account for the appeal that Stanley has for audiences, and thus does not adequately comprehend how Williams' complex dramaturgy creates a peculiarly modern form of tragic experience that opens like an "abyss" out of comedy[4] (Durrenmatt 255). Unlike Arthur Miller, who contributed to the (problematic) definition of his own *Death of a Salesman* as a tragedy, Williams himself has commented in various interviews on both tragic and comic elements in *Streetcar*. In this essay, then, I propose to examine how Williams' subtle handling of the relations between weeping and cackling create *A Streetcar Named Desire* as tragicomedy, a genre that offers its audience a less cathartic, more ambiguous and disturbing kind of theatrical experience than tragedy might, but also an experience better suited to the needs and tastes of audiences in mid-to-late twentieth-century America. *Streetcar*'s tragicomic genre, I would suggest, is one reason for the play's continuing vitality and contemporaneity in the theatre. The tragicomic opposition in *A Streetcar Named Desire* inheres most obviously in the conflict between Blanche and Stanley. Just as Blanche represents the soul, culture, and death (the moth drawn to the candle) and Stanley (the "*gaudy seed-bearer*" [29]) the body, the primitive, and life, so Blanche seems to embody the play's tragedy and Stanley its comedy. However, the tragic and the comic are related in a much more integral and complicated way than this rather diagrammatic account of the play suggests. Both Blanche and Stanley are tragicomic figures, and *Streetcar* is richly ambiguous: it presents a sensitive, tormented woman cast out from her final refuge, deprived of her last hope of happiness, and brutally destroyed by her crude brother-in-law and/or a down-to-earth working man defending his home and his masculinity from a neurotic, snobbish intruder who would destroy both and indeed almost succeeds. Williams has said that "the meaning of the play" is that Blanche, "potentially a superior person," is broken by the "falsities" of society and also that "the meaning of the play" is that Stanley "does go on" with Stella at the end (Devlin 81, 275). But it might equally be true to say that Stanley has to "go on," though his sexuality and his family life are forever tarnished, and that Blanche in some sense escapes, if only into madness, on the arm of her last kind stranger, the Doctor. Throughout the play Williams carefully balances the audience's sympathies between Blanche and Stanley by his orchestration of tragic and comic effects, producing finally not the catharsis of tragedy but instead the richly stimulating discomfort that is characteristic of the endings of tragicomedies.

Blanche is at the center of *Streetcar*'s tragic action and also the focal point for much of its comedy. She is tragic in her attempt to expiate her guilt over her young husband's death and to find consolation in "intimacies with strangers" (118), and in her self-destructive sexual game-playing with Stanley that leads him finally to rape her. I do not wish to suggest that anything Blanche does excuses Stanley for the crime of rape, but rather that her own complicity in bringing it about produces the tragic inevitability of her downfall ("We've had this date with each other from the beginning!" [130]) and makes Blanche a tragic figure rather than merely a victim.

Despite her tragic trajectory, however, Blanche is in many ways a comic character. Underscoring in various interviews the comedy of *Streetcar*, Williams has focused particularly on Blanche, describing her as "funny" and as having a "comic side, her little vanities, and her little white lies"; as "a scream"; and as "really rather bright and witty" (Devlin 277, 285, 316). If we ignore the comic perspective created both by Williams' attitude to Blanche and by Blanche's ironic detachment from her own behavior, as a tragic persona Blanche is too febrile and too self-indulgent to evoke the kind of emotional identification that an audience typically feels with the sufferings of a tragic protagonist. But Williams' comedy cuts into and allows the audience to laugh at Blanche's fantasies, her vanity, her selfishness, her hypocrisy about her drinking, and even her aggressive sexuality. By presenting the weaknesses that contribute to her downfall in a comic light, Williams creates in the audience a degree of critical detachment from Blanche but also protects her from the audience's disapprobation by making her vanity and her role-playing endearing to us though annoying to Stanley. By also giving her an intelligent and even comic apprehension of her own tragic situation, Williams ensures that Blanche has the capacity to engage the audience's sympathetic understanding. Paradoxically, then, it is as a comic rather than as a tragic character that Blanche wins the audience's sympathy for her tragic situation.

One of the chief ways in which Williams creates almost simultaneous engagement with and detachment from Blanche is through her theatricality. As C.W.E. Bigsby has pointed out, Blanche "is self-consciously her own playwright, costume designer, lighting engineer, scenic designer and performer"; she enacts "southern belle, sensitive virgin, sensuous temptress, martyred daughter, wronged wife" (4). Since Blanche in some sense is all of these roles, she quite appropriately elicits the audience's sympathy for herself in each character. But the theatricality of her behavior also serves to block complete identification and create the critical distance needed for a comic response to the performance as well as a tragic response to the persona.

Today we tend to associate the blocking or partial blocking of empathy with Brecht. Brecht certainly has taught us to understand and appreciate the theatrical uses of detachment, and his own *Verfremdungseffekte* has contributed to the repertoire of distancing devices available in late twentieth-century theatre. But the manipulation of dramatic engagement and detachment to create complicated audience responses long precedes Brecht's work. It is a defining characteristic of both Renaissance and modern tragicomedy. Both Shakespeare and Beaumont and Fletcher in their tragicomedies often use a dramatic style that is at once moving and absurd: Leontes's expressions of jealousy in *The Winter's Tale*, for example, or Arbaces's internal conflict over committing, supposedly, incest in *A King and No King*. And, similarly, in a modern tragicomedy, *The Wild Duck*, Ibsen creates in Hjalmar Ekdal a comic character who sees himself as tragic. The audience is moved by the genuinely tragic nature of Hjalmar's plight, the death of his daughter, not because of his self-regarding, pseudo-tragic posturing, which is indeed comically alienating, but because his absurdity throughout the play has rendered him endearing and thus sympathetic.[5]

As a comic character Blanche is more complex than Hjalmar. She understands herself, as Hjalmar does not understand himself, and thus solicits as well as elicits laughter. We are wryly amused when she is being "bright and witty," in some of her turns of phrase ("epic fornications" [43]), for example, and in the way she plays up to and with Mitch. "I guess it is just that I have-old-fashioned ideals!" she tells Mitch, rolling her eyes to express the absurdity of any such sexual reticence on her part. Sometimes, seeing Blanche through Stella's eyes, we laugh in a good-natured way at her foibles. After she grandly orders Stella not to clean up after Stanley, Stella asks, "Then who's going to do it? Are you?" Blanche replies in comic shock, "I? I!" (66). The punctuation says it all.

Most often the audience both laughs at and pities Blanche's behavior. Her attempts to hide her drinking, for example, become a running joke, a comically obvious form of role-playing to save appearances. Blanche gushes to Stella in the first scene, "I know you must have some liquor on the place! Where could it be, I wonder? Oh, I spy, I spy" (19), even though she has already had a drink and carefully washed her glass. Later she tells Mitch, "I'm not accustomed to having more than one drink" (54). When we consider, however, that Blanche drinks to forget her past and to make living in Stanley's apartment bearable; that she hides her drinking because she needs to maintain a ladylike image if she is to persuade Mitch, whom she sees as her last hope of salvation, to marry her, then the behavior we have laughed at becomes pitiable. Pirandello's definition of "humor" (essentially tragicomedy) is helpful here. We move from the *perception of the opposite* (that Blanche's behavior is the opposite of what she pretends to be), which produces laughter, to the *feeling of the opposite* (recognizing the reasons for Blanche's behavior), which creates sympathy (Pirandello 113); our laughter at Blanche and our pity for her are thus inextricably bound together, producing a quintessentially tragicomic response. By scene nine when Mitch knows the truth (at least Stanley's truth) about her, Blanche's pretence of abstemiousness has become more painful than funny: "Here's something. Southern Comfort! What is that, I wonder?" (115). The joke is the same, but the audience no longer laughs.

Another comic motif that turns tragic is Blanche's insistence on behaving like a southern lady in an environment ignorant of and even hostile to any such elegant manners. As she walks through the room where the men are playing poker in the play's last scene, Blanche says, "Please don't get up. I'm only passing through" (138). "Please don't get up" is an exact repetition of what she gaily says to the poker players in scene three when Stella and she return home before the game is over (48). On the earlier occasion Stanley's comeback emphasises the comic inappropriateness of Blanche's expectation of gracious manners in his home: "Nobody's going to get up, so don't be worried" (48). Blanche's repetition of her earlier line underscores how she has been unwilling and unable to change her behavior to fit her new circumstances. Her inability to change, however, is not only an example of Bergsonian comic rigidity but also expresses a tragic commitment to values and traditions—art, poetry, and music (72), "beauty of the mind and richness of the spirit and tenderness of the heart" (126)—that are not relevant in Stanley's world but are finer than anything that might replace them. Blanche's repetition of "Please don't get up" (this time most of the men do stand) superimposes on the audience's memory of the earlier comic exchange between herself and Stanley a sense of sadness and loss, reinforced by her self-deprecating addition "I'm only passing through." This tragicomic use of repetition with variation is typically Chekhovian.[6]

The most overtly comic elements in *Streetcar* are the exchanges between Blanche and Stanley, such as the one I have just discussed, that underscore the oppositions between them and often take on the force of repartee. When Stanley asks Blanche how much longer she is going to be in the bathroom, she tells him, "Possess your soul in patience!"; Stanley quickly responds, "It's not my soul, it's my kidneys I'm worried about" (102). This exchange, little more than vulgar verbal humor in itself, here represents the classic conflict between soul and body, the sublime and the grotesque, whose union, Victor Hugo suggested, produces the modern genre of tragicomedy (Hugo 357–61). Stanley transforms Blanche's fine phrase and her spiritual, therapeutic use of the bathroom for cleansing that is symbolically regenerative (giving her "a brand new outlook on life" [105]) into a physical need to use the bathroom for purposes of evacuation. The spiritual sublime becomes the physical grotesque.

Since the sparring couple is a staple of romantic comedy, the relationship between Blanche and Stanley provokes both ready laughter and uneasy anticipation of their (quasi-incestuous) coupling. Their diverse comic styles, however, appropriate to the personality, attainments, and way of life represented by each, emphasize the unlikelihood of any rapprochement between them. Blanche's comedy is intellectual and playful, consisting in flirtation, conscious role-playing, and irony directed at others and also at herself, emphasising at once her resilience and her vulnerability. Stanley's humor, by contrast, is always self-aggrandizing; it consists in physical horseplay (smacking Stella on the thigh to assert his ownership of her [48]), crude jokes dealing with bodily functions that draw attention to his own body, or literal-minded sarcasm that can be as cruel as it is funny. Stanley's aggressive humor can, of course, be interpreted as a mark of his own vulnerability.

Early audiences sympathized with Stanley because they identified with a working man defending his home from an invader who despises him and everything he stands for and because of the charm and sensitivity that Marlon Brando brought to the part (Clurman 72–80; Spector). They were prepared to laugh with him at Blanche's expense, as Stanley repeatedly takes her down a peg or two. He refuses to accommodate her fine airs or to flirt with her or to allow her to gain any sexual advantage over him; he reduces her fantasies to sober facts; and he sees through all of her pretences, often in a wry, humorous way: "Liquor goes fast in hot weather" (30). As the play progresses Stanley's humor at Blanche's expense becomes more cruel. When Blanche corrects Stanley, saying that her millionaire is from Dallas, not Miami, Stanley undercuts her fantasy with the retort "Well, just so he's from somewhere!" (124). Their repartee pungently expresses the opposition between Blanche's fantasy world and Stanley's world of facts. Sometimes Williams develops this tragicomic opposition throughout a whole scene, creating a counterpoint between reality and fantasy, death and life. In scene seven Stanley plans to give Blanche a one-way ticket out of town, while offstage Blanche, happy for once in anticipation of seeing Mitch, sings "Paper Moon," a song about the make-believe nature of love and happiness. In scene eleven Blanche, depending on the kindness of strangers, leaves for a kind of death in the asylum, while the community of men play a game of poker with its implications of raw male sexuality: "This game is seven-card stud" (142).

The most important tragicomic opposition in the play is that between desire and death. Desire, says Blanche, is the opposite of death (120). Rather than constructing any such simple dichotomy between desire and death in *Streetcar*, however, Williams renders desire tragicomic and makes desire and death identical as well as opposites. Stanley, the *"gaudy seed-bearer"* (29), who smashed the light bulbs on his wedding night, who is forever taking off his shirt, and who plans to wave his "brilliant pyjama coat ... like a flag" when he hears that his son is born (125), possesses a comic satyr-like sexuality that is life-giving when he impregnates Stella, but death-giving when he rapes Blanche. Blanche's sexuality seems to her an escape from death—from "the bloodstained pillow-slips" (119) of her dying relatives—but actually leads her to it. After a sexual encounter with a young male student, Blanche is sent away by her school principal, Mr. Graves. Arriving in New Orleans, she takes a streetcar named Desire, transfers to Cemeteries, and arrives at Elysian Fields. Both psychologically and symbolically, Blanche's sexual experiences lead her on a journey to death.[7]

According to Lyle Leverich, Williams "once said that desire is rooted in a longing for companionship, a release from the loneliness that haunts every individual" (347). So it is with Blanche. As Blanche describes her sexual promiscuity to the uncomprehending Mitch in scene nine, Williams powerfully elicits the audience's sympathy for the terrible loneliness and the need to forget the death of her husband and the grotesque, drawn-out deaths of her relations that drove Blanche into self-destructive "intimacies with strangers." Blanche's condition, to which her guilt for the death of her husband and her own desperate need have brought her, exemplifies a tragic boundary of the human spirit, worked out in psychosexual terms. However the need that drives Blanche is not to be explained simply in such terms. It is rather a more existential loneliness and a more metaphysical need that impel her and other Williams characters into self-destructive behavior. As Bigsby remarks, "The irony which governs the lives of his protagonists, whose needs are so patently at odds with their situation, is less a social fact than a metaphysical reality" (39). Bigsby finds in Williams's work a strong affinity with the "absurd."

Indeed, while the need that drives Blanche's sexual behavior retains its tragic and metaphysical force, Williams often presents the particular manifestations of her sexuality as comic and even mildly grotesque. The comedy of sex is most obvious in the scenes (three and six) in which Blanche plays with Mitch. The comedy of the two scenes arises out of the interplay between a knowing Blanche, who can flatter Mitch into believing in her "old-fashioned ideals" (91), and a fumbling Mitch, concerned about his jacket, his sweat, and his weight, who is easily dazzled by Blanche's charms. Some of Blanche's lines seem to convey a sophomoric wink at the audience, as when, knowing that Mitch cannot understand French, she asks him, "Voulez-vous coucher avec moi ce soir?" (88). In these scenes we laugh with Blanche. But in the scenes in which she tries unsuccessfully to play similar sexual games with Stanley, we are obliged to view her more objectively. Stanley induces the audience, if not quite to laugh at Blanche's expense, yet to become uncomfortably critical of her behavior. When Blanche sprays Stanley with her perfume, for example, he responds, "If I didn't know that you was my wife's sister I'd get ideas about you!" (41).[8]

Williams evokes an even more complex response to Blanche's behavior with the Young Man, who calls to collect money for *The Evening Star* (scene five). This tense scene, a reenactment of Blanche's tragic attraction to boys that cost her her teaching job, exists at the border of the terrible and the farcical. Williams uses expressionist techniques both to convey the drama Blanche imagines occurring and to comment on it. The visual and aural imagery of the scene is intensely sexual: it is dusk and *"a little glimmer of lightning"* plays about the building (82); blues music is heard in the background; Blanche asks the young man to light her cigarette. Though literally only a shy, polite newspaper boy who is comically eager to leave, the unnamed Young Man symbolically takes on the sinister role of Blanche's nemesis. In the list of characters the Young Man is referred to as a Young Collector, reminding us perhaps that everything, even the evening star (as Blanche jokes), must eventually be paid for. Blanche's overt desire for the Young Man threatens to disrupt any future she might have with Mitch; she only just manages to control herself and let the boy go with one kiss.

Despite the scene's disturbing quality, there is, nonetheless, an element of comedy in Blanche's self-consciously predatory use of *double entendres*: "You make my mouth water" (84), referring both to the young man and his cherry soda. Blanche herself is able to adopt a comic stance towards her own sexuality, and it is this self-awareness that gives a tragic dignity to her sexual obsessions. She mocks even the horror of her life at the Flamingo and Mitch's disgust with her promiscuity by satirically calling the hotel where she brought her "victims" the "Tarantula Arms" (118), an allusion that is lost on Mitch. This scene (nine) is quintessentially tragicomic. Williams makes Mitch's sexual obtuseness, at which we have previously laughed, destroy any hope Blanche might have for a secure future when, unable to see her as anything other than a whore, Mitch rejects her as unfit to be his wife. Blanche is finally destroyed by both Mitch's sexual diffidence and Stanley's sexual predatoriness, both of which Williams initially presents as comic.

The play's last scene, depicting the consequences of Stanley's rape of Blanche, counterpoints life and death in an even more disturbing tragicomic mix.[9] Blanche's mental breakdown is not, of course, a literal death, but Williams evokes the idea of death as at once absurd, terrifying, and in Blanche's imagination at least a prelude to resurrection. Blanche imagines dying at sea from "eating an unwashed grape" (136). Her fantasy of being "buried at sea sewn up in a clean white sack and dropped overboard—at noon—in the blaze of summer—and into an ocean as blue as ... my first lover's eyes!" (136), spoken against the sound of the cathedral chimes, suggests purification, peace, and resurrection: "That unwashed grape has transported her soul to heaven" (136). This echo in Blanche's fantasy of one of the defining features of Renaissance tragicomedy—the resurrection motif—is given a certain objective warrant by the sound of the cathedral chimes, but it is also countered by the appearance of the Doctor and especially the Matron—"*a peculiarly sinister figure*" (139)— who have come to take Blanche to the asylum and whom Williams presents expressionistically as death figures.[10]

The play's contrary ending, depicting the life that "has got to go on" (133), in Eunice's words, is at best problematic, at worst another kind of death in life. *Streetcar* allows its audience to experience neither tragic catharsis from Blanche's destruction nor comic satisfaction that Stanley "does go on" with Stella. In fact, the continuation of their life together is the most appalling thing about the play's ending and in that sense more truly moral than the ending (in which Stella says that she will never return to Stanley) imposed by the censors on the 1951 film version. Stella implicitly knows that Blanche was telling the truth about Stanley's raping her, even though she also knows that in order to go on living with Stanley, she must not believe it. At the end we see her crying "*luxuriously*" (142) with Stanley's hand in her blouse, a prelude to sex. But now more than ever sex seems to be a narcotic.[11] The ending of *Streetcar* is as horrifying, as disturbingly tragicomic, for Stanley and Stella as it is for Blanche. Though Blanche has "lost" and Stanley has "won" whatever game they were playing, the outcome for each remains ambiguous. Blanche may have found a terrible release in fantasy; Stanley's relationship with Stella is forever tarnished.[12] For the audience, even Stella's baby, who should be a sign of new life and hope (like the children who are reunited with and reunite their parents in Shakespeare's late tragicomedies), is symbolically linked through his blue blanket with Blanche, whose final outfit is "the blue of the robe in the old Madonna pictures" (135).[13] Thus the baby reminds us of Blanche's essential innocence and vulnerability and that his birth coincided with her destruction, and Stanley's.

In *Streetcar* Williams entertains such conventional elements of comedy as marriage, birth, and reunion but gives them all a tragic twist. The wished-for marriage (between Blanche and Mitch) is abortive, the birth occasions rape, and the reunion (of Stanley and Stella) remains horrifyingly ambiguous. Through these distortions of comic conventions Williams creates the moral and aesthetic discomfort that is a defining characteristic of tragicomedy.

Apart from obviating the problems in writing tragedy in the modern age, tragicomedy provided Williams with the most effective way to explore the darker regions of human sexuality since tragicomedy allows for the expression of both the painful and the absurd in sexual experience as well as the creation of a peculiar relationship between sex (carnal, life-giving, and thus comic) and death (tragic). Desire may be the opposite of death, just as comedy is the opposite of tragedy, but in *A Streetcar Named Desire* tragicomedy fuses an emotionally charged and psychologically acute symbiosis between them.

Notes

1. A shorter version of this essay was given at MLA in Toronto in December, 1997.

2. Williams's acknowledged master was Chekhov (Devlin 114). He was also impressed by the "quick interchange of comedy and tragedy" in O'Casey's *Juno and the Paycock* (Leverich 344).

3. On Williams's laughter see Leverich 112, 202, 240, 562.

4. Adler discusses the early critical reception of *Streetcar* as tragedy (47–50). See also the essays by Harwood and Cardullo ("Drama of Intimacy and Tragedy of Incomprehension"). Roderick discusses the play as tragicomedy but focuses more on the juxtaposition than on the integration of tragic and comic elements.

5. See Foster, "Ibsen's Tragicomedy: *The Wild Duck*."

6. See Foster, "The Dramaturgy of Mood in *Twelfth Night* and *The Cherry Orchard*."

7. For a discussion of the play's symbolism see Quirino.

8. For a good discussion of the sexual relationship between Blanche and Stanley, especially Blanche's sexual game-playing, see Davis (60–102).

9. Cardullo points to the importance throughout *Streetcar* of images of "birth and death, of rebirth and death-in-life" ("Birth and Death in *A Streetcar Named Desire*").

10. Schvey sees the end of the play as "an expression of spiritual purification through suffering" (109); Adler comments, "Blanche leaves the stage a violated Madonna, blessed by whatever saving grace insanity/illusion can provide" (46); and Schlueter points out that the John Erman film of *Streetcar* (1984), starring Ann-Margret and Treat Williams, ends with a view of the cathedral and the sound of its chimes, suggesting a "sacramental context for Blanche's wish for purification" (80). Leverich comments that Williams "used the passage from crucifixion to resurrection as a constant theme in his work" (582).

11. Williams describes Stella as exhibiting an "*almost narcotized tranquility*" (62) after a night of sex, following violence, with Stanley.

12. Bigsby comments, "Even Stanley now has to live a life hollowed out, attacked at its core" (46).

13. On color symbolism in Streetcar see Schvey. Cardullo provides a good discussion of the baby ("Drama of Intimacy and Tragedy of Incomprehension," 153, n.5).

Works Cited

Adler, Thomas P. *A Streetcar Named Desire: The Moth and the Lantern*. Boston: Twayne Publishers, 1990.

Bigsby, C.W.E. *Modern American Drama, 1945–1990*. Cambridge: Cambridge UP, 1992.

Burks, Deborah G. "Treatment Is Everything: The Creation and Casting of Blanche and Stanley in Tennessee Williams' 'Streetcar'." *Library Chronicle* 41 (1987): 17–39.

Cardullo, Bert. "Drama of Intimacy and Tragedy of Incomprehension: *A Streetcar Named Desire* Reconsidered." Tharpe 137–53.

———. "Birth and Death in *A Streetcar Named Desire*." Kolin 167–80.

Clurman, Harold. *Lies Like Truth*. New York: Grove P, Inc., 1958.

Davis, Walter A. *Psychoanalysis, Modern American Drama, and the Audience*. Madison: U of Wisconsin P, 1994.

Devlin, Albert J. *Conversations with Tennessee Williams*. Jackson, MS: UP of Mississippi, 1986.

Durrenmatt, Friedrich. "Problems of the Theater." *Plays and Essays*. Ed. Volkmar Sander. New York: Continuum, 1982. 231–62.

Foster, Verna A. "The Dramaturgy of Mood in *Twelfth Night* and *The Cherry Orchard*." *MLQ* 48 (June 1987): 162–85.

———. "Ibsen's Tragicomedy: *The Wild Duck*." *Modern Drama* 38 (Fall 1995): 287–97.

Harwood, Britton J. "Tragedy as Habit: *A Streetcar Named Desire*." Tharpe 104–115.

Hugo, Victor. Preface to Cromwell (1827) *European Theories of the Drama*. Ed. Barrett H. Clark, rev. Henry Popkin. New York: Crown Publishers, 1965. 357–70.

Kolin, Philip C., ed. *Confronting Tennessee Williams's A Streetcar Named Desire*. Westport, CT: Greenwood P, 1993.

Leverich, Lyle. *Tom: The Unknown Tennessee Williams*. New York: Crown Publishers, 1995.

Pirandello, Luigi. *On Humor*. Introd. and trans. Antonio Illiano and Daniel P. Testa. Chapel Hill, NC: U of North Carolina P, 1960.

Quirino, Leonard. "The Cards Indicate a Voyage on *A Streetcar Named Desire*." Tharpe 77–96.

Roderick, John M. "From 'Tarantula Arms' to 'Della Robbia Blue': The Tennessee Williams Tragicomic Transit Authority." Tharpe 116–25.

Schlueter, June. "'We've had this date with each other from the beginning': Reading toward Closure in *A Streetcar Named Desire*." Kohn 71–81.

Schvey, Henry I. "Madonna at the Poker Night: Pictorial Elements in Tennessee Williams's *A Streetcar Named Desire*." *Costerus: From Cooper to Philip Roth: Essays on American Literature* ns 26, edited by J. Bakker and D.R.M. Wilkinson (1980). Rpt. in *Tennessee Williams's A Streetcar Named Desire*. Ed. Harold Bloom. New York: Chelsea House Publishers, 1988. 103–109.

Shaw, Bernard. "Tolstoy: Tragedian or Comedian?" *The London Mercury* IV (1921): 31–34.

Spector, Susan. "Alternative Visions of Blanche Dubois: Uta Hagen and Jessica Tandy in *A Streetcar Named Desire*." *Modern Drama* 32 (1989): 545–60.

Tharpe, Jack, ed. *Tennessee Williams: A Tribute*. Jackson, MS: UP of Mississippi, 1977.

Williams, Tennessee. *A Streetcar Named Desire*. New York: New American Library, 1947.

ANNETTE J. SADDIK

Critical Expectations and Assumptions: Williams' Later Reputation and the American Reception of the Avant-Garde

"The job of the theatre critic is first of all to determine what the human significance of a particular play or performance is. In doing this he evaluates it. Every play or performance has a certain quality or 'weight' of life in it. The critic must try to define its essence and place it in some personal or traditional scale of values which the reader in his turn is permitted to judge."

> —Harold Clurman, introduction to *Lies Like Truth*

"There is actually a common link between the two schools, French and American, but characteristically the motor impulse of the French school is intellectual and philosophic while that of the American is more of an emotional and romantic nature. What is this common link? In my opinion it is most simply definable as a sense, an intuition, of an underlying dreadfulness in modern experience."

> —Tennessee Williams, introduction to Carson
> McCullers's *Reflections in a Golden Eye*

In a 1975 interview with Charles Ruas, Williams denied any allegiance with other playwrights or other schools of thought in drama, insisting that the "different" forms of his later period were entirely his own:

From *The Politics of Reputation: The Critical Reception of Tennessee Williams' Later Plays*: pp. 135–150. © 1999 by Associated University Presses, Inc.

I'm quite through with the kind of play that established my early
and popular reputation. I am doing a different thing, which is
altogether my own, not influenced at all by other playwrights
at home or abroad, or by other schools of theatre. My thing is
what it always was, to express my world and experience of it in
whatever form seems suitable to the material.[1]

Although Williams claimed that his later style was unique, he did often
hail Samuel Beckett along with Harold Pinter and Edward Albee as major
playwrights whose work he greatly admired,[2] and several critics have
pointed out interesting parallels between Beckett's work especially and
Williams' experimental plays. Therefore, since these playwrights were doing
work similar to what Williams was doing in the second half of his career,
it is certainly worthwhile to explore how they were received, both by the
reviewers and by the critics, in order to illuminate further the extent to which
Williams' reputation may be a product not of what he actually achieved but
of the assumptions and biases of those who evaluated his plays.

   Those evaluating Williams' later plays have often discussed them in
Beckettian terms. James Coakley saw Williams exhibiting what has become
known as a Beckettian view of the world as early as *Camino Real*, which was
first performed in New York within a few months after *Waiting for Godot*
was presented in Paris. Although *Godot* appeared in book form in 1952 (in
French), it premiered in Paris in January 1953, and *Camino Real* had its first
performance in March of that year.[3] Coakley, writing in 1977, argued that
the "central perception" of *Camino Real* is that "life is no more than 'dim,
communal comfort' eroded by change; values are illusory, perpetually in
transit. How, in short, is one to live?"—a perception which he claimed is
characterized by "a despair worthy of Beckett, priding itself upon no more
than the black honesty of its vision."[4]

   In *The Two-Character Play*, most obviously, Williams was aiming for a
more Beckettian kind of drama, one that deliberately challenges orthodox
notions of expression and meaning. George Niesen asserts that "The
Beckettian echoes in *The Two-Character Play* are striking,"[5] and goes on to
catalogue similarities between Williams' play and several of Beckett's works,
including *Endgame* and *Waiting for Godot*:

The set itself, the freezing, dimming "state theatre of a state
unknown" (p. 313), the "prison, this last theatre" (p. 364), with
its solitary slit of a hole in the backstage wall, is right out of
Endgame. Felice's description of his own play, "It's possible for a
play to have no ending in the usual sense of an ending, in order

to make a point about nothing really ending" (p. 360), and his statement, "With no place to return to, we have to go on" (p. 316) apply equally to *Waiting for Godot*.[6]

Similarly, C. W. E. Bigsby draws attention to the parallels between *Out Cry* (*The Two-Character Play*) and the plays of Beckett, Pinter, and Albee, pointing out that

> movement is reduced to a minimum—physical stasis standing as an image of constraint, as a denial of clear causality and as an assertion that the real drama operates in the mind (which reinvents the past, translates experience into meaning and imposes its own grid on experience, denying death and acting out its own necessary myth of immortality).... The incompletions of the set underline the deconstructive thrust of the play which is a drama of entropy in which character, plot and language slowly disintegrate.[7]

Like Beckett's works, Williams' plays discussed in chapter three—*I Can't Imagine Tomorrow*, *In the Bar of a Tokyo Hotel*, and *The Two-Character Play*—defy realistic expectations of character, plot, action, and language in an attempt to raise central questions about the nature of reality and the role that language plays in its representation. In the same vein as plays such as *Waiting for Godot* and *Endgame*, Williams' later work focuses on the concept that language is the medium through which reality is constructed and defined rather than directly expressed. The typical situation presented in these plays involves characters who are trying to escape from a language which is neither an accurate nor a satisfying expression of their thoughts and desires. Yet the realization that language, however flawed, is the only means of conceiving their realities and themselves, traps them in the endless need to continue speaking. Therefore, a simultaneous frustration with and dependence on dialogue creates the "tension" in both Beckett's and Williams' plays, which experiment with the paradox of linguistic existence. While the purpose of discourse in realistic drama is typically the attempt directly to communicate truth or convey rational meaning, in the type of experimental drama discussed above discourse serves primarily as a diversion from the silence that would signal the annihilation of the characters.

In Beckett's works, communication often occurs through means other than language. In *Molloy*, for example, a work which takes the unreliability of language to an extreme, Molloy communicates with his mother by knocking on her skull.[8] In *Waiting For Godot*, dialogue, rather than being a vehicle for communication, is consciously used to occupy Gogo and Didi while they wait and divert their attention from the alternative—the silent void that signifies death. They often opt for language over action, telling stories to pass the time[9] rather than hanging themselves, even though the later activity would promise them the physical pleasure of sexual erection.[10] In *Endgame*, Nagg and Nell communicate with each other by knocking on their trash bins and rattling the cans. It is linguistic play, rather than the attempt directly to communicate meaning through language, which drives the action in Beckett's works. Clov asks Hamm, "What is there to keep me here?" and Hamm replies, "The dialogue."[11] Michael Vanden Heuvel points out that "Play, Beckett suggests, ultimately functions as a 'just' refusal of powerlessness and chaos because, despite its painful exertions, it remains a source of momentum."[12]

Similarly, for Williams, it is precisely the dialogue of *The Two-Character Play*—both Williams' play and the play-within-a-play in which the characters perform—that saves them from the silence they both desire and dread and enables them to "go on":

> *Clare.* [Overlapping.] Stop here, we can't go on!
> *Felice.* [Overlapping.] Go on!
> *Clare.* [Overlapping.] Line!
>   (5:345)

Clare and Felice realize that although language is an inaccurate, unreliable, and essentially arbitrary construct in its relation to truth and meaning, it is all they have to define and affirm their existence. At the end of the play, when they are feeling trapped and it seems as though there's "nothing to be done" (5:366), Felice suggests that they "Go back into the play" (5:366), that is, the play-within-the-play. Like Beckett's characters, it is the only way for them to go on. In *Endgame*, Clov expresses his dissatisfaction with existing linguistic structures, telling Hamm "I use the words you taught me. If they don't mean anything any more [sic], teach me others. Or let me be silent."[13] The present language is not useful anymore as far as expressing truth is concerned, but the silence is worse. Even though there is "nothing to say,"[14] Hamm pleads with Clov to "Say something"[15] before he goes. Similarly, in *The Unnamable* the voice states, "Unfortunately I am afraid, as always, of going on,"[16] yet the fear of silence is even greater than the fear of continuing: "I shall never be silent. Never."[17] Therefore the impulse is finally "I can't go on, I'll go on."[18]

Despite the striking dramaturgical parallels between Beckett's work and many of Williams' later plays, both reviewers and critics reacted very differently to the two playwrights. Overall, the reception of Beckett's plays in the United States was much warmer than that of Williams' similar experimental dramas, which were of course never fully accepted by either reviewers or critics. Although American reviewers initially resisted Beckett's unconventional style, they eventually applauded his art as valid and original. The critics hailed Beckett's work from the beginning as mature, avant-garde, and philosophically engaging.

In 1957 a composer living in Chicago, Warren Lee, used the example of Beckett's reception in the United States to address what he saw as the cultural biases evident in the American critical reaction to theater and to literature in general which does not "divert and amuse." Although he uses the term "critics," Lee is unequivocally referring to the group I've designated as "reviewers." He insisted that his article, "The Bitter Pill of Samuel Beckett," written for the *Chicago Review*, was intended "less as a defense of Beckett (which isn't needed) than as an exposition of what he is saying."[19] Lee believed that

> A discussion of [Beckett's] "bitter pill" and the reasons for taking it will suggest critical standards that are sorely needed in this country. With a long-standing reputation for inhospitality to the best in contemporary literature, the Wealthy Man runs the risk of spinning idly in the shallows while the main currents of European thought pass by.[20]

Lee associates the "Wealthy Man" with the American public, and puts forth the notion that

> The Wealthy Man, who has no fear, will usually choose a literature that diverts and amuses. His closest association with meaning will be in writing that agrees with him and tells him what a fine fellow he is. Thus, for instance, *The King and I* and *The Moon is Blue* each enjoyed longer runs on Broadway than all of O'Neill's plays together.[21]

By contrast, Lee argues,

> The Anxious Man, on the other hand—the man who has fear, or at least doubt will often prefer meaning and interpretation to diversion and ornamentation. (Not always, to be sure—but at least often enough to warrant the distinction). He also selects books that agree with him and that corroborate his values, but in a broader sense of the word, corroborate. And he may even undertake to hear the opposition once in a while.[22]

Lee associates the "Anxious Man" with a more European sensibility and understanding of literature. While it is not entirely clear what signifies "meaning" for Lee, he proposes that "It is the first premise of this essay that the primary value of literature is 'meaning'—*then* ornament."[23]

Lee's article is essentially a complaint about the commodification of theatrical and literary criticism in the United States and the unwillingness of the comfortable American "Wealthy Man" to accept a kind of literature—and specifically drama—which is not easily accessible and pleasantly entertaining, and which does not reinforce positive American cultural myths and values. Lee calls criticism an "essential commodity" in this country and believes that criticism, when "functioning properly, should bridge the gap between author and audience—discerning good literature, and expounding it when necessary." He argues, however, that in the categories of tragedy and tragicomedy, American critics "have accomplished a succession of impressive failures—failing on one hand to perceive fine writing, and then being unable to account for it after it has arrived." His argument is obviously applicable to the reviewers' reactions to the work of Williams and Beckett, and Lee does specifically mention both these authors. He hails *Camino Real* along with *The Iceman Cometh* as examples of the "fine writing" that American reviewers and critics failed to perceive, and argues for the superiority of the original—albeit more pessimistic—version of act 3 in *Cat on a Hot Tin Roof*, as he tries to illustrate some reasons for these errors in critical judgement:

> Many reasons come to mind. First, we are the Wealthy Man, isolated and safe. We can ignore certain melancholy truths—and even exert pressure to make sure they won't be brought up by authors: cf. the difference between *Camino Real* and *Cat on a Hot Tin Roof*—and, worse, the inferior version of Act III of the later, which Williams was persuaded to use.[24]

Lee goes on to discuss (with disdain) the "bafflement" of the American press when *Waiting for Godot* reached the States in 1956:

> Recently an important writer appeared in the person of Samuel Beckett, an Irishman writing in French; and the event proved to be a perfect occasion for American critics to demonstrate their theoretical limitations. Lacking proper equipment, most of those who acknowledged Beckett's appearance sounded like so many versions of Wolcott Gibbs, saying "Somehow the meaning of the piece eluded me." In general they were baffled (and offended)—particularly by Beckett's play, *Waiting for Godot*.[25]

Lee's contention that members of the American critical establishment are "theoretically limited" and that they (as well as American audiences) seek "diversion and amusement" in theater and literature in general, is one which often proved to be true in the case of Williams' later work as well as some of his less "sensitive" and "benign" earlier plays. Once we slide from theater/literature to film, the American critical bias for the safe, the morally right, and the pleasant becomes blatantly obvious. We only have to witness how Hollywood altered the endings of both *The Glass Menagerie* and *A Streetcar Named Desire*—ensuring that its audiences would be subjected to as little unpleasantness as possible—in order to conclude what American criticism values in its art/entertainment (in Hollywood, the distinction is already blurred). The atrocious conclusion of the film version of *Menagerie* showed Laura happily adjusted to society—fortified rather than destroyed as a result of the experience with Jim—and excitedly awaiting the arrival of a new gentleman caller who presumably will be the answer to her (and Amanda's) prayers. The film version's altered ending of *Streetcar*, while more subtle, was still clearly an effort to force the conclusion to correspond with American morality. Of course, especially in the case of *Streetcar*, and especially during the 1950s, Hollywood was also contending with the Roman Catholic Legion of Decency and was forced to consider its influence where sexual or other "inappropriate" film content was concerned. Williams' sexually suggestive film *Baby Doll* (1956), for example, was condemned by both the Legion of Decency and Francis Cardinal Spellman as "immoral," generating a great deal of controversy. Both the Motion Picture Code and the New York State Board of Censors, however, ultimately approved the film for release after Elia Kazan agreed to a number a excisions. While Williams' ending of *Streetcar* has Stella sobbing "luxuriously" and "with inhuman abandon" in Stanley's arms as he "voluptuously, soothingly" comforts her, kneeling beside her while "his fingers find the opening of her blouse" (1:419), at the end of the Hollywood version Stella directly reacts to the brutality Stanley has shown throughout the film—his striking of her on the poker night, for example, and his cruelty to Blanche. She sweeps her baby into her arms, tells Stanley to never touch her again, and goes up to Eunice's house for protection from this brute of a man. He is justly punished for his evil, Stella exhibits strength, morality, and independence, and the audience is satisfied. Never mind that in the play the fact that Stella stays with Stanley despite all that has come between them is a central aspect of the power that lies in the sensuality of their relationship. The play's ambivalence concerning whether she is acting out of weakness or strength, and whether she is right or wrong to stay with him, adds to the complexity and effectiveness of the ending, but the moral implications of these issues were too dangerous and controversial for the standard Hollywood mentality.

In *Lies Like Truth*, Harold Clurman wrote of the tendency of reviewers to avoid addressing the connection between the disturbing issues that are brought to light in American drama (he specifically mentions Williams and Beckett) and the recognition of these issues in American culture at large. The American tendency, he argues, is to dismiss the distressing "pessimism" of certain plays as "incomprehensible" in order to avoid confronting it in our own culture:

> We do not say that we cannot abide the pessimism in *Camino Real* (it is not pessimistic but romantic); we say it is incomprehensible. We do not confront the core of *Godot*'s bitterness; we say it is unintelligible. We do not object to the brutality in Shakespeare because we do not actually relate to Shakespeare: he represents "poetry"—which may be translated as high-minded entertainment.
>
> The tendency then is to retreat from the essence of every serious play even when we applaud it, so that we may think of it simply as an amusement. Thus, though we may prize *A Streetcar Named Desire* as an absorbing show, we generally avoid saying what it signifies to the American scene.[26]

The reviewers' rejection of disturbing aspects of Williams' early work which Clurman brings out and, I would argue, of the more pessimistic message and unconventional style of his later work, was rooted in the fundamental expectations of an established theater criticism which reflected American political values and assumptions of the 1950s and early 1960s.

The reviewers who established Williams' early reputation but regarded his later work with disdain were divided in their reactions toward *Waiting for Godot* when it hit New York in 1956. While the group as a whole essentially admitted that the "intellectualism" of the play was beyond their ken, some reviewers were, as Eric Bentley puts it, "respectful towards what was not fully understood," while others, like Walter Kerr for example, found "something of a scandal in the very existence of difficulty."[27] Kenneth Tynan described the response of the New York press to *Godot* as "baffled, but mostly appreciative," and informed his readers that the play's reception was prefigured by "an advertising campaign in which the management appealed for 70,000 intellectuals to make its venture pay."[28] Beckett's reputation as an "intellectual" was established primarily through his association with Joyce and the avant-garde. In 1957 A. J. Leventhal wrote of Joyce's influence on

Beckett in *The Listener*, but he asserted that "Beckett is in a sense a more intellectual writer than Joyce and his jousting with words has a background of erudition deeper, one suspects, than that of the Master—the *cher maître* of the *avant garde* of the 'twenties and 'thirties in Montparnasse."[29]

Walter Kerr, like several of his colleagues, seemed to take offense at what he saw as Beckett's pretentious intellectualism and insensitivity to "what goes on in the minds and hearts of the folks out front," and wished that Beckett were more "in touch with the texture of things." He wrote in the *New York Herald Tribune* that "*Waiting for Godot* is not a real carrot; it is a patiently painted, painstakingly formed plastic job for the intellectual fruitbowl."[30] John Chapman complained in the *Daily News* that "Thinking is a simple, elementary process. *Godot* is merely a stunt," and in the *Daily Mirror* Robert Coleman wrote that "The author was once secretary to that master of obfuscation, James Joyce. Beckett appears to have absorbed some of his employer's ability to make the simple complex."[31] In London, W. A. Darlington called *Waiting for Godot* "a queer play which nobody pretends to understand very clearly."[32]

The more "respectful" press, while praising the philosophical seriousness of the play and the artistic validity of the writer, were nonetheless inclined to point out that *Waiting for Godot* was a puzzling piece, and certainly not for all tastes. In a 1956 review for the *New York Times*, Brooks Atkinson called *Godot* "a mystery wrapped in an enigma," but went on to praise it as "an allegory written in a modern tone" that incorporates symbolism which, although elusive, "is not a pose." Beckett's drama, he decides, "adumbrates—rather than expresses—an attitude towards man's experience on earth." From the beginning of his review, Atkinson brings up Beckett's association with Joyce, and he looks to Beckett's French and Irish predecessors for an interpretation of his message, claiming that Beckett's "acrid cartoon of the story of mankind" is forged through a combination of Sartre's "bleak, dark, disgusted" point of view, and Joyce's "pungent and fabulous" style. Atkinson's piece abounds with bewilderment and even dislike concerning the drama itself, remedied by praise for the sheer physicality of the acting. Although he calls *Godot* an "uneventful, maundering, loquacious drama," he hails Bert Lahr in the role of Gogo as an actor "in the pantomime tradition who has a thousand ways to move and a hundred ways to grimace in order to make the story interesting and theatrical, and touching too." Overall, Atkinson concludes that Beckett is a "valid writer," and that although *Godot* is a "'puzzlement' ... Mr. Beckett is no charlatan.... Theatregoers can rail at it, but they cannot ignore it."[33]

Audiences, however, did not always agree. Kenneth Tynan points out that when *Godot* was performed in London in 1955, "many of the first-night audience found it pretentious."[34] When the play reached the United States, the first Miami audiences were "bitterly disappointed" after the enormous build-up the play received from abroad, and walked out of the theater in disgust.[35] By the time the play reached Broadway some months later, however, New York audiences were generally appreciative, but, like Atkinson, were largely responding to Bert Lahr's "noble performance."[36]

Atkinson's reaction to Beckett's second play, *Endgame*, was similar. He starts off his 1958 review by crediting the director and the actors with the play's artistic success.[37] Lewis Funke's 1962 review of the same play proclaims that "whatever else may be said of Beckett, of his personal attitudes toward life, of his lack of hope, no one can deny that he possesses an artist's witchcraft. He is able to weave spells in the theatre." Like Atkinson, Funke believed that "The Theatre of the Absurd is not for the general taste. Nor, however, can it be denied."[38]

These reviewers reacted to Beckett's avant-garde contemporaries—such as Harold Pinter—in much the same way, but there was less controversy overall concerning the acceptance of Pinter's work since Beckett had paved the way for the "Theatre of the Absurd" in Britain and the United States. In *Thirty Plays Hath November*, Walter Kerr writes that "Every playwright whose work is genuinely original goes through a trial period of resistance and doubt, followed by a time of advancing rumor. On his first exposure to Broadway, with *The Caretaker*, Pinter had been banished after a short run."[39] Just as with Beckett's introduction to New York, however, there were champions of Pinter's Broadway debut. In 1961 Harold Taubman wrote in the *New York Times* that

> Out of a scabrous derelict and two mentally unbalanced brothers Harold Pinter has woven a play of strangely compelling beauty and passion. "The Caretaker," which opened last night at the Lyceum, proclaims its young English author as one of the important playwrights of our day... A work of rare originality, "The Caretaker" will tease and cling to the mind. No matter what happens in the months to come, it will lend luster to this Broadway season.[40]

British reviewers were often also ambivalent about Pinter's works overall—in a review of *The Homecoming* in 1965, B. A. Young wrote that "London's critics ... were generally disappointed by the play"[41]—but he was eventually accepted in Britain and the United States to the point where even Walter Kerr considered himself a "dedicated Pinterite."[42]

Clearly the reviewers had expectations and prescribed standards for judging drama which blatantly affected their evaluation of both the unconventional plays of Beckett (and the other dramatists) which were becoming popular in the late 1950s, and Williams' similar later plays. After an initial period of outrage, however, reviewers were willing to give Beckett and Pinter the benefit of the doubt when faced with plays which baffled their conventional expectations, while the same courtesy was never given to Williams. Factors such as Beckett's overwhelming success abroad, his association with Joyce and with the established tradition of French existentialism, and finally pressure from the intellectual community at large led to an acceptance of and eventually enthusiasm for Beckett and those playwrights who followed him. Atkinson wrote in 1958 that "Although it is impossible to construct a story or theme out of 'Endgame,' after the manner of realistic drama, Mr. Beckett's point of view is adumbrated in the dialogue. Life is meaningless, he says."[43] Furthermore, Atkinson's comparisons of Beckett's dramas with the work of Joyce and Sartre—and later with "a Picasso abstraction "[44]—are typical of the associations that aided in building Beckett's reputation as a serious artist. When Williams, however, "adumbrated" the same point of view through his dialogue, the reviewers stopped at "baffled" and concluded that Williams was either drugged, burnt-out as a writer, or unsuccessfully trying to imitate Beckett.

The critics' reactions to the work of Beckett and Pinter were from the beginning clearly more enthusiastic and admiring than that of the reviewers. Like the reviewers, they often referred to Beckett's intellectual background, specifically his association with Joyce. John Gassner called *Waiting for Godot* "Beckett's Joycean masterpiece,"[45] and praised the philosophy behind Beckett's repetitious and minimalistic language:

> In drama of the absurd, language has once more been undercut by moody repetitions that make progression of feeling and thought impossible; this is apparent even in such well-written plays by Samuel Beckett as *Krapp's Last Tape*, *Endgame*, and *Happy Days*. In some of these, words, which have been the carriers of ideas in the theatre ever since Aeschylus, have even been subordinated to mechanical sounds and movements as a preferable means of communication.[46]

Gassner decided that both Beckett and Pinter were writing plays which "provided a concentration of mature feeling with worthy skill and control that set them apart from other new plays as products of a virtually different

world of theatre than the customary commercial product." He applauded the
New Yorker's description of *Happy Days* and *Waiting for Godot* as "mysterious,
frightening, funny and altogether remarkable."[47]

Eric Bentley believed that *Waiting for Godot* was an "important play,"
yet he felt that while Beckett's voice was "interesting," it was "not quite ...
individual" nor "new" since "Mr. Beckett is excessively—if quite inevitably—
overinfluenced by Joyce." Bentley insisted that "one is tempted to think that
Irish literature, even when it is written in French, as Beckett's play was, is
cut from those coats of many colors, *Ulysses* and *Finnegan's Wake* [sic]."[48]
Overall, however, Bentley defended Beckett's dramaturgy, and called *Godot*
"a landmark":

> *Waiting for Godot* seems antidramatic in that garrulity is the all-
> but-declared principle of its dialogue. These men talk to kill time,
> talk for talking's sake. It is the opposite of *azione parlata*, which
> implies "a minimum of words, because something important is
> going on." Here we seem to have a maximum of words because
> nothing at all is going on—except waiting.
>
> But this is a big exception, and it saves Beckett's play. It makes
> no difference that the waiting may be for nothing. Here is a play
> with a very slight Action, with only the slightest movement from
> beginning to middle to end, and yet there is an Action, and it
> enables us to see the totality, not as undramatic, but as a parody
> of the dramatic.[49]

In *The Theatre of Revolt*, Robert Brustein called Beckett "the most gifted"
of the theatre of the absurd dramatists,[50] and in 1956 Kenneth Rexroth wrote
in *The Nation* that

> Beckett is so significant ... because he has said the final word
> to date in the long indictment of industrial and commercial
> civilization which began with Blake, Sade, Hölderlin, Baudelaire,
> and has continued to our day with Lawrence, Céline, Miller, and
> whose most forthright recent voices have been Artaud and Jean
> Genet.[51]

When Kenneth Tynan reviewed *Godot* at its London debut, he asserted that
"It forced [him] to reexamine the rules which have hitherto governed the
drama; and, having done so, to pronounce them not elastic enough. It is
validly new."[52] Like the other critics, Tynan enthusiastically explored and
defended Beckett's dramaturgy and his philosophy:

By all the known criteria, Samuel Beckett's *Waiting For Godot* is a dramatic vacuum. Pity the critic who seeks a chink in its armour, for it is all chink. It has no plot, no climax, no *dénouement*; no beginning, no middle, and no end. Unavoidably, it has a situation, and it might be accused of having suspense, since it deals with the impatience of two tramps, waiting beneath a tree for a cryptic Mr. Godot to keep his appointment with them; but the situation is never developed, and a glance at the programme shows that Mr. Godot is not going to arrive. *Waiting for Godot* frankly jettisons everything by which we recognize theatre. It arrives at the custom-house, as it were, with no luggage, no passport, and nothing to declare; yet it gets through as might a pilgrim from Mars.[53]

The critics more closely allied with the academic community were similarly writing in praise of Beckett's philosophical position and his dramaturgical style. As early as 1955 Edith Kern wrote in *Yale French Studies* that "It is Beckett's genius to have found the simple word, the absurdly comical situation to express his thoughts on man's place in the universe."[54] She asserts that "by all traditional standards *Waiting for Godot* is not a play" since "It has no action and thus completely lacks what Aristotle considered the most essential element of a successful play," there is "no character development" and no "plot or any kind of suspense." In spite of this she believes that "author and director manage to convey to the spectator a sensation of high drama, of a tragic fatality wedded to laughter which hides behind the exuberance of slapstick."[55] Kern concludes her article with the grand evaluation that

> Beckett's characters in this play glorify ... the all-surpassing power
> of human tenderness which alone makes bearable man's long and
> ultimately futile wait for a redeemer and which, in fact, turns out
> itself to be the redeemer of man in his forlornness.[56]

The critics' evaluations of Pinter were, like those of the reviewers, similar to their evaluations of Beckett. Gassner writes that *The Caretaker*

> is a haunting work as well as an exciting one; even the humor
> is wry and enigmatic.... *The Caretaker*, regardless of my minor
> dissatisfactions with the work, coheres for me magically and
> makes sense as a poetic (though not necessarily "anagogical")
> realization of a "feeling" about humanity. It is possible, I would
> conclude, to derive gratifications from Pinter's play on both
> literal and imaginative, or *reflective*, levels.[57]

Arthur Ganz praised Pinter as well, claiming that he "has known as much as any modern playwright the appeal of the liberated self. He has sensed, and embodied in the plays, that impulse toward the unlimited expansion of the ego, toward dominance, luxury, action, possession, sensual gratification." Ganz even went so far as to align Pinter with "the first great modern playwright," Henrik Ibsen, on the basis that they share "a kind of grim humor ... [and] an essentially ambiguous view of the human condition," despite their very different styles.[58]

While the work of avant-garde playwrights such as Beckett and Pinter was praised by the critics as innovative, intelligent, and philosophical, Williams' similar experiments were, of course, dismissed by them as failures most of the time. The critics were hailing dramaturgical qualities in Beckett's work that were clearly present in Williams' later plays, but they were not willing to grant Williams the intellectual capabilities that would enable him to produce a serious work of art in the tradition of the avant-garde. Precisely the same qualities that the critics praised in Beckett and Pinter's work, they condemned and complained about in Williams' later plays. Gassner's contention that in Beckett's plays, as well as in other works in the tradition of drama of the absurd, "language has once more been undercut by moody repetitions that make progression of thought and feeling impossible" could just as easily be applied to Williams' *I Can't Imagine Tomorrow*, *In the Bar of a Tokyo Hotel*, and *The Two-Character Play*.[59] Apparently for Gassner, Williams was more a part of the "customary commercial product" which, unlike the plays of Beckett and Pinter, did not provide "a concentration of mature feeling with worthy skill and control."[60] Similarly, Bentley's description of Beckett's dramaturgy in *Waiting for Godot* as "a parody of the dramatic,"[61] and Tynan's praise for *Godot* as an artistic success which "gets through" despite the fact that it is a "dramatic vacuum" which "frankly jettisons everything by which we recognize theatre," are qualities which many later plays of Williams exhibit.[62] In Williams' case, however, his dramaturgy was not recognized as a deliberate attempt to undermine traditional convention; rather, he was criticized for failing to uphold those very conventions "by which we recognize theatre"— or at least the essentially realistic, commercial theater for which Williams was known.

Overall, it was Beckett's reputation as an "intellectual" from the beginning of his career which anticipated the critics' reactions to his work and helped establish him within the elite circle of serious avant-garde writers which also welcomed Pinter and Albee. Williams, on the other hand, was excluded from this elite circle primarily on the basis of his early reputation. The critics were never prepared to take Williams seriously. From the beginning of his career they looked upon him as the pop hero of Broadway, and they were not about to budge from that position long enough to form a careful evaluation of his later work. This attitude is clearly illustrated in an anecdote concerning John Simon, who is generally known for his vicious attacks on playwrights and performers rather than for overly praiseful criticism. When Simon—who went on to become the drama critic for *New York* magazine—was a student at Harvard University, he wrote a rave review of *A Streetcar Named Desire* for the *Harvard Advocate*. The editorial board "thought he must be crazy for his enthusiasm" and consequently he lost his job.[63] While at times the critics did recognize the power and originality of the plays which were in general spurned by the reviewers, they still maintained their own assumptions, and set of prescribed standards concerning Williams' work. They had serious reservations concerning the artistic validity of a playwright who was so well established on Broadway and in the popular American cinema, and therefore were often inclined to casually dismiss Williams' later plays as either pretentious and empty philosophical ramblings or weak and superficial imitations of Beckett's style.

The overall consensus of the critics during the second half of Williams' career was (similar to the reviewers) that either he was so exhausted from his indulgences with drugs and alcohol that he was unable to think coherently, or that in his twilight years he must be running out of ideas for new plays and was therefore desperately and pathetically trying to imitate the popular avant-garde drama of his younger contemporaries. Even some of Williams' personal acquaintances felt this way. Spoto writes that when Williams was working on *The Two-Character Play*, his friends saw his new offering as "a strange dialogue for two characters that suggested ... an imitation of Pirandello or Pinter."[64] And when Vassilis Voglis, an artist who knew Williams socially for several years, claimed that Williams "turned to Beckett's *Godot* for his *Two-Character Play* and to other plays by other writers later" after "he lost contact with his roots,"[65] the implication is, once again, that Williams was no longer able to write originally and so was engaging in simple imitation of the newer successful artists. These remarks are emblematic of the critics' attitude toward his later work, an attitude which combines scorn with pity. Essentially, the response from Williams' friends and acquaintances to resemblances between his later work and the new drama contemporary with it was the assumption that Williams must be getting desperate, since he couldn't possibly be "intellectual" enough to turn his hand at "serious" drama.

In his later years, Williams was defeated before he ever began; reviewers tended to exhibit hostility toward experimental drama in general, and Williams never had a chance to be taken seriously in the first place by the critics. His later reputation, therefore, tells us more about the critical biases in the popular and academic press in this country than about Williams' work per se. In most critical texts on theater and drama, Williams is hailed as one of America's greatest playwrights, but he is referred to as if he died after *The Night of the Iguana*. The later plays are mentioned only in passing, if at all, and then usually with either brutal disdain or pity for the loss of talent in the great artist who, by the 1970s, was perceived as having been reduced to a babbling, drugged-out, dirty old man—capable of expressing himself only through the lewd ramblings of his *Memoirs*.

NOTES

1. Devlin, Conversations with Tennessee Williams, 284–85.

2. Ibid., 98, 137.

3. *Waiting for Godot*, however, was not performed in the United States until 1956.

4. James Coakley, "Time and Tide on the Camino Real," in Bloom, *Modern Critical Views: Tennessee Williams* (New York: Chelsea House, 1987), 98.

5. Niesen, "The Artist against the Reality," 106.

6. Ibid., 107.

7. Bigsby, "Valedictory," 132–33.

8. Samuel Beckett, *Molloy, Malone Dies, The Unnamable* (New York: Grove Press, 1955), 18.

9. Samuel Beckett, *Waiting For Godot* (New York: Grove Press, 1954), 9.

10. Ibid., 12.

11. Samuel Beckett, *Endgame* (New York: Grove Press, 1958), 58.

12. Vanden Heuvel, *Performing Drama/Dramatizing Performance*, 90.

13. Beckett, *Endgame*, 44.

14. Ibid., 81.

15. Ibid., 79.

16. Beckett, *Molloy, Malone Dies, The Unnamable*, 302.

17. Ibid., 291.

18. Ibid., 414.

19. Warren Lee, "The Bitter Pill of Samuel Beckett," *Chicago Review* 10:4 (1957): 79.

20. Ibid., 79–80.

21. Ibid., 77.

22. Ibid., 78.

23. Ibid.

24. Ibid.

25. Ibid., 79.

26. Clurman, *Lies Like Truth*, 15.

27. Bentley, *What Is Theatre?*, 297.

28. Tynan, *Curtains*, 272.

29. A. J. Leventhal, "Samuel Beckett, Poet and Pessimist," *The Listener* 57 (9 May 1957): 747.

30. Quoted in Bentley, *What Is Theatre?*, 298.

31. Ibid., 297.

32. W. A. Darlington, *New York Times*, 13 November 1955.

33. Brooks Atkinson, *New York Times*, 20 April 1956, 21:2.

34. Tynan, *Curtains*, 101.

35. Martin Esslin, *The Theatre of the Absurd* (1961; reprint, New York: Penguin Books, 1980), 40.

36. Tynan, *Curtains*, 272.

37. Brooks Atkinson, *New York Times*, 30 January 1958, 18:3.

38. Lewis Funke, *New York Times*, 12 February 1962, 27:1.

39. Walter Kerr, *Thirty Days Hath November* (New York: Simon and Schuster, 1969), 41.

40. Howard Taubman, *New York Times*, 5 October 1961, 42:3.

41. B. A. Young, *New York Times*, 4 June 1965, 38:8.

42. Kerr, *Thirty Days Hath November*, 45.

43. Brooks Atkinson, *New York Times*, 16 February 1958, 2:1:1.

44. Brooks Atkinson, *New York Times*, 29 April 1956, 2:1:2.

45. John Gassner, *Dramatic Soundings* (New York: Crown Publishers, 1968), 113.

46. Ibid., 692.

47. Ibid., 503.

48. Bentley, *What Is Theatre?*, 301.

49. Eric Bentley, *The Life of the Drama* (New York: Atheneum, 1964), 100–101.

50. Robert Brustein, *The Theatre of Revolt* (Boston: Little, Brown, and Company, 1964), 377.

51. Kenneth Rexroth, "The Point Is Irrelevance," *The Nation* (14 April 1956): 325.

52. Tynan, *Curtains*, 103.

53. Ibid., 101.

54. Edith Kern, "Drama Stripped for Inaction: Beckett's *Godot*," *Yale French Studies* 14 (1955): 45.

55. Ibid., 41–42.

56. Ibid., 47.

57. Gassner, *Dramatic Soundings*, 506–7.

58. Arthur Ganz, "Mixing Memory and Desire: Pinter's Vision in *Landscape, Silence, and Old Times*," in *Pinter: A Collection of Critical Essays*, ed. Arthur Ganz (Englewood Cliffs, NJ.: Prentice Hall, 1972), 177–78.

59. Gassner, *Dramatic Soundings*, 692.

60. Ibid., 503.

61. Bentley, *The Life of the Drama*, 101.

62. Tynan, *Curtains*, 101.

63. John E. Booth, *The Critic, Power, and the Performing Arts* (New York: Columbia University Press, 1992), 116.

64. Spoto, *Kindness of Strangers*, 297.

65. Vassilis Voglis to Donald Spoto, 22 September 1983, quoted in Spoto, *Kindness of Strangers*, 297.

SELECT BIBLIOGRAPHY

Abrams, M. H. *A Glossary of Literary Terms*. Orlando: Harcourt Brace Jovanovich, 1993.
Beckett, Samuel. *Endgame*. New York: Grove Press, 1958
———. *Molloy, Malone Dies, The Unnamable*. New York: Grove Press, 1955.
———. *Waiting For Godot*. New York: Grove Press, 1954.
Belsey, Catherine. *Critical Practice*. New York: Methuen, 1980.

Bentley, Eric. *The Dramatic Event*. New York: Horizon Press, 1954.

———. *In Search of Theatre*. New York: Alfred A. Knopf, 1953.

———. *The Life of the Drama*. New York: Atheneum, 1964.

———, ed. *The Theory of the Modern Stage*. Baltimore: Penguin Books, 1968.

———. *What Is Theatre?* 1968. Reprint, New York: Limelight Editions, 1984.

Bigsby, C. W. E. "Valedictory." In *Modern Critical Views: Tennessee Williams*, edited by Harold Bloom, 131–49. New York: Chelsea House, 1987.

———. *Modern American Drama, 1945–1990*. Cambridge: Cambridge University Press, 1992.

Bloom, Harold, ed. *Modern Critical Views: Tennessee Williams*. New York: Chelsea House, 1987.

Booth, John E. *The Critic, Power, and the Performing Arts*. New York: Columbia University Press, 1992.

Boxill, Roger. *Tennessee Williams*. London: Macmillan, 1988.

Brooks, Charles B. "Williams' Comedy." In *Tennessee Williams: 13 Essays*, edited by Jac Tharpe, 173–88. Jackson: University Press of Mississippi, 1980.

Brustein, Robert. *Critical Moments*. New York: Random House, 1980.

———. *Seasons of Discontent*. New York: Simon and Schuster, 1965.

———. *The Theatre of Revolt*. Boston: Little, Brown, and Company, 1964.

Bryer, Jackson R., ed. *Conversations with Lillian Hellman*. Jackson: University Press of Mississippi, 1986.

Clurman, Harold. *The Collected Works of Harold Clurman*. Edited by Marjorie Leggatt and Glenn Young. New York: Applause Books, 1954.

———. *Lies Like Truth*. New York: Macmillan, 1958.

Coakley, James. "Time and Tide on the *Camino Real*." In *Modern Critical Views: Tennessee Williams*, edited by Harold Bloom, 95–98. New York: Chelsea House, 1987.

Devlin, Albert J., ed. *Conversations with Tennessee Williams*. Jackson: University Press of Mississippi, 1986.

Diamond, Elin. "Mimesis, Mimicry, and the "True-Real." *Modern Drama* 32 (March 1989): 58–72.

Leverich, Lyle. *Tom: The Unknown Tennessee Williams*. New York: Crown, 1995.

Levine, George. *The Realistic Imagination*. Chicago: University of Chicago Press, 1981.

Nathan, George Jean. *The Theatre Book of the Year 1944–45*. New York: Alfred A. Knopf, 1945.

Nelson, Benjamin. *Tennessee Williams: The Man and His Work*. New York: Ivan Obolensky, 1961.

Niesen, George. "The Artist against the Reality in the Plays of Tennessee Williams." In *Tennessee Williams: 13 Essays*, edited by Jac Tharpe, 81–111. Jackson: University Press of Mississippi, 1980.

Patraka, Vivian M. "Lillian Hellman's *Watch on the Rhine*: Realism, Gender, and Historical Crisis." *Modern Drama* 32 (March 1989): 128–45.

Prenshaw, Peggy W. "The Paradoxical Southern World of Tennessee Williams." In *Tennessee Williams: 13 Essays*, edited by Jac Tharpe, 3–27. Jackson: University Press of Mississippi, 1980.

Rader, Dotson. *Tennessee: Cry of the Heart*. New York: Doubleday, 1985.

Rexroth, Kenneth. "The Point is Irrelevance." *The Nation* (14 April 1956): 325–28.

Reynolds, James. "The Failure of Technology in *The Glass Menagerie*." *Modern Drama* 34 (December 1991): 522–27.

Riddel, Joseph N. "*A Streetcar Named Desire—Nietzsche Descending.*" In *Modern Critical Views: Tennessee Williams*, edited by Harold Bloom, 13–22. New York: Chelsea House, 1987.

Savran, David. *Communists, Cowboys, and Queers: The Politics of Masculinity in the Works of Arthur Miller and Tennessee Williams.* Minneapolis: University of Minnesota Press, 1992.

Smith, Bruce. *Costly Performances: Tennessee Williams: The Last Stage.* New York: Paragon House, 1990.

Spoto, Donald. *The Kindness of Strangers: The Life of Tennessee Williams.* New York: Ballantine Books, 1985.

St. Just, Maria. *Five O'Clock Angel.* New York: Alfred A. Knopf, 1990.

Taylor, Harry. "The Dilemma of Tennessee Williams." *Masses and Mainstream 1* (1948): 51–56.

Tharpe, Jac, ed. *Tennessee Williams: 13 Essays.* Jackson: University Press of Mississippi, 1980.

Tynan, Kenneth. *Curtains.* New York: Atheneum, 1961.

Vanden Heuvel, Michael. *Performing Drama/Dramatizing Performance.* Ann Arbor: University of Michigan Press, 1991.

Watt, Ian. *The Rise of the Novel.* London: Chatto and Windus, 1957.

Wilder, Thornton. *Three Plays.* New York: Harper and Brothers, 1957.

Williams, Dakin and Shepard Mead. *Tennessee Williams: An Intimate Biography.* New York: Arbor House, 1983.

Williams, Tennessee. *Collected Stories.* New York: Ballantine Books, 1985.

———. *Memoirs.* New York: Doubleday and Company, 1975.

———. *Out Cry.* New York: New Directions, 1973.

———. Introduction to Carson McCullers's *Reflections in a Golden Eye.* New York: Bantam Books, 1967.

———. *The Theatre of Tennessee Williams.* 8 vols. New York: New Directions, 1971–92.

———. *Where I Live: Selected Essays by Tennessee Williams.* Edited by Christine R. Day and Bob Woods. New York: New Directions, 1978.

Zola, Émile. "Naturalism in the Theatre." 1881. Reprinted in *The Theory of the Modern Stage*, edited by Eric Bentley, 315–72. New York: Alfred A. Knopf, 1953.

FRANK BRADLEY

Two Transient Plays:
A Streetcar Named Desire *and* Camino Real

Tennessee Williams chose to introduce the public to *A Streetcar Named Desire* by focusing attention on the "spiritual dislocation" he felt on the heels of his most abrupt and dramatic *coup de théâtre*—his sudden success and notoriety in the wake of *The Glass Menagerie* ("Success" 3). In an article entitled "On a Streetcar Named Success" which appeared in *The New York Times* a few days before *Streetcar*'s opening,[1] Williams described his awkward assumption of a public identity, "an artifice of mirrors," which alienated him from his private and relatively anonymous identity as a literary struggler "clawing and scratching along a sheer surface and holding on with raw fingers" (1). He described himself as:

> [...] snatched out of virtual oblivion and thrust into sudden prominence, and from the precarious tenancy of furnished rooms about the country I was removed to a suite in a first-class Manhattan hotel. (1)

It was as if he'd walked across *Camino Real*'s plaza from the skid row Ritz Men Only to the plush Siete Mares. Yet as disorienting as his new accommodations were (his famous destruction of hotel rooms might be seen as a means of resurrecting the spiritual comfort of his clawing and scratching

From *Tennessee Williams: A Casebook*, edited by Robert F. Gross: pp. 51–62. © 2002 by Routledge.

years), the deeper "spiritual dislocation" had more to do with language and relationships than physical environs:

> I soon found myself becoming indifferent to people. A well of cynicism rose in me. Conversations all sounded like they had been recorded years ago and were being played back on a turntable. Sincerity and kindliness seemed to have gone out of my friends' voices. I suspected them of hypocrisy. (3)

Success alienated him. Only when he returned to a state of relative misfortune, hospitalized "in pain and darkness" after one of many serious eye operations, did Williams once again hear "sincere ... kindly voices with the ring of truth" (9). In order to stabilize his self-image vis-à-vis those of his friends, he had to suffer. Restored through suffering, he then sought a more deliberate experience of dislocation:

> I checked out of the handsome suite at the first-class hotel, packed my papers and a few incidental belongings, and left for Mexico, an elemental country where you can quickly forget the false dignities and conceits imposed by success, a country where vagrants innocent as children curl up to sleep on the pavements and human voices, especially when their language is not familiar to the ear, are soft as birds'. My public self, that artifice of mirrors, did not exist here and so my natural being was resumed. (9)

From the Siete Mares back to the Ritz Men Only—it was here in a Mexican village, a place of soft voices, unfamiliar language, and innocent vagrancy, that Williams found refuge from an alien public self imposed upon him and achieved restoration of a private "natural" one. Here in Mexico, in what he called "a final act of restoration," he resumed work on a play he called *The Poker Night*, which later became *A Streetcar Named Desire*. Sometime between his Mexican restoration and his writing about it he began work on another piece, originally called *Ten Blocks on the Camino Real* (agent Audrey Wood initially cautioned him to put it away, out of sight), which in 1953 became a longer play with a shorter title, set in an imaginative Mexican setting no doubt inspired by his restorative experience (Murphy 64). A transient from a broken home, a seeker of sincerity, and a writer who throughout his professional career sought accommodation to homelessness,[2] Williams attempted in these two plays to dramatize the rescue of a private self from a degraded collection of imposed public identities which, like the posh hotel rooms that he often trashed, repulsed him as they attracted him.

Although "On a Streetcar Named Success" casts Williams's attempted rescue of a private identity in a personal light, of greater significance to a study of Williams's works and of twentieth-century drama is the dramaturgical dimension of his effort. Far from typical examples of bourgeois domestic drama, both *Streetcar* and *Camino Real* nonetheless cannot be analyzed without reference to the bourgeois dramatic tradition of which they, like a number of twentieth-century plays from Chekhov to Miller, signal the collapse. The central figures of both plays—Blanche DuBois, Don Quixote, and Kilroy—are, like Williams, itinerants who seek in their own ways the "sincere ... kindly voices with the ring of truth," voices which once were the hallmark of bourgeois domestic drama.

Peter Szondi's analysis of an early theorist of domestic drama, Denis Diderot,[3] throws light on some of the significant dramaturgical issues with which Williams struggled in *Streetcar* and *Camino Real*. Szondi draws from Diderot the contrasting dramatic principles of *tableau*, roughly defined as a stable, interior family display whose purpose was to express visually and verbally the family members' feelings for one another in a free and protected private space; and the *coup de théâtre*, or the unexpected and often capricious reversal of fortune characteristic of a pre-modern world governed by the fickleness of absolute rulers who had the power to impose motivation from without. Diderot's points were that a new drama for a newly emergent middle-class audience needed to find a way to reflect and express the condition of its audience truthfully, that the principle of the *coup de théâtre* belonged to a dying order, and that the *tableau*, belonging as it did to the private, domestic world of the paterfamilias, "secluded from the public area, and therefore also from the state and from politics in general," was the appropriate dramatic expression of the middle class (Szondi, *Tableau*, 334).

As Szondi points out, Diderot was greatly concerned with the concept of dramatic *vérité* or "true speech," which might roughly be described as truth, with overtones of sincerity. The point of Szondi's analysis of early bourgeois drama is that, as Diderot recognized, social conditions brought on by the rise of the middle class had changed the dramatic rules by which *vérité* could be manifested on stage from the expression of "great passions" to "the realistic representation of the author's own social surroundings" (*Tableau*, 325). The realistically represented social surrounding was, of course, the middle class interior, governed by rationalism, whose purpose it was to keep at bay the unforeseen capricious events which had governed the earlier drama.

In his *Theory of the Modern Drama*, Szondi analyzes another aspect of dramatic *vérité* in a changing social and dramatic landscape. He refers to the Drama[4] as a product—born in the Renaissance and perfected in the domestic dramas of the eighteenth century—of "a newly self-conscious being who

... sought to create an artistic reality within which he could fix and mirror himself on the basis of interpersonal relationships alone" (7). To Szondi, the Drama is absolute, "conscious of nothing outside itself," distinguished by "[t]he absolute dominance of dialogue," which "reflects the fact that the Drama consists only of the reproduction of interpersonal relations" (8). The domestic Drama orients its characters, and its spectators, according to a dialogic bond which forms a community built upon a family model. Dramatic *vérité* is produced and reinforced via the mutual interaction of the domestic *tableau*, whose demands of realistic detail and accuracy grew throughout the Drama's period of ascendancy, and the intersubjective dialogic bond of characters whose private space, the space for such dialogue, is protected by the walls of the home.

That Diderot and Williams represent the alpha and omega of domestic drama is nowhere more clearly seen than in the common search for *vérité* for Williams the "sincere ... kindly voices with the ring of truth"—amid widely differing conditions. A product of a broken home whose life was marked by transience, Williams sought a means of expressing truth and sincerity on a stage in which the home, the site of dialogic bonding, had virtually collapsed. His project, then, was the same as Diderot's—how to express dramatic *vérité* in a transitional period, when old forms had collapsed and new ones had not yet defined themselves.

In the distant background of *A Streetcar Named Desire* can be seen a home which produced the *vérité* of Diderot's drama. Since Stella's departure from Belle Reve the Du Bois family home in Mississippi, life there under Blanche's stewardship had undergone a series of degradations, from the "long parade to the graveyard," (261) to the "epic fornications" (284) for which inheritance was exchanged. Despite the fact that Blanche herself had participated in the latter (in recent years Belle Reve was declared "out of bounds" to a nearby army camp) (361), the ancestral family home remained the site of one of the few periods in Blanche's life when she was—as a child—more "tender and trusting" than anyone (376). But this brief reference stands as a mere precursor to a recent history of degradation which has pushed Blanche out of the home onto a series of conveyances, from Laurel to New Orleans, from the streetcar named Desire to the one called Cemeteries, and finally to Elysian Fields.[5] Her search for companionship, in the person of the least sexually identified man in the play, Mitch, a level-headed fellow from a stable home, devoted to his mother, merges together all of the elements missing from her recent history, elements once displayed in Diderot's domestic *tableau*— stability, intersubjectivity, and a cessation of the capricious reversals of the *coup de théâtre*. If Blanche's libido at times turns her into "Dame Blanche," whose "intimacies with strangers" set her adrift, her value system remains essentially that of a daughter seeking the protection of the family bond and its domestic walls (386). As she says, rather desperately, to her sister, "I want to rest! I want to breathe quietly again!" (335).

As the title suggests, *Streetcar* embraces the metaphor of movement, or more specifically, public transit, in order to engage the question of dramatic *vérité* in a world in which private relations have become problematic. The companionship which Blanche seeks must find a means of expression and enactment in a stage environment which has shaken the home's foundation and thereby blurred distinctions between private and public.

Although the home in *Streetcar*—the Kowalski apartment—still stands, it does so largely in the character of an environmental antagonist to Blanche. Her chief problem in the dirty, crowded, and oppressive apartment is that she is subject to too many personal disclosures at the hands of too many strangers, and on terms not her own. The apartment crowds a number of people into a very small space; and is itself surrounded by other spaces of intrusive activity which condition it. The location of the Hubbel apartment upstairs, the flimsiness of walls, and the necessity of open windows to combat the New Orleans heat and humidity guarantee that the Kowalskis and the Hubbels will never be free from each other. As if this weren't enough, Williams adds the device of making the back wall of the apartment transparent at times so that we might be reminded of the conditioning of the action within by a larger outside context, as he describes during the scene which immediately precedes the inevitable "date" that Blanche and Stanley have "had with each other since the beginning":

> Through the back wall of the rooms, which have become transparent, can be seen the sidewalk. A prostitute has rolled a drunkard. He pursues her along the walk, overtakes her and there is a struggle. A policeman's whistle breaks it up. The figures disappear. (399)

Voices and sounds from the outside keep intruding on attempted "private" dialogues: Blanche asks Stella if she may "speak plainly" her opinions of Stanley's brutishness, at which point the loud sound of a train approaching temporarily makes hearing her impossible (322).

Inside the apartment there are no doors between rooms, and there are only two rooms. Its inhabitants must undress in view of each other. Nothing is safe from another person's scrutiny in such a space. It is significant that Stanley's first penetration of Blanche's privacy happens largely as a result of space and proximity: because there is literally no place for Blanche's trunk to be stored, it must remain throughout the play in a high-traffic area in Stanley and Stella's bedroom, vulnerable to Stanley's rough dissection as he hurls about the room the remaining vestiges of her private life—her dresses, furs, jewelry, and love letters (273–274). That Blanche's bed is in the most public place of all—a kitchen, where Stanley and his friends play poker—serves as a constant reminder of her all-too-public past while at the same time it visually reinforces the problem of her present lack of privacy. To lack privacy is to be exposed to multiple and often conflicting outside influences. To be public is to be impure, and every space in this setting is impure. Even the home's most private space, the bathroom, does uncomfortable double duty: Blanche's periodic rejuvenating baths occur in the same space where Stanley and his friends urinate.

As was the case in Diderot's time, the domicile in Williams's world reinforces the value system of its paterfamilias. Stanley's explanation of the Napoleonic code suggests that everything in the apartment bears his mark. By this principle alone he appears far better accommodated to living in crowded conditions which blur the distinction between private and public. He is a man of the present, well-adjusted to an instrumental world which has no time for Blanche's ornate literary discourse, but insists on laying his cards on the table (279). But if the environment of Elysian Fields antagonizes Blanche, her mere presence antagonizes Stanley. He feels the pressure of having his space violated by a stranger, as he complains to Stella:

> God, honey, it's gonna be sweet when we can make noise in the night the way that we used to and get the colored lights going with nobody's sister behind the curtains to hear us! (373)

To lack privacy in this broken home is to lack the ability to speak purely (even if, in Stanley's case, speaking purely means nothing more than making noise), to disclose oneself with completeness and sincerity, and on one's own terms. Speech is inevitably compromised in this instrumental space; the search for *vérité* the "sincere ... kindly voices with the ring of truth," takes place on grounds that make its achievement virtually impossible to enact.

Compromised language, no longer capable of manifesting the intersubjective bond that Blanche desires, becomes in *Streetcar* as menacing and disorienting as the alien environment in which she wanders. A literary figure (she was an English teacher) set loose in a brutal and instrumental world, Blanche bears witness to a trail of broken meanings which intensify her fragmentation. Her arrival at the Kowalski apartment in the opening scene betrays a naïve faith in words to mean what they say in a crude world governed by insincere relations. She stands bewildered that the reality of her destination, Elysian Fields, contradicts the literary image of paradise that she had heretofore accepted; she uncomprehendingly mutters to the stranger Eunice that "they mustn't have—understood—what number I wanted" (246). As one who spent a teaching career trying to "instill a bunch of bobbysoxers and drugstore Romeos with a reverence for Hawthorne and Whitman and Poe" (302), Blanche relies upon the literary reference in order to help stabilize her in disorienting surroundings, as she describes her reaction to Elysian Fields to Stella:

> Never, never, never in my worst dreams could I picture—Only Poe! Only Mr. Edgar Allan Poe!—could do it justice! Out there I suppose is the ghoul-haunted woodland of Weir! (20)

Yet as much as Blanche relies upon the literary reference to give orientation, such reference has itself become degraded in her world. Her life in Laurel was characterized by linguistic disjunctions, between the name of "Belle Reve" and its "epic fornications" and "long parade to the graveyard," between "English teacher" and "spinster," "Flamingo" and "Tarantula Arms," "Sister Blanche" and "Dame Blanche, "lover" and "degenerate," to name but a few. Little wonder then, that the object of her search is a cessation of what has become a long journey of dislocations. A "restful" bond with Mitch, who carries with him as a memento of a former romance a cigarette case with Blanche's "favorite sonnet by Mrs. Browning" might, in Blanche's mind, resurrect the power of language to keep an unstable, possessive, and libidinous world at bay, as it no doubt would have in Diderot's day (297). But Blanche's past, which buried the private identity she seeks to restore, that of the daughter of the family more "tender and trusting" than anyone, under the public mask of a profligate, becomes a means by which Stanley can banish what he perceives as her ornate pretensions and return to his household its pure language, a language of ecstatic shrieks and violent shouts, a language to which his wife, unlike her sister, seems well accustomed.

If *Streetcar*'s broken *interieur* gives rise to a powerful dramatic experience that crushes its heroine's attempt to resurrect a domestic *tableau*, it does so by recognizing that at the core of the play's conflict is a conflict of language. The language of *vérité* which Williams found in the Kowalski house was a language of brutal directness, "laying ... cards on the table" and adding one's shrieks to the noisy public atmosphere of the French Quarter, where everyone seems within sight and earshot of everyone else (279). By abandoning the interior altogether in *Camino Real*, Williams carried his search for *vérité* more directly into the public sphere. As he did with *Streetcar*, Williams took the opportunity prior to *Camino Real*'s premiere to draw a connection between his private struggle for expression and the pubic outcome of such expression.

His *New York Times* article of March 15, 1953[6] focuses his search for dramatic *vérité* on the problem of how to communicate theatrically the private vision of one who, having squeezed the remaining dramatic potential from a broken home, had reached a more confident accommodation to homelessness, and was endeavoring to discover a new, post-domestic theatrical language. He wanted to share his "sensation of release" with audiences he knew would be challenged by the experimental language of *Camino Real* (419). He wrote that the play seemed, more than any other work he had written, "like the construction of another world, a separate existence" (419). He suspected that this "separate existence" would be a bit hard to swallow for spectators who might not wish to leave the familiarity of the home and its conventional languages, spectators whom he accused of being "a little domesticated in their theatrical tastes":

> A cage represents security as well as confinement to a bird that has grown used to being in it; and when a theatrical work kicks over the traces with such apparent insouciance, security seems challenged and, instead of participating in its sense of freedom, one out of a certain number of playgoers will rush back out to the more accustomed implausibility of the street he lives on. (422)

Williams surely had in mind here a suburban American street nothing like the one he gives us in *Camino Real*. The play's setting is a transitional space, a "port of entry and departure" with "no permanent guests" (503). It reflects Williams's own itinerancy, *en route* between various points of reference—the Siete Mares and the Ritz Men Only; the known and the unknown (the *terra incognita* beyond the back wall of the plaza); and life and death, the latter made present by ever hovering Streetcleaners, whose job it is to collect corpses for scientific dissection. The plaza is distinguished by its absolute proscription of private relations. Serious conversations are forbidden, and every encounter is public, from the exhausted conversations of Marguerite Gautier and Jacques Casanova to the pickups of the Baron de Charlus (469). The presence of Gutman as a menacing authority figure whose role doubles as epic narrator continually reminds denizens of the plaza and the spectators of the play that everything in this place has an audience. Kilroy's occasional escapes into the auditorium similarly remind spectators of the public nature of the play.

As is the case with *Streetcar*, *Camino Real* casts a glance back to an abandoned home which was once capable of producing intersubjective meaning. When Don Quixote, a transient like Blanche, arrives in the plaza, he refers back to a more fulfilling time in his past, drawing attention to the bit of faded blue ribbon on the tip of his lance, which he keeps as a remembrance of *vérité*:

QUIXOTE: It ... reminds an old knight of that green country he
lived in which was the youth of his heart, before such singing
words as Truth!
SANCHO: [panting] —Truth
QUIXOTE: Valor!
SANCHO: —Valor
QUIXOTE: [elevating his lance] Devoir!
SANCHO: —Devoir ...
QUIXOTE: —turned into the meaningless mumble of some old
monk hunched over cold mutton at supper! (433–434)

Soon after this exchange Sancho leaves Quixote, setting in motion
the play's theme of a search for companionship. Quixote falls asleep in order
to dream:

... a pageant, a masque in which old meanings will be remembered
and possibly new ones discovered, and when I wake from this sleep
and this disturbing pageant of a dream, I'll choose one among its
shadows to take along with me in the place of Sancho ... (437)

The quest for companionship is related to the quest for meaning
which here, unlike in *Streetcar*, holds out the possibility for something new.
Given the abandonment of the home and the possibility of private relations,
there is in fact some pressure for "new meanings" to provide a basis for the
companionship which Don Quixote seeks. Williams wrote *Camino Real* in
order to discover what these new meanings, the new basis for dramatic *vérité*,
might be.

The new companion with whom Quixote bonds at the end of the play is
an archetypal character, the all-American boxer Kilroy, who, like Quixote, is a
drifter who has left a once fulfilling home. Kilroy hit the road because of a bad
heart, "as big as the head of a baby," which compelled him to leave his "real
true woman;" he became scared that "a real hard kiss would kill me!" (456).
In Quixote's dream, which constitutes the play-within-the-play, Kilroy learns
from the exiled Jacques Casanova that "the exchange of serious questions and
ideas ... is regarded unfavorably here" (472); is forced to put on a clown wig
and play the role of patsy for Gutman; wins an evening with Esmerelda, a
prostitute whose virginity is restored with each new moon (532); undergoes
a ritual murder at the hands of the Streetcleaners (577); and finally, after
having his solid-gold heart pulled from his chest in an autopsy, is pronounced
the only sincere "Chosen Hero" of the Camino Real (583). Declared sincere,

Kilroy joins the awakened Quixote and walks with him out of the plaza into the "terra incognita" visible beyond the upstage wall (591). If at the play's conclusion Williams give us a sign that a sincere, bonding relationship has been accomplished, we are left to figure out what its conditions are and what has made it possible.

Recalling Williams's own post–*Glass Menagerie* Mexican restoration which revived his private self with the soft sound of an unfamiliar language, and taking a cue from Quixote's nostalgia for a time and place when companionship was stable and words meant something, it can be inferred that the new theatrical language of *vérité* which Williams sought to express in *Camino Real* must both embrace the strange and overcome it. The play embraces the strange by reasserting, boldly, the force of the *coup de théâtre*— the sudden, capricious reversal of fortune which the domestic *interieur* helped protect against. *Camino Real* is punctuated by sudden reversals by which Williams was able to "give ... audiences my own sense of something wild and unrestricted that ran like water in the mountains" (*Camino Real*, 420). The world of *Camino Real* is governed by caprice; but if the *coup de théâtre* of classical drama reflected the arbitrary power of an absolute ruler, that in *Camino Real* reflects nothing more than the playwright's sense that life is a "wild and unrestricted" ride, the source of which is obscure. The most striking example of this is the "Fugitivo," a "non-scheduled" flight which appears on "orders from someone higher up" (500). The Fugitivo is a means of escape which is offered as a hope, but it cannot be controlled or bought, as we learn from Marguerite's futile efforts to bribe the pilot. A fanciful *coup de théâtre*, the Fugitivo arrives without warning (even Gutman, who seems in control of most of what goes on, is irate that he isn't told of its immanent arrival [512]), creates havoc by turning people against each other in a mad rush for its doors, and reinforces the status of the play's characters as helpless objects of some outside agency. In its own way, the Fugitivo is as brutal a theatrical agent as Stanley Kowalski; by disrupting the *tableau*, it reinforces the victimization of those who would engage it.

Williams was clearly attracted to this kind of theatrical communication, as attested by his writings during the 1940s and early 1950s on the need for a new "plastic theatre" to replace the "exhausted theatre of realistic conventions," a theatre of "unconventional techniques" which might find "a more penetrating and vivid expression of things as they are" (Adler 28). Writing specifically about *Camino Real* Williams celebrated the theatrical power of the visual symbol, which he called "nothing but the natural speech of drama," able "to say a thing more directly and simply and beautifully than it could be said in words" (421). Here, it seems, the poet in Williams who sought a restoration of verbal sincerity ran into conflict with the stage manipulator impatient with the theatrical inefficiency of words. "Symbols," he wrote in reference to *Camino Real* "are the purest language of plays" (422). As an example, he described the battered portmanteau full of Jacques Casanova's "fragile mementoes" which, when hurled from the balcony of the Siete Mares, signals his eviction:

> I suppose that is a symbol, at least it is an object used to express
> as directly and vividly as possible certain things which could be
> said in pages and pages of dull talk. (422)

Symbols and objects are vivid and penetrating; talk is dull. Tzvetan Todorov, in discussing Friedrich Creuzer's description of the symbol, noted the power of the symbol to have an effect of "lightning that in one stroke illuminates the somber night," and "a ray that falls straight from the obscure depth of being and thought into our eyes, and that traverses our whole nature" (217). The *vérité* of the symbol strikes with the power of the *coup de théâtre*. Despite the efforts of Williams, Blanche, and Don Quixote to resurrect the restful companionship of the past built on intersubjective dialogue, greater sincerity on Williams' stage, whether in Stanley's home or on the plaza of *Camino Real*, speaks the language of an instrumental world. The scene which precedes the Fugitivo, that which culminates with Lord Byron's exit into *terra incognita*, puts the question of theatrical language into stark relief. Byron is the literary center of the play-within-the-play. A poet who, like Williams, is concerned with his own powers of expression, he has been living for some time at the Siete Mares, where he has lost his inspiration: "The luxuries of this place have made me soft. The metal point's gone from my pen, there's nothing left but the feather" (503). He speaks of an "old devotion" to something which he doesn't name (504), and then proceeds to tell the story of the burning of Shelley's corpse on the beach at Viareggio. As he describes Shelley's heart being removed from his body, "snatched out—as a baker would a biscuit," the gross materiality of it all strikes him like a coup:

> I thought it was a disgusting thing to do, to snatch a man's heart
> from his body! What can one man do with another man's heart?
> (506)

At this point Jacques, in another moment which exploits the power of the visual symbol to communicate efficiently, twists, crushes, and stamps on a loaf of bread, exclaiming, "He can do this with it!" (506). Byron then counters this demonstration with a speech which pays homage to the poet's vocation:

[...] to influence the heart in a gentler fashion than you have made your mark on that loaf of bread. He ought to purify it and lift it above its ordinary level. For what is the heart but a sort of [...] instrument!—that translates noise into music, chaos into—order [...]—a mysterious order! (507)

Byron goes on to note how his poet's vocation had become obscured by the vulgar materiality of the world, its wealth, "baroque facades," and "corrupting flesh," which he attributes to a "passion for declivity" in the world (507–508). He now plans to leave this corrupting place, to set sail for Athens, where he hopes to revive within himself "the old pure music" of the poet (508). He will depart "from my present self to myself as I used to be" by first crossing *terra incognita* (503).

Byron is an example for Don Quixote and Kilroy, whose departure at the play's conclusion signals an achievement of companionship while avoiding answering the question of what makes companionship possible and dramatically representable. Given the suffering that Kilroy must still undergo after Byron's departure—his near escape from the Streetcleaners in Block Eleven; his encounter with Esmerelda in Block Twelve that mocks the very idea of conversation and intercourse, climaxed by a chanted repetition of "I am sincere" as he lifts Esmerelda's veil (562); his capture and dissection by the medical students, one of whom holds aloft his solid gold heart (581); and finally, his having a slop jar dumped on him (587)—it seems clear that the signs of companionship that Williams wishes to dramatize consist in a mutual recognition of one's victimization at the hands of manipulative, "rugged" forces which, like the experience of life in *Camino Real*, cannot be controlled. Given this state of things, companionship cannot be intersubjectively represented; it can only be referred to, much like the hope of recovering lost meanings. What binds Don Quixote and Kilroy is the common recognition that one goes on, with a tolerant smile, in the face of inevitable suffering in a world in which actions speak louder than words (589).

If Byron, Quixote, and Kilroy hold out the promise of "new meanings," we are no closer to finding out what these meanings may be at the end of the play than at the beginning. This is the continuing romantic quest carried by a literary figure identified with persistence in the face of lost causes. The final line of the Esmerelda's bedtime prayer, "let there be something to mean the word *honor* again," echoes Quixote's nostalgic reminiscence about the "green country" of the youth of his heart when words like "truth," and "valor," meant something (586). Williams is still searching for what that may be in a stage which, like the Mexican town to which he retreated after *The Glass Menagerie*, has none of the familiar reference points provided by the home.

The only things he seems confident of are that these meanings existed in the past, that we were better off when they existed, and that the only way to find them again is to traverse an open landscape that is as empty as a desert. In the meantime, his embrace of the language of the "plastic" theatre ensures that the quest for new/old meanings will be nothing but quixotic. If Williams's Mexican restoration resurrected a sense of private integrity in the face of an insincere world, it did so by reaching an accommodation to a stage on which the representation of private meaning, and private life, became impossible.

NOTES

1. Also reprinted in the Signet New American Library edition of *Streetcar Named Desire*.

2. See, for example, Leverich, or Williams's own *Memoirs*.

3. "*Tableau* and *Coup de Théâtre*: On the Social Psychology of Diderot's Bourgeois Tragedy (with Excursus on Lessing)."

4. Szondi capitalizes the term.

5. Thomas P. Adler has denoted the fluid structure of *Streetcar*, signified by Blanche's line "I'm only passing through": "Blanche's opening line about disembarking from a series of ... conveyances introduces the notion of a journey. Virtually her last line in the play, "I'm only passing through [...]," concludes the metaphor and confirms the spectators' sense that Williams builds his action around the image of an alienated, isolated wanderer seeking some kind of human connection (20)."

6. Reprinted in the New Directions edition of *Camino Real*.

WORKS CITED

Adler, Thomas P. A. *A Streetcar Named Desire: The Moth and the Lantern*. Boston: Twayne, 1990.

Leverich, Lyle. *Tom: The Unknown Tennessee Williams*. New York: Crown, 1995.

Murphy, Brenda. *Tennessee Williams and Elia Kazan:: A Collaboration in the Theatre*. Cambridge: Cambridge University Press, 1992.

Szondi, Peter. "*Tableau* and *Coup de Théâtre*. On the Social Psychology of Diderot's Bourgeois Tragedy." Trans. Harvey Mendelsohn. *New Literary History* 92 (1980): 323–43.

———. *The Theory of the Modern Drama*. Trans. Michael Hays. Minneapolis: University of Minnesota Press, 1987.

Todorov, Tzvetan. *Theories of the Symbol*. Trans. Catherine Porter. Ithaca: Cornell University Press, 1982.

Williams, Tennessee. *Camino Real*. Volume 2 of *Theatre*. New York: New Directions, 1971: 417–591.

———. *Memoirs*. New York: Doubleday, 1972.

———. "On a Streetcar Named Success." *A Streetcar Named Desire*. *New York Times* Nov. 30, 1947, sec. 2: 1, 3.

———. *A Streetcar Named Desire*. Volume 1 of *Theatre*. New York: New Directions, 1971: 239–419.

PHILIP C. KOLIN

The Family of Mitch:
(Un)suitable Suitors in Tennessee Williams

Perhaps more frequently than any other American playwright, Tennessee Williams knew the promise and the pain of (un)suitable suitors. His *Memoirs*, letters, essays, and even paintings record his mismatched liaisons; the roll call of suitors rejected by Williams or rejecting him is long and includes Pablo Rodriguez-Gonzales, Kip Kiernan, and all the boys of desire whose anatomies he temporarily cruised to dispel loneliness. Frank Merlo stands out as the bright exception. Turning his courting performances into text, Williams energized many of his dramatic works—and his fiction, too—around the quest for suitors and the disappointment their discovery effected.

Unsuitable suitors—failed gentleman callers, if you will—are obsessively persistent in Williams's imagination. Some of these suitors are spectral— Miss Lucretia Collins's lover in *Portrait of a Madonna*; Shep Huntleigh in *A Streetcar Named Desire*; and Merriwether in Williams's one-act play, *Will Mr. Merriwether Return from Memphis?* Their invisibility is a sign of phantom, unattainable desire. Sailors, the quintessentially unanchored lovers, also appear often as ill-fated suitors—Blanche's analogue from whom she asks directions in the acting script of *Streetcar*; the drunken paramours whom Violet entertains in *Small Craft Warnings*; and the predatory sailor of vicious and vulgar carriage in *Something Cloudy, Something Clear*. Serafina in the *Rose Tattoo* knows the type all too well when she asks her daughter's boyfriend, the

From *Magical Muse: Millennial Essays on Tennessee Williams*, edited by Ralph F. Voss: pp. 131–146. © 2002 by the University of Alabama Press.

sailor Jack Hunter: "What are you hunting, Jack?" Ironically, Sailor Jack in *Not About Nightingales* is the first casualty of cruel Warden Whalen's attack on desire in Williams's early play (1938). Few suitors, if any, in Williams offer honest love, commitment. Jake Torrence is the most mean-spirited suitor Lady ever had. Bill is rapacious and cruel in *The Long Good-bye*, trying to get sex from Joe's sister and denouncing her when she refuses. Another Bill, the aging stud in *Small Craft Warnings*, delivers a selfish paean to "Junior" (his penis), which seems more wish fulfillment than accomplishment.

The most famous group of unsuitable suitors belongs to what might be termed the "Family of Mitch," after Harold Mitchell in *Streetcar*. They share a repertoire of similarities, chief among which is that their narratives of self compete with and become emasculated in the plays in which they appear. These unsuitable suitors suffer from interrupted/incomplete sexuality, branding them as representatives of a desire that is fathomable, disappointing. Characteristically, Williams portrays their attempts within sacramental symbolism. Unsuitable suitors are caught in anticipated but ultimately annihilated epiphanies, made emblematic through Williams's numerous connections between the sacred and the profane. I would like to explore in some detail here the ways in which Williams develops and then radicalizes unsuitable suitors by focusing on Jim O'Connor in *Glass Menagerie*, Mitch, Alvaro Mangiacavallo in *The Rose Tattoo*, and Chicken Ravenstock in *Kingdom of Earth*.

I

Incomplete/interrupted sexuality is at the very center of Williams's most famous gentleman caller, Jim O'Connor in *The Glass Menagerie*, Williams's memory play. But *Menagerie* is Jim's memory play, too, for he tries to recall and to recuperate his image as a lover/powerfully sexual man that the script undermines. Jim's performances of hyperbolic virility are driven by his narratives of boundless masculinity. He brags to Laura that, when he was in school, "I was beleaguered by females in those days" (218) and reminisces that with his manly voice he "sang the lead baritone in that operetta" *The Pirates of Penzance*, not sensing the incongruity between the diminutive ("operetta") and his sexual self-importance. Believing that his manly ambition was effectively realized through public speaking, Jim thought he would go to the White House, the male seat of power, but he ended up at the shoe factory. His masculine hubris governs his ersatz courtship of Laura. Jim injects several illocutionary anatomical references to his manly physique. Although the remark is made in a "gently humorous" way, when he tries to get Laura to drink some wine—a frequently used male ploy to seduce a woman Jim brags,

"Sure I am superman" (210). Earlier, narrator Tom mocks Jim's superhuman ego: "He always seemed at the point of defeating the law of gravity" (190). Performing his manhood before Laura in the candlelit room, Jim boasts: "Look how big my shadow is when I stretch" (225). His fatuous shadowed self conflicts with the reality of pettiness in which he is enclosed. Even Jim's expletives attempt to reinforce his masculinity—"Why man alive" (221). "My interest happens to lie in electro-dynamics," he informs the gullibly adoring Laura as if to substantiate in language a sexual dynamism he can only fabricate.

Yet *Menagerie* includes another version of Jim's reality, not the shadow script he offers to Laura, but one that interrogates his sexual inadequacies, revealing him as a fabulist of desire. Williams deflates Jim's own representations of manhood, unpacking into the script of *The Glass Menagerie* the problematics of the gentleman caller's virility. No icon of male sexual beauty, Jim is "medium homely." His masculinity is underwritten by bovine femininity when he claims that he is as "comfortable as a cow!" (212). In that he is an advocate of chewing gum, Jim's mastication, not Tom's, further confirms the bovine in his repertoire. Appropriately, Jim is a shipping clerk, not one of the workers who make or manufacture, twice removing him from manly labor. Deflecting Jim's tauted masculinity again, Williams often situates Jim within a context of failed light and power. His self-announced manly expertise in "electro-dynamics" is futile when it comes to restoring the lights in the Wingfield apartment—"All the fuses look o.k. to me." Although he may have been cast as a hero in *The Torch*, Jim never lived up to the manly dreams of leadership that this publication augured. In signing Laura's copy of this contract of undelivered promises, Jim shows how ineffectual his manhood is. *The Torch* and the pen he uses to sign it—faint phallic tropes— mock his failed accomplishments. Like the old *Torch*, Jim is burned out, only pretending a passionate future. A perfect fetish of his inadequate manhood is the candelabra that he carries into the living room; as Amanda recalls, it "was melted a little out of shape," just like Jim, whose manly bravado dissolves into comic reality. Carrying such a melted symbol of light and fire, Jim, as Roger Boxill points out, "does not fulfill the role of redeemer" (75), still another indictment of his manliness.

Jim's self-proclaimed sexuality is further devalued in his (un)intentionally parodying courting rituals, all of which point to a disabling interruption of love. He is out of place in a romantic setting of shadows, candlelight, music, and dancing—tropes indicting his, and not just Laura's, diminished performance. Though claiming expertise about the technical world, Jim knows little about wooing. As a courtier, he is clumsy, awkward, gauche; he is a poseur in love. The gestures of his faux courtship are interruptive.

No elegant, smooth dancer, "he moves about the room in a clumsy waltz." As he dances with Laura, "they suddenly bang into the table, and the glass piece on it falls to the floor. Jim stops the dance." One of the most blatant attacks on Jim's virility comes from his own lips; he twice refers to himself as a "stumblejohn" after inappropriately kissing Laura. Jim is indeed the inept, stumbling john, or man in search of sex. After kissing her, "he coughs decorously and moves a little farther aside"—again interrupting the space and spirit of romance. Further breaking any love spell, he "fishes in his pocket for a cigarette" and then for a piece of gum, for, as he says, "my pocket's a regular drugstore" (229). Props of amorous engagement, gum (freshened desire) and the cigarette (seduction) become signs of evasion, disruption. Jim's fatuous discourse on these objects in his pockets interrupts the performative amorous script that he initiates and the desire-starved Amanda directs. As he fumbles in his pockets, Jim physicalizes both the banality and the concealment of his romantic overtures.

Structurally, the entire episode with Laura is an interruption in Jim's involvement with Betty, to whom he is engaged; he leaves Betty out of the picture and meets Laura and then returns to her after he breaks Laura's heart "I hope it don't seem like I'm rushing off. But I promised Betty that I'd pick her up at the Wabash depot.... Some women are pretty upset if you keep 'em waiting" (234). The script hints that Jim's future relationship with the impatient Betty will be uxorious—"I've got strings on me" (229). He will learn much more about what Amanda labels "the tyranny of women" (234). Jim's temporary tryst with Laura, then, says as much about his future love relationship as hers; both face alienation.

Williams invests the script heavily in religious symbolism to deflate Jim's sexual heroics, to underscore a failed epiphany for him as well as for Amanda and Laura. In setting and trope, Williams relates sacred to secular. The lighting is both romantic and sacramental, the one fusing with the other. The melted candelabra comes ironically from the "Church of Heaven's Rest" (210). The "Blue Roses" and "a floor lamp of rose colored silk" contribute to the aura of sacramentality Williams creates around Jim's courtship of Laura. Music drifts in from the Paradise Dance Hall across the street. Amanda, too, contributes to the sacramentality of the moment in action and allusion. Hiding behind the kitchenette curtains, she behaves like a giddy angel at the Annunciation or, even more ironic, one of the foolish virgins (she is presented as "Amanda as a girl" on one screen) waiting for the bridegroom of the biblical parable. But Jim does not cooperate with the biblical subject, despite her bringing in macaroons and fruit punch (secular, romantic communion) after his unholy kiss. Drinking the punch, Amanda exclaims: "Oooo! I'm baptizing myself!" (232). In fact, Jim undercuts any expected sacramental revelation or epiphany. "The holy candles on the altar of Laura's face have been snuffed out" (230) by his antiepiphanic revelation of his approaching marriage to Betty. The long-waited redeemer leaves for uxoriousness, and in his wake, two foolish virgins—Laura and Amanda—inherit a bleak, loveless future, a triangulation of the lost.

II

In *Streetcar*, Mitch also repeatedly projects an incomplete/interrupted sexuality in word and act, the hallmarks of the unsuitable suitor. Significantly, when he asks Blanche whether he may have a kiss, she responds: "Why should you be so doubtful?" Mitch's doubt, though, is a consequence of his insufficient sexuality. As Elia Kazan rightly pegged him in his *Streetcar* "Notebook," Mitch's "spine" is that of a "mama's boy," neither man nor boy, caught somewhere in between, incomplete. William Kleb wisely refers to Mitch's "arrested adolescence, even sexual confusion." Like a child, Mitch even looks sensitive, unmanly. No wonder Blanche calls him "angel puss," her most salacious epithet. Among his male friends, Mitch—the boy/man—is comically harangued for his unmanly ways; he needs a "sugar tit." He is accused of saving his poker winnings in a piggy bank for his mother. Occupationally, his sexual incompleteness is suggested by his work in the "spare parts department" at Stanley's plant. During the poker game, Mitch twice says, "Deal me out" (51, 52), separating himself from male sport. Domestically he is still caught in his mother's apron strings, metonymically represented in the Kazan film of 1951 by his leaving the washroom (Blanche's domain) still holding a towel, something literally left out that should have been left in. The incompetent wooer, Mitch is suspended between the worlds of desire and dependence, trapped in diminishment.

Mitch's language also demonstrates his sexual incompleteness—his lack of originality, psychic wholeness, integrity. He often leaves his sentences unfinished and even speaks without the benefit of connective syntax—"You ... you ... you ... brag ... brag ... bull ... bull" (131). Another indication of Mitch's insecurity and lack of confidence is his awkward reliance on the language of trite, conventional romance in wooing Blanche. He is so invested in the antiquated symbology of romance that it is easy for Blanche to trap, and then undercut, him. Among three of Mitch's many examples of stilted romancespeak are (1) "in all my experience I have never known any one like you" (87), a pickup line that serves as wonderful bait for Blanche's hook; (2) "you may teach school but you certainly are not an old maid" (56); and (3) perhaps his most disjunctively melodramatic line—"You need somebody.

And I need somebody, too. Could it be—you and me, Blanche?" (96), cycling Mitch's banal sensitivity through the doubtful interrogative, the tentative.

Mitch's passing status in Blanche's life as well as his liabilities as a suitor are epitomized at the end of scene 5—Blanche "blows a kiss at [the newspaper boy] as he goes down the steps with a dazed look. She stands there dreamily after he has disappeared. Then Mitch appears around the corner with a bunch of roses" (84). A young, dashing rosenkavalier leaves Blanche's life as Mitch, the retreaded rosenkavalier, enters late, almost as an ominous second thought. Quite literally, Mitch is a runner-up who will run out of time in Blanche's world. His roses will be replaced by the Mexican woman's *flores*, the florilegia of grief.

Mitch's props of love are equally incomplete, cues to his amorous incompetence and failure. Blanche too easily snares him by asking for a cigarette (Murphy), thus giving Mitch an opportunity to recount his narrative about the deceased girl who loved him and then to produce the silver cigarette case with the poetic inscription "I shall love thee better after death." Mitch's past love affairs, like this one with Blanche, ended in defeat. He will never know recrudescence. He smokes Luckies, a choice that ironically and bluntly indicts him as "never getting lucky in love" and suggests that all sorts of sexual rituals/overtones go unfulfilled. The cigarette case he carries is equivalent to Blanche's trunk, the remnants of his former life—dead, unresurrectable. Mitch's narrative of self contains too many ghostly lacunae.

Scene 6, which might be entitled "The Date's Over," contains two pejorative symbols of Mitch's sexual folly, his inability to be a whole man. Coming home from his date with Blanche on Lake Pontchartrain, Mitch "is bearing, upside down, a plaster statue of Mae West, the sort of prize won at shooting galleries and carnival games of chance" (85). Williams could not have found a more salient reminder of Mitch's sexual ineptitude than the shabby relic of the queen of burlesque, the boastful, domineering woman of hyperbolic assignations fueling male fantasies in the 1930s and 1940s. Like the statue, all of Mitch's sexual ardor and sexual plans are upside down, an icon of his failures. He has not won a prize of merit at the shooting gallery (phallic implications noted). Instead, his upside-down Mae West suggests that Mitch does not know how to shoot or that his shot is limp, sexually. For his foolish efforts he has won the most appropriate prize symbolizing the Blanche he courts—a woman who pretends to eschew Mae West's vulgarity but who has engaged in the type of sexual escapades for which the burlesque diva was infamous. Romantic possibility and the fulfillment of desire are upside down, topsy-turvy in Mitch's world. In the acting version of *Streetcar*, Kazan substituted a Raggedy Ann doll for the Mae West statue, a change that also marginalized Mitch as a complete adult man. The message: men don't carry dolls.

In the second set of symbols in scene 6, Blanche's purse and keys are involved. "See if you can locate my door-key in this purse," instructs Blanche, using sexual shorthand as old as Chaucer—keys = phallic; purse = vagina. "Rooting in her purse," Mitch comes up with the wrong key ("No, honey, that's the key to my trunk which I must soon be packing"). Searching some more, he utters another line of characteristic interrogative tentativeness, "This it?" As if she were reaching a sexual climax, Blanche shouts, "Eureka. Honey you open the door" (86). Through this calculatingly realistic stage business, Williams broadcasts to an attentive audience that Blanche is out with a man who cannot find a key and cannot carry a woman (Mae West) the right way because he is forever trapped by/in spare parts, held captive to a castrating matriarchy.

When Mitch does attempt physical intimacy, he is a fumbling clown whose actions are repeatedly interrupted, at first comically but then tragically for him and for Blanche. Mitch's desire is severed from sexual competence. When he is parked at the lake with Blanche, she allows him to kiss her but to go no farther—"It was the other little-familiarity—that I—felt obliged to—discourage" (87). Mitch's sexual advances are not only discouraged but disrupted. When he lifts her up a few minutes later, still with his "hands on her waist" (90), Blanche again, though politely, says first "release me" and then "I said unhand me, sir." "He fumblingly embraces her. Her voice sounds gently reproving" (91), halting Mitch's awkward journey toward intimacy. In between these two failed attempts to become sexual with Blanche, Mitch is thwarted, mocked in his overtures. Blanche coquettishly says in French, "Voulez-vous coucher avec moi ce soir?"—a line omitted from the Kazan film by the censors—knowing that he does not understand French. (Ironically, the audience may know that he could not do what she asks even if he did understand.) Mitch is no student of the language of love. When he begs to lift her, she taunts him using an allusion to one of the greatest victims of foolhardy love. "Samson. Go on and lift me!" Like his biblical antecedent, Mitch is shorn of strength, satiety; he will lose whatever sexual promise of success he anticipates, thanks to Blanche and his own blindness. Claiming adherence to "old-fashioned ideals," Blanche "rolls her eyes, knowing he cannot see her face." At the end of this playlet in the middle of scene 6, Blanche histrionically sighs like a lovelorn maiden, while the disconnected Mitch can only "cough," two gendered gestures of amorous interruption. Mitch's cough represents male capitulation and isolation after a failed attempt; Blanche's sigh is an expression of feigned female longing, forced desire. Like Jim in *Glass Menagerie*, Mitch's cough marginalizes/derhapsodizes his wooing.

In scene 9, Mitch's interrupted sexuality turns tragic, violent. Revisiting his date after the date—he is always a victim of poor self-timing—Mitch replays tragically the comic interlude of scene 6. Once more he "places his hands on her waist and tries to turn her about" (120). In this repetitive behavior Mitch again misses closure; he is caught in disruption, denounced desire. When Blanche asks him, "What do you want?" and he replies, "What I been missing all summer," Mitch admits his lack of connection, his miserable luck in love, the numerous times he started but failed—"Fumbling to embrace her" (120). Mitch's gestures are the signatory of interruption; a fumble is a failed attempt. When Blanche offers him the only way he can complete his amorous quest "Then marry me, Mitch!"—he refuses not with an explanation based on his feeling, a sign of wholeness, but with an appeal to maternal jurisprudence— "You're not clean enough to bring in the house with my mother." Blanche screams, stopping Mitch in his tracks and conclusively interrupting his final attempt to get lucky. "With a startled gasp, Mitch runs and goes out the door, clatters awkwardly down the steps and around the corner of the building" (121). This event is scripted in interrupted motion—*gasping, clattering, hiding around a corner*—graphically reducing Mitch from a beau to a petty thief or arsonist, foiled in his botched quest for manhood and easily frightened out of purpose by Blanche's three monosyllables—"Fire! Fire! Fire!"

Time and sex are destructively intertwined for an unsuitable suitor like Mitch. His sexual clock is not in keeping with Blanche's, nor is hers with his. Blanche's love clock is kept by the Pleiades, undulating according to celestial harmony. The ill-suited suitor Mitch, however, takes the "owl car" home (85). He is not on the same track as Blanche; neither of them connects. She won't go out with him on Sunday afternoons, and his mother is alarmed about Blanche's biological clock. Mitch tells Blanche that "my mother worries because I am not settled" (94), yet paradoxically, when he is ready to settle down, Blanche is not, and vice versa. His first words in scene 6—"I guess it must be pretty late—and you're tired"—are the most (unconsciously) prophetic pronouncements that Mitch makes about Blanche. When he bursts into Stanley's apartment in scene 9, Mitch, drunk and disheveled, is greeted by Blanche's temporal unreadiness—"Just a minute." A few lines later Blanche tries to redeem time and love again: "She offers him her lips. He ignores it and pushes past her into the flat" (113). Pushing past her, Mitch will not wait for a kiss. Their schedules, like their lips, are not synchronous. When she was playing hard to get, she reproved Mitch for too much intimacy in scene 6. What Mitch wanted then, Blanche, desperate, offers in scene 9, but at this point the stakes for Mitch have both gone high and disappeared.

Throughout his encounters with Blanche, Mitch is plagued by expected but failed epiphanies. Like Jim O'Connor, he experiences an annihilated epiphany, sensing the arousal of passion but not experiencing its consummation. As in *The Glass Menagerie*, the unsuitable suitor's lack of sexual connectedness is tied to imagery both secular and sacred in *Streetcar*, diffusing body and soul. Nowhere is this link clearer for Mitch than at the end of scene 6 when, suggesting the inevitability of commitment, Blanche utters one of the most famous lines in the play—"Sometimes—there's God—so quickly" (96). The eternal (God) for Mitch is short-circuited by the ephemeral (quickly) as he moves away from Blanche, signaled beautifully by Williams's use of dashes. The ultimate failed epiphany is recorded in Blanche's reference to the cathedral bells, "the only clean thing in the Quarter." As she leaves with her new beau/gentleman caller—the courtly doctor dressed in black—Blanche proceeds off the stage as if she were a triumphant bride going on her honeymoon, leaving the inconsolable Mitch, the failed suitor, to contemplate his loss, spiritually and physically, with his head down on the bastion of male gamesmanship, the poker table. Interestingly, Jessica Tandy's Blanche in 1947 suggested a bride—she wore a white veil and a white dress as she exited with the doctor—while in the John Erman *Streetcar* of 1984, Ann-Margret's Blanche was driven away with her new gentleman caller in a stately black car headed right for the St. Louis Cathedral in the distance, its spire welcoming her as it might some heavenly bride preparing for a heavenly climax.

III

Alvaro Mangiacavallo in the *Rose Tattoo* is the quintessential comic unsuitable suitor, the generic embodiment of the type. Serafina sees him as a ridiculous version of her handsome and romantic husband Rosario—"My husband's body with the face of a clown." A creature of mental and physical deformities for Serafina, Alvaro is the grandson of the village idiot, a "buffooe," "cretino" (394), a "paintetela." His ears stick out, he is short, he hitches his shoulders in nervous agitation, traits that call attention to his status as the buffoon. When Serafina first sees Alvaro, he is "sweating and stammering," and he later makes ridiculous sounds like a bird. He physicalizes awkwardness, a fumbling sexuality.

Alvaro's sexual potency is weakened, interrupted, as was Jim's and Mitch's. If Rosario was the priapic benefactor of fruitfulness, Alvaro is frequently portrayed as unregenerative. Though at one point Alvaro is called "one of the glossy bulls," and he vows to give Serafina endless nights of pleasure, his behavior suggests otherwise. When he first appears onstage, Alvaro receives a comically painful priapic injury. The salesman who runs Alvaro off the road, and whom this "Macaroni" dares to challenge, "brings his knee up violently into Alvaro's groin. Bending double and retching with pain, Alvaro staggers over" to Serafina's porch. After this altercation, Alvaro weeps profusely, admitting that "crying is not like a man" (355). Later, attempting to persuade Serafina to make love, Alvaro professes that his fingers are so cold from a lack of love that "I live with my hands in my pocket," a masturbatory allusion and gesture. But then he "stuffs his hands violently into his pants' pockets, then jerks them out again. A small cellophane wrapped disk falls on the floor, escaping his notice, but not Serafina's." She indignantly asks whether that was "the piece of poetry" Alvaro claimed to offer her. For Serafina, Mangiacavallo's rubber symbolizes interrupted love, sex without passion's juices, an insult to both her lustiness (she does "glance below the man's belt freely" [Robinson 31]) and her protective prudery. The condom is also a sign of Alvaro's less than manly amor, which puts him in stark contrast to the diurnally fruitful and sanctified Rosario.

The most salient instance of interrupted love occurs in the last scene of *Rose Tattoo*, where Alvaro, drunk and disoriented, is accused of trying to rape Rosa, a hilarious analogue to the tragic encounter that Mitch had with Blanche in scene 9 of *Streetcar*. The parallels are many and once again marginalize Alvaro's lovemaking. Like Mitch, Alvaro is chased for his life by Serafina, who screams "Fire"—as Blanche did—and who beats him. The scene is both grotesque and comic, all at Alvaro's expense. It should be "played with the pantomimic lightness ... of an early Chaplin comedy," according to Williams's stage direction (405). Being denied Mitch's flurry of forcefulness, Alvaro is even further deromanticized. He is a comically weakened Mitch.

Alvaro's position as the ungentlemanly caller is part of the larger psychic narrative of replication in the *Rose Tattoo* that contributes to the cycle of interrupted/incomplete sexuality. Imitation, copying, is the dynamic of this Williams play. Estelle gets a rose tattoo copied on her chest to brand herself as Rosario's *inamorata*; Serafina copies dress patterns and also reifies, imaginatively, her husband's rose on her chest; Alvaro, too, apes Rosario by having the patronymic emblem of Serafina's first husband emblazoned on his chest and, further, by wearing Rosario's shirt, given to him by Serafina. In the process, Alvaro invests in a feminine version of a man. He becomes a copy of a copy by imitating the women who are imitating Rosario, an act that amounts to a feminization of Alvaro's masculine agency, the deromanticizing of the Don Juan (masculine) amor he proffers to Serafina. Like Jim and Mitch, too, Alvaro arrives with prior experience in love, further casting him as a casualty in imitation. He gave his previous girlfriend "a zircon instead of a diamond. She had it examined. The door slammed in my face" (377).

Alvaro is presented as the zircon lover, cheap, laughable, gender voluble. Not surprisingly, the emblematic bird of the play is the polly, the parrot, the totem of squawking mimesis.

My reading of Alvaro is squarely in keeping with the standard received opinion of the gentleman caller in *The Rose Tattoo*. Yet this Williams comedy is more subversive than festive. He alters and radicalizes this character type, establishing Alvaro as among the first strain of the valorized ungentlemanly callers. Forever the champion of the underdog, Williams is the apostle of transformation. Alvaro is the loser who becomes a winner, a character in Williams's performative rhetoric of investing the other with power, just as he does Chicken Ravenstock as suitor in *Kingdom of Earth*, as we shall see. Through Alvaro, Williams both fictionalizes and celebrates the instability of Otherness, the character who does most textual violence to the conventional image of male sexual prowess. In *Rose Tattoo*, Williams marshals his resistance to conventional romantic nostalgia by disrupting the romantic hegemonies that Rosario represents and, even in death, insists upon. Through Alvaro, Williams attacks a complacent audience's romantic assumptionality and consumption.

By disrupting and resisting the vestigia of romanticism in the Rosario script, Alvaro is significantly redeemed through an act of unremembering, ejecting the expectations the script encourages Serafina to harbor. As Rosa implores her gentleman caller, Jack Hunter: "I want you not to remember" (399), that is, to disregard Serafina's command to abstain from sex. Unremembering is precisely what Serafina (and we as audience) must do with Alvaro's literary/theatrical heritage as the unsuitable suitor. We must erase the clown image as we simultaneously reject the dashing allure of a romantic Rosario implanting roses—fictional or tattooed—in his lovemaking. As he does politically in *Camino Real*, Williams dislodges nostalgia from representation. Thwarting any audience's proclivity to valorize Rosario and depreciate Alvaro, Williams reconfigures our notion of the romantic. Love for Serafina, like love for Williams, comes from unexpected quarters. E. E. Cummings's poem "The Balloon Man"—rather than "Cara Mia"—could serve as Alvaro and Serafina's love song. As in the other unsuitable suitor plays, Williams invokes the religious in *Tattoo* perhaps most overtly. Serafina's prayers to the Virgin are efficacious. Through the power of Her son, Mary brings Serafina's heart back to life again. Once Serafina exorcises the Rosario lie/nostalgia from her memory and comes back into real time by accepting Alvaro, she can escape the past and recoup love, an act of unremembering analogous to our unremembering that her new honeymoon lover was the grandson of the village idiot. Serafina's Alvaro is Tennessee Williams's Frank Merlo.

IV

Even more than Alvaro, Chicken Ravenstock in *Kingdom of Earth* may be the most ungentlemanly suitor in the canon. A mixed breed, or "wood's colt," Chicken is "someone with colored blood." He and his half brother, the landowning pale white Lot, had the same white father, but Chicken's mother was "very different," marginalized racially. The quintessential black man, Chicken cannot buy liquor, is forbidden to have relations with white women, and is dismissed as "untutored"—hardly romantic assets in Williams's bigoted Two River County. Branded a "misfit," an "outsider," a sexual deviate, Chicken has one of the strongest libidos in the canon. Don Rubicam observed that Chicken "had the sexual appetite of a satyr." He is unashamedly priapic with his hip-hugging boots and overt sexual gestures. At one point, Chicken "consciously or not drops one of his large, dusky hands over his crotch, which is emphasized, pushed out by his hip boots" (144). He carves lewd words into the kitchen table and bluntly probes his and others' sexual backgrounds. But what most infuriates critics is that Chicken receives fellatio from a white woman between acts 2 and 3.

Chicken's role as unholy suitor plays out within one of Williams's perpetual triangles—in this instance two men (Lot and Chicken) and one woman (Myrtle, the white "bride" whom Lot brings home). Triangulation in Williams always leads to disruption of the conventional. Myrtle is the female linchpin around whom the brothers' rivalry oscillates. Lot lures Chicken back to the family estate with the promise that if he comes back to work, Lot will include him in the inheritance, and Lot gives him a paper to that effect. But Lot changes his mind, arguing that he would turn over the family estate to a white woman he has known barely a few days—and whom he denigrates as a "whore"—rather than see his "colored" half brother get the land. To defraud Chicken, Lot instructs Myrtle: "Get Chicken drunk but get drunk yourself, and when he passes out, get this legal paper out of his wallet, tear it to bits and pieces, and burn 'em up." If Myrtle does this, "Then as my wife, when I die, the place will be yours, go to you" (168). She is to do this in Chicken's domain, the black servant's kitchen, a place that links him with cooking, subservience, and shadows.

Like Alvaro, Chicken's liminal status sets him apart as a special Williams suitor who succeeds, the critics' disgust notwithstanding. In Williams's theater of unsuitable suitors, Chicken powerfully thwarts, even threatens, an audience's expectations about courtship, marriage, union. Yet Williams boldly shows Lot's inferiority as a suitor by contrasting him with Chicken's actions. Lot, the spoiled aristocrat, diseased, is a tubercular transvestite whose own sexuality (and hence suitability as a lover) is intentionally linked to the satanic: "Lot remains in the wicker chair, still smoking with his mother's ivory holder and wearing now her white silk wrapper. His 'Mona Lisa' smile is more sardonic and the violent shadows about his eyes are deeper" (177). Secluded in his whites-only parlor, Lot can offer Myrtle only "the sexless passion of the transvestite" (212), the perverse pleasure of a lifeless Narcissus.

As he did to discredit Jim and Mitch but to valorize Alvaro, Williams contextualizes Chicken's actions within the sacramental promise of a fulfilled, not annihilated, epiphany. Unlike Jim or Mitch, Chicken's raw sexuality and blunt courtship are, in Williams's radicalization of the (un)suitable suitor, imprinted with a procreative and proleptic biblical seal. In fact, Williams invokes several biblical narratives—epiphanic validations—to valorize Chicken. One of these clearly relates to Noah and the Flood, in which Chicken is cast as the survivor/savior. At play's end, when Lot is dead, Chicken saves Myrtle from the flood and participates Noah-like in the rechristening of the farm, affirming, "Floods make the land richer" (183). Closely associated with the flood, of course, is the fall of Sodom and Gomorrah—Lot's empire. But unlike Lot's wife, Myrtle does not look back and is redeemed/recuperated through her new husband Chicken. The second biblical narrative on which Williams draws to situate Chicken in an epiphanic light is that of Adam and Eve. Chicken is the new man, the rechristened Adam. And paradoxically, the "whore" for Chicken will become the new Eve, the mother of succeeding generations of Ravenstocks who will own the kingdom of earth as men and women of color. "Always wanted a child from an all-white woman," announces Chicken.

In this religious context, sex becomes a means of salvation for Chicken and Myrtle. The so-called perverse act between Myrtle and Chicken takes on almost a religious quality rather than something unnatural, revolting, or suspicious. Sex is not interruption, as for Jim or Mitch, but continuation. Their lovemaking is the *summum bonum* for a postlapsarian world. As Chicken says, "There's nothing in the world, in the whole kingdom of earth, that can compare with one thing, and that one thing is what's able to happen between a man and a woman, just that thing, nothing more, is perfect. The rest is ... almost nothing" (211). The way Myrtle's response is described in one stage direction speaks volumes about a comedic conclusion: "Myrtle is still on a chair so close to the table that she's between his boots, and she looks as if she had undergone an experience of exceptional nature and manipulation" (203). Thanks to Chicken, she has had an epiphany of her own. Foster Hirsch eloquently comments on the secularization of Williams's sacramental vision: "The approach of the orgasmic flood coincides with Chicken's inheritance of the land. The flood symbolized the full release of the 'lust' body" (10).

As Williams's plays progressed, he took the unsuitable suitor farther and farther away from the conventional—Jim or Mitch—and into new, bold, revolutionary directions, Alvaro and Chicken being the two leading examples.

In the course of this evolution, though, Williams retained or radicalized the symbolism of disrupted sex and annihilated epiphanies that helped him to create the characters who sought but rarely captured love.

WORKS CITED

Boxill, Roger. *Tennessee Williams*. New York: St. Martin's Press, 1987.

Hirsch, Foster. "Sexual Imagery in Tennessee Williams's *Kingdom of Earth*." *Notes on Contemporary Literature* 1.2 (1971): 10–13.

Kazan, Elia. "Notebook for *A Streetcar Named Desire*." In *Directors on Directing: A Source Book of the Modern Theatre*, edited by Toby Cole and Helen Krich Chinoy. 2d (rev) ed. Indianapolis: Bobbs-Merrill, 1976.

Murphy, Brenda. *Tennessee Williams and Elia Kazan: A Collaboration in the Theatre*. Cambridge: Cambridge University Press, 1994.

Robinson, Marc. *The Other American Drama*. New York: Cambridge University Press, 1994.

Williams, Tennessee. *Glass Menagerie*. In *The Theatre of Tennessee Williams*. Vol. 1. New York: New Directions, 1971.

———. *Kingdom of Earth*. In *The Theatre of Tennessee Williams*. Vol. 5. New York: New Directions, 1971.

———. *Rose Tattoo*. In *The Theatre of Tennessee Williams*. Vol. 2. New York: New Directions, 1971.

———. *Streetcar Named Desire*. In *The Theatre of Tennessee Williams*. Vol. 1. New York: New Directions, 1971.

GEORGE HOVIS

"Fifty Percent Illusion": The Mask of the Southern Belle in Tennessee Williams's A Streetcar Named Desire, The Glass Menagerie, and "Portrait of a Madonna"

> After all, a woman's charm is fifty percent illusion.
> —Blanche DuBois, *A Streetcar Named Desire*

> For conjure is a power of transformation that causes definitions of "form" as a fixed and comprehensible "thing" to dissolve.
> —Houston Baker, Jr., *Modernism and the Harlem Renaissance*

Tennessee Williams achieved his early success largely on the strength of his unforgettable female leads, the southern belles of *The Glass Menagerie* and *A Streetcar Named Desire*. They are strong, articulate, assertive—and yet often tender and vulnerable. They are women who are acutely aware of being watched and heard because they have been reared in a culture with a strict decorum for the accepted behavior of its women. Because the belle can only be understood by considering her in a specific historical context, it is necessary to examine the cultural pressures that have provoked her performances. A comparative examination of Lucretia Collins of "Portrait of a Madonna," Amanda Wingfield of *The Glass Menagerie*, and Blanche DuBois of *A Streetcar Named Desire* shows how the role of the belle has perpetuated the possibilities both for victimhood and for survival. Amanda and Blanche adopt the role of the belle in an effort to survive within a social milieu in which they are disempowered. Unlike Lucretia, they both adopt the role as a means of literal

From *The Tennessee Williams Literary Journal* 5, no. 1 (Spring 2003): pp. 11–22. © 2003 by *The Tennessee Williams Literary Journal*.

survival by securing economic and social stability. More importantly, in the case of Blanche, she performs subtle transformations in the role of the belle and thereby effects a revolution within the gender consciousness of Williams's audience.

Ironically, a striking comparison can be made between the dilemma faced by these socially privileged belles and the situation of black men and women in much of this century's black American literature. During the long decades before feminism and civil rights, both blacks and white women found themselves in discursive situations at a marked disadvantage, speaking and behaving according to rules that were forced upon them. In *Modernism and the Harlem Renaissance*, Houston Baker examines the crisis of voice in interracial discourse during the Jim Crow era and the problem of black speakers, who were politically disempowered and who therefore necessarily had to develop methods of subterfuge, of illusion and deception, in order to speak and be heard. Baker identifies the minstrel mask as the form taken by black speakers seeking some measure of freedom, safety, and leverage in interracial discourse. Like the guise of the belle, however, the minstrel mask is not the creation of the wearer so much as the creation of the interlocutor with whom the wearer is engaged. White speakers misappropriated elements from black vernacular and black culture and then exaggerated and arranged them "into a comic array, a mask of *selective memory* [...] Designed to remind white consciousness that black men and women are *mis-speakers* bereft of humanity—carefree devils strumming and humming all day" (21). The occurrence of masking is more prevalent in the literature of twentieth century black male writers than in the work of black women. In *Moorings and Metaphors: Figures of Culture and Gender in Black Women's Literature*, Karla Holloway finds that the writings of black men and women fundamentally differ in that the men concentrate on individual ways of acting, while the women focus on shared ways of speaking. Holloway argues that this distinction is based not simply on sociological factors but on the fact that black male writers have adopted white male modernist assumptions about the self in relation to a community. In portraying his southern belles as alienated performers, Tennessee Williams similarly views them from perhaps a distinctly male point of view. Like his contemporaries Richard Wright and Ralph Ellison, Williams inherits from the male tradition of Anglo-American modernism a preoccupation with isolation, a factor which was, of course, heightened by his sexual orientation.

In the Jim Crow era, black male speakers consistently needed to reassure white men of black powerlessness before proceeding to negotiate for a position of relative power. Baker promotes Booker T. Washington as the foremost black American leader during Reconstruction and attributes Washington's success—in both oral address and in his autobiography, *Up*

From Slavery—to Washington's ability to "master the form" of minstrelsy (25–36), his ability to convince his white benefactors that blacks posed no threat to the ascendancy of the white male ego. Likewise, belles recognized the necessity of pacifying their men with recognizably subservient, sexually passive behaviors. In the unreconstructed South, both white women and black men were often recognized not as fully complex individuals but as representatives of a type; both the servant and the belle were reified as platonic ideals with a kind of static purity of form that would allow them reliably to serve as objects to white male subjects. In his *The Mind of the South*, W. J. Cash observes the Southern white man's obsessiveness over the utter purity of his women: "'Woman!!! The center and circumference, diameter and periphery, sine, tangent and secant of all our affections!' Such was the toast which brought twenty great cheers from the audience at the celebration of Georgia's one-hundredth anniversary in the 1830's" (87). While the white "massa" was down in the slave quarters regularly indulging his own sexual appetite, his wife was securely ensconced in the big house upholding the virtues of the Old South. In compensation for denying her own libidinal needs, she was made the emblem of moral virtue. Cash remarks: "There was hardly a sermon that did not begin and end with tributes in her honor, hardly a brave speech that did not open and close with the clashing of shields and the flourishing of swords for her glory. At the last, I verily believe, the ranks of the Confederacy went rolling into battle in the misty conviction that it was wholly for her that they fought" (86–87). Of course, the world of Williams's dramas is not the Old South but his contemporary America, an ethnically and culturally heterogeneous urban world, a setting in which Williams's belles appear comically out of place. As a remnant of the antebellum South, their presence serves to reenact the dynamics of that earlier culture within a contemporary context and thereby critiques both the earlier culture and its continuing presence in the contemporary world. In particular, Williams targets the unjust sexual mores of Southern society, mores which he shows to be virtually identical to those he finds throughout his contemporary America.

As Faulkner had, Tennessee Williams recognized the psychic damage done to Southern women by this stereotype of the belle and its attendant demand of sexual purity. As with Faulkner's Miss Emily and Rosa Coldfield, Miss Lucretia Collins of "Portrait of a Madonna" is a "middle-aged spinster" (109), who remains fixated upon her frustrated sexuality well past her prime. The daughter of an Episcopal minister, Lucretia is a woman who has long borne the brunt of her culture's puritanism. Since the death of her mother fifteen years earlier, she has remained isolated in a run-down "moderate-priced" apartment in a northern city, and she has evidently given up the weekly meetings at the church, so that now her only society is her limited contact with the building's landlord and elderly porter. As the play opens, we see an alarmed Lucretia telephoning her landlord to report that she has lately been the recurrent victim of a man who has been forcing his way into her bedroom for the purpose of "indulging his senses!" (109). Lucretia is wearing the negligee she has been saving since girlhood in her hope chest, and the stage directions consistently confront us with the comically grotesque image of a faded belle performing the actions of a young woman: "*Self-consciously she touches her ridiculous corkscrew curls with the faded pink ribbon tied through them. Her manner becomes that of a slightly coquettish but prim little Southern belle*" (114). Her manner is both "coquettish" and "prim," demonstrating the war raging inside her between libidinal energies and puritan repressions. The coquettish manner is designed to assure the prospective suitor that she is capable of sexuality, and the primness assures him that she is nevertheless virginal, waiting for the appropriate suitor. This position of waiting, of utter passivity, is the target of Williams's satire. In her middle age, with time running out, Lucretia grows desperate of waiting and so conjures for herself the fantasy of the man whom she loved in her youth. Night after night, she has imagined that he has forced himself upon her, and now she believes herself pregnant with his child. In a series of digressions, she relives her youthful attachment to Richard and her loss of him to a rival belle, a woman who was likely less sexually repressed than she. Appropriately, Lucretia lost her beau on a Sunday school faculty picnic.

Indeed, her sexual nature is repeatedly considered in relation to the church. In the opening scene when Lucretia phones her landlord to report that she has been raped, she says, "I've refrained from making any complaint because of my connections with the church. I used to be assistant to the Sunday school superintendent and I once had the primary class. I helped them put on the Christmas pageant. I made the dress for the Virgin and Mother, made robes for the Wise Men. Yes, and now this has happened, I'm not responsible for it, but night after night after night this man has been coming into my apartment and—indulging his senses!" (109). At the end of the play when the doctor and nurse from the state asylum come to take her away, she exclaims, "I know! [*Excitedly*] You're come from the Holy Communion to place me under arrest! On moral charges!" (125). Ironically, her words contain the truth that, at least on a figurative level, she is being institutionalized because of a sexual crime. She has been allowed to carry on in her delusions without disturbance for fifteen years; it is only when she affronts her limited society with the possibility of sexuality, even if it is imagined, that she is denied her freedom. The porter serves as the voice of this society and restores social order at the end of the play by denying any actual sexual transgression, when he says, "She was always a lady, Doctor, such a perfect lady" (125).

As in Faulkner's "A Rose for Emily," Williams shocks us with the disparity between the facade of the belle and her psychological reality. Unlike Emily, however, Lucretia is an impotent belle, the victim of her society's sexual mores. We are likely to agree with the porter, who tries to convince the elevator boy that Lucretia is more "pitiful" than "disgusting" (113–14). She is pitiful because she is unable to gain the necessary critical distance from her culture that would allow her to reject the imposition of its moral judgments. For a moment at least, she is capable of this rejection, and, as she is being carried away to the asylum, she shouts out that her child will receive a secular education so that "it won't come under the evil influence of the Christian church!" (123). This denouncement comes only in a moment of passion and derives from an emotional core that periodically eclipses her rational self. On a deep libidinal level she is autonomous, but on a rational level Lucretia is dominated by her culture. This lack of rational autonomy, of self-awareness, dooms her to victimhood.

Lucretia Collins's behaviors bear a striking resemblance to those of Amanda Wingfield and Blanche DuBois. All three women are constantly and acutely aware of how they are being perceived by men. Each is aware that she is beyond what her culture considers to be her "prime" and therefore engages in an elaborate scheme of denial, which involves a repetition of some critical moment from the past that marks a missed opportunity. Both Lucretia and Amanda seem to be reliving their debuts, reenacting the ritual that is designed to ensure their sexual and economic gratification. Like Lucretia in her hope-chest negligée, Amanda dons the party dress she wore while being courted as a girl at Blue Mountain, and Blanche puts on the gown and rhinestone tiara that she likely wore to the Moon Lake Casino the night her husband killed himself. Each costume is comically grotesque and out of place and thus serves as a theatrical device to remind us how each woman is trapped in a moment that passed her by years before. Perhaps the most important comparison among these women is that each feels she has been cheated, that her society has not lived up to its end of the bargain. Each has played the role of the belle without receiving the promised economic and psychosexual compensation; instead of standing amid her family surveying acres of cotton from a porch lined with columns, each woman is alone and destitute, relying upon "the kindness of strangers" and alienated family members for her bare existence.

In contrast to Lucretia, however, one feels a power, a sense of control—and a sexuality—in Blanche and Amanda that is absent from the more religiously orthodox Lucretia. Considering Lucretia's narrative of the Sunday school picnic when Richard briefly "put his arm around her," it is difficult to imagine that, even in her "prime," she ever managed to overcome the sexual repressions of her minister father. More importantly, she has never sufficiently questioned the forms of behavior expected of her as a woman. She may be emotionally outraged, but she never rationally distances herself from the role of the belle she unconsciously adopts. By contrast, with Amanda and even more so with Blanche, we see a character who may be trapped in the role of the belle but one that recognizes the entrapment. Rather than naïvely and passively expecting the deference and protection of the men around them, Blanche and Amanda relentlessly extract the expected behaviors by constantly reminding the men of the social contract of chivalry in the South and demanding the appropriate ritualized behaviors.

This problem of self-consciousness is central to both the belle and the minstrel. Richard Wright feared the adoption of masking behaviors as simply a capitulation to the expectations of white America. Throughout his autobiography, *Black Boy*, Wright explains that he survived and managed to find a writing voice precisely because he was relatively successful in avoiding situations that required him to ape the subservient behaviors of the "dumb nigger" universally expected by whites in the Jim Crow South where he grew up. For Wright, to engage in masking was to give up the struggle for equal rights. Conversely, Houston Baker argues that, during the early decades of this century, masking behaviors were the most viable form of resistance available to blacks. He sees the mastery of the forms of minstrelsy as the mode of disguising revolutionary content in the pacifying sounds of nonsense: "The mastery of form conceals, disguises, floats like a trickster butterfly in order to sting like a bee" (50). Williams's feelings about masking appear to fall somewhere between those of Wright and Baker. While he dramatizes masking as a possible mode of revolution (especially with Blanche), his maskers tend to martyr themselves for their cause. Like Wright, Williams recognizes the chief danger of masking to be the performer's loss of the ability to distinguish the difference between the performance and reality. *Streetcar* ends with a deluded Blanche, who seems to retreat to fantasy as irrevocably as the prematurely senile Lucretia in "Portrait." Throughout most of the play, however, Blanche demonstrates a much more controlled performance in which she calculates the effect of her performance on her various audiences (principally Mitch, Stanley, and Stella).

By contrast, Stella dispenses with the role of the belle and speaks candidly to her husband, trusting him to respect her openness with commensurate tenderness and honesty. Stella fled Belle Reve and the example of her older sister perhaps because she recognized the dangers of performance. Unfortunately, Stella fails to recognize the dangers of *not* performing. Unlike Blanche's, Stella's passivity is real, and Stanley takes advantage of it by intermittently bullying her and by virtually denying her a voice in the affairs of their home. He invites his drinking buddies over for poker nights and ignores her objections. He physically and emotionally abuses her, even when she is pregnant—and afterward, to the chagrin of Blanche, Stella returns home to forgive and make love to her husband. When Stanley ultimately betrays Stella's trust by raping her sister while Stella is in labor at the hospital, Stella passively accepts Stanley's denial of Blanche's report and even acquiesces to his demand that her sister be institutionalized for her delusions. Williams seems to be acknowledging that, even in the postwar melting pot of regional and ethnic traditions, America is no less chauvinistic than the Old South and that for women to deny the uneven gender dynamics is naively to accept a position of powerlessness.

The contrast between Blanche and Stella is mirrored by the relationship between Amanda Wingfield and her daughter Laura in *The Glass Menagerie*. Like Stella, Laura is incapable of adopting the role of the belle. Her intense sexual frustration combined with her father's abandonment and her mother's tyranny have produced such a fragile sense of self that she is utterly incapable of the kind of projection required in the coquettish behaviors Amanda prescribes. It would be easy to succumb to a simple and sentimentalized reading of *Menagerie* in which Laura is seen as her mother's victim and Amanda as selfishly wishing only to relive her youth through her daughter's courtship. However, if Amanda is less capable than her son, Tom, of appreciating Laura's "true self," it is because Amanda recognizes her daughter's inability to survive in the world outside their apartment. There is a strong naturalistic element in all of Williams's drama, and the world of *Menagerie* is perhaps his most Darwinian. We should hear less malice than desperation in Amanda's voice when she warns her daughter of the possibilities awaiting her:

> So what are we going to do the rest of our lives? Stay home and watch the parades go by? [...] What is there left but dependency all our lives? I know so well what becomes of unmarried women who aren't prepared to occupy a position. I've seen such pitiful cases in the South—barely tolerated spinsters living upon the grudging patronage of sister's husband or brother's wife!—stuck away in some little mousetrap of a room—encouraged by one in-law to visit another—little birdlike women without any nest— eating the crust of humility all their life! (852)

Amanda understands the social and economic realities of their world, and, by modeling the role of the belle, she attempts to teach her daughter an important survival technique.

Like Laura, Blanche was vulnerable as a girl. Stella explains to Stanley, "You didn't know Blanche as a girl. Nobody, nobody, was tender and trusting as she was. But people like you abused her, and forced her to change" (136). Blanche changed by developing an outer self that served to protect her inner self from scrutiny and judgment. She tells Stella, "I never was hard or self-sufficient enough. When people are soft—soft people have got to shimmer and glow—they've got to put on soft colors, the colors of butterfly wings, and put a—paper lantern over the light. [...] It isn't enough to be soft. You've got to be soft *and attractive*" (92). One might also remark that Blanche is not only attractive but manipulative, aggressive, and domineering. In her article "Destructive Power Games: A Study of Blanche DuBois and Amanda Wingfield," Nancy O. Wilhelmi criticizes Blanche's obsessions with surfaces as well as her relationships based "on dominance rather than intimacy, on one person's victory rather than the success of both individuals" (33). Wilhelmi appreciates how such power dynamics inevitably lead to exploitation and how Blanche perpetuates her own victimization by engaging in such a "game of deception" (33). However, Wilhelmi stops short of exploring the complexities of victimization at work in *Streetcar*. She denies Blanche an awareness of her interior life or an understanding of the history that has shaped her behaviors. Wilhelmi calls attention to Blanche's duplicity with Mitch and says that "Even the game that Blanche has been playing is a lie: she wants to marry Mitch not because she loves him but because she wants to secure her future. She betrays herself by not recognizing her own worth, as an intelligent and sensitive woman" (34–35). It is perhaps a serious misreading of the play to suggest that Blanche is actually interested in marrying Mitch at all. Someone as complex and perceptive as Blanche would likely not be interested in someone as dull and simple as Mitch, at least not for long. Blanche remarks to Mitch that no one can be sensitive without having suffered, and certainly one of the few commonalties between them is an acquaintance with suffering and death. Yet Mitch's suffering for his mother and the girl who died is simple and pitifully conventional by comparison to the complex and imaginative articulation of suffering that Blanche has managed.

As with all her other "intimacies with strangers," including her recent string of escapades in Laurel, there is a doubleness about Blanche's involvement with Mitch. In each case, she seems less interested in the affair for its own sake than in the ritual of romance in its relation to her first love, the defining relationship of her life. In easily the most tender moment between them, Blanche divulges to Mitch the history of her early marriage: "When I was sixteen, I made the discovery—love. All at once and much, much too completely. It was like you suddenly turned a blinding light on something that had always been half in shadow, that's how it struck the world for me"

(114). She explains how she came to learn of her husband's homosexuality and how she reacted to it by pronouncing the judgment that precipitated his suicide: "It was because—on the dance floor—I'd suddenly said—'I saw! I know! You disgust me ...' And then the searchlight which had been turned on the world was turned off again and never for one moment since has there been any light that's stronger than this—kitchen—candle" (115). If Blanche's neurotic avoidance of sunlight is considered in relation to this passage, then her obsession with colored lights reveals more than a paranoia about the marks of age. The sun, like a searchlight, too easily penetrates her facade of self-control and discloses the naked truth of guilt and loss that she spends her life alternately obsessing about and trying to avoid. The artificial colored lights that Blanche habitually manipulates in order to create an atmosphere conducive to the awakening of libidinal desire serve as a reminder that any love she experiences will only be a pale counterfeit of her young marriage. In reenacting the ritual of romance, however halfheartedly, Blanche is resurrecting the spirit of her first love. After apologizing for her lack of interest during their date to the amusement park, she invites Mitch into her flat, lights a candle, pours each of them a shot of liquor, and declares, "We're going to be very Bohemian. We are going to pretend that we are sitting in a little artists' cafe on the Left Bank in Paris!" (102). Blanche's involvement with Mitch here is essentially autoerotic; she is interested in the moment only for the possibility of projecting fantasies that stem from her first introduction to Bohemia with her poet husband. Similarly, she recognizes the possibilities for imaginatively evoking the past when she flirts with the newspaper boy and asks him, "Don't you just love these long rainy afternoons in New Orleans when an hour isn't just an hour—but a little piece of eternity dropped into your hands—and who knows what to do with it?" (97–98). Desire is the key to eternity; by kissing the young newspaper boy, she reenacts her passion for her late husband, who died when both he and Blanche were very young.

True to her Southern gothic nature, Blanche is a character overwhelmed by the past, both her own past and a familial and cultural past. Just as her present involvement with Mitch must be considered in relation to her first romantic attachment, all of her sexual experience must be considered in relation to the sexual history of Belle Reve and of the plantation South. In giving herself to the young soldiers who come drunken to the front lawn of Belle Reve, Blanche is reenacting the sexual attraction she felt for her young husband, but she is simultaneously revenging herself upon the self-indulgent sex lives of her "improvident grandfathers and father and uncles and brothers," who "exchanged the land for their epic fornications" (44). In explaining to Stella the loss of Belle Reve, Blanche says, "The four-letter word deprived us of our plantation" (44). One is left to guess at the degree to which Blanche's own extravagances helped precipitate that loss. In mimicking the sexual indulgence of her male forebears, she aggressively dismantles the gender roles that subject women to passive victimhood. The loss of Belle Reve, the "beautiful dream," becomes an objective correlative for the collapse of a hypocritical tradition that depends upon the belle's sexual purity, a tradition designed to perpetuate the exclusive sexual freedom of aristocratic men. As a consummate belle, Blanche has to realize the psychic and economic damage that such a collapse will deal her, and so her participation in the demise of Belle Reve must be seen at least in part as masochistic, perhaps as a sort of penance for her acquiescence to that same conservative and exclusionary tradition of sexual mores that led to her homosexual husband's suicide.

Two historical sources serve as sufficient context for Blanche's rebellion. In her *Incidents in the Life of a Slave Girl*, Harriet Jacobs candidly describes the sexual abuses of slave masters, which were silenced even in the quarters during slavery: "The secrets of slavery are concealed like those of the Inquisition. My master was, to my knowledge, the father of eleven slaves. But did the mothers dare to tell who was the father of their children? Did the other slaves dare to allude to it, except in whispers among themselves? No, indeed! They knew too well the terrible consequences" (367). Armed with reports of slavery's atrocities such as those described in *Incidents*, detractors of the Confederacy launched an assault on the notions of honor and chivalry so highly prized by Southern aristocracy. The South reacted with a collective denial that only intensified after the loss of the Civil War. W. J. Cash recognized the central role of the belle in this cultural denial. The Yankee, Cash says, had to "be answered by proclaiming from the housetops that southern Virtue, so far from being inferior, was superior, not alone to the North's but to any on earth, and adducing southern Womanhood in proof" (86). Cash explains that the history of inhumanity and rape practiced by plantation owners was categorically denied, a denial that was "enforced under penalty of being shot"; furthermore, the "fiction" of sexually pure Southern women developed to help shore up this denial (86). The moral superiority of the South, then, depended upon the sexual purity of its women.

It is this cultural fiction that Blanche attacks. She delights in transgressing Southern decorum and mocking the chauvinistic gender dynamics of her culture that deny women sexual initiative and forgive men their excesses. After being informed by Stanley about Blanche's sordid past at the seedy Flamingo Hotel in Laurel, Mitch confronts Blanche with the charges, and, after initially defending herself, she sadistically delights in her refusal to be judged by him:

> BLANCHE. Flamingo? No! Tarantula was the name of it! I stayed
> at a hotel called The Tarantula Arms!

MITCH [*stupidly*]. Tarantula?

BLANCHE. Yes, a big spider! That's where I brought my victims.
[*She pours herself another drink*] Yes, I had many intimacies with
strangers. After the death of Allan [...] here and there in the
most—unlikely places—even, at last, in a seventeen-year-old
boy but—somebody wrote the superintendent about it—"This
woman is morally unfit for her position!"
[*She throws back her head with convulsive, sobbing laughter. Then she
repeats the statement, gasps, and drinks.*]
True? Yes, I suppose—unfit somehow—anyway. (146–47)

Not surprisingly, Mitch is unprepared for such an unreserved affront
to his sense of decorum, but he is not the only male threatened by Blanche's
assertive sexuality. For all that might be remarked about Stanley's animal
sexuality, he is actually quite conventional in his attitudes toward women. He
relishes the sexual jokes and innuendo at the table with his poker buddies, and
he is unfazed by the rumor of his friend Steve's infidelity with a prostitute at
the Four Deuces, but he would not even consider the possibility of infidelity
among their wives. Clearly he expects Stella's undivided attention and her
utter fidelity. He is even shocked by Blanche's coquettish flirtations with him.
After she playfully sprays him with her perfume, he says, "If I didn't know
that you was my wife's sister I'd get ideas about you!" (41). Though he openly
proclaims his right to relax around his home in any stage of undress that suits
him, he shows intolerance for Blanche's exhibitionism. In the third scene when
Stanley leaves the poker game and violently intrudes into the bedroom to
turn off the radio Blanche is playing, he finds her sitting in the chair wearing
only a pink silk brassiere and a white skirt, and he ambivalently responds with
a mixture of desire and uneasiness: "*Stanley jumps up and, crossing to the radio,
turns it off. He stops short at the sight of Blanche in the chair. She returns his look
without flinching. Then he sits again at the poker table*" (55). There is the vaguest
sense of a confrontation in this scene, one that foreshadows the more violent
confrontations to come.

   If Blanche were recognizably and openly a prostitute, then she would be
much less threatening to Stanley. Because she is both "whore" and belle, she
occupies a liminal space in which labels are less easily affixed. Blanche wears the
mask of the belle both to appease and to shock; it is the fluidity of the form
that allows her to exploit conventional ideas about feminine sexuality. Of the
transformative powers of masking, Houston Baker writes, "Conjure's spirit work
moves behind—within, and through—the mask of minstrelsy to ensure survival,
to operate changes, to acquire necessary resources for continuance, and to cure
a sick world" (47). In both the literature of black America and in Williams's

dramas, masking subverts the notion of culturally fixed identities. In creating a situation where two antithetical identities coexist in one person, masking creates the possibility for a range of multiple identities. For both black Americans in the Jim Crow South and for women before the advent of feminism, masking provided a liberating sense of freedom to people who had been objectified and categorized and thereby denied the basic right of self-determination.

Of course, one cannot overlook the subtext of homosexual guilt and the problem of passing for "straight" that underlies the main drama. Like Blanche, Williams was intimately familiar with the sexual prohibitions and the obsession for labels that accompanied Southern society. Like Blanche, he lived a life divided between the world of accepted society and that of Bohemia. In his *Memoirs* he records the shock of certain society friends in New Orleans when he came out to them about his homosexuality. He describes a party he and his lover-roommate threw in their apartment located in the Vieux Carre, an area where, he says, their debutante guests had probably never been before, an area seen as dissolute by "the Garden District mothers." Upon discovering that Williams and his roommate shared a bed that "was somewhere between single and double," the debutantes "began to whisper to their escorts, there were little secretive colloquies among them and presently they began to thank us for an unusual and delightful evening and to take their leave as though a storm were impending" (100). Significantly, the debutantes—not their male escorts—take the initiative to preserve social decorum. Like their Garden District mothers, these young women bear the responsibility of perpetuating their society's sexual norms. In Blanche DuBois, Williams creates a belle who comes to recognize—at least subconsciously—the damage caused by such a preservation of the status quo: the death of her husband, the loss of Belle Reve, and the loss of her own liberty. If Blanche does not explicitly serve as a surrogate for Williams, then she certainly represents his interests as a gay male who is ostracized and judged by mainstream America.

Like Belle Reve, Blanche has outwardly progressed toward a state of increasing dissolution, but inwardly she moves toward a more definite sense of self, one determined by her identification with the homosexual husband whom she unfairly judged and pushed toward suicide. The dearest possessions among the souvenirs she carries in her trunk as all the tangible proof of her existence are the love letters she received from her poet husband, and she protects these letters from her intrusive brother-in-law with as much (or more) determination than she demonstrates when protecting her own body:

> BLANCHE. Now that you've touched them I'll burn them!
> STANLEY. What do you mean by saying you'll have to burn them?

> BLANCHE. Poems a dead boy wrote. I hurt him the way that
> you would like to hurt me, but you can't! I'm not young and
> vulnerable any more. But my young husband was and I—never
> mind about that! Just give them back to me!
> STANLEY. What do you mean by saying you'll have to burn
> them?
> BLANCHE. I'm sorry, I must have lost my head for a moment.
> Everyone has something he won't let others touch because of
> their—intimate nature [...]. (42–43)

This scene reveals both the earliest demonstration of her intense identification with her husband and the hint that she anticipates the rape that marks the climax of the play. Later she tells Mitch that Stanley "hates me. Or why would he insult me? The first time I laid eyes on him I thought to myself, that man is my executioner! That man will destroy me, unless—" (111). The fact that she recognizes the threat Stanley poses complicates her flirtation with him. Indeed, the question of their relationship has generated a vast diversity of readings. Perhaps she believes that as long as she maintains his sexual interest, if not his respect, then he will not "destroy" her or put her out onto the street. Perhaps, on the other hand, by provoking in Stanley an inappropriate sexual interest, Blanche expects to expose the degree of his crudeness and thereby gain control over him—in the same way that he wishes to unmask and dominate her. Their ongoing battle is largely one of name calling and labeling. He calls her "loco," "nuts" (121), and she calls him a "Polack" (22), "primitive" (39), an "animal" and "ape-like" (83). Before he rapes her, Stanley pursues a campaign of slander in an effort to ostracize her from the allegiance she enjoys from Stella and Mitch. Upon learning of her behaviors at the Flamingo and the subsequent scandal at the high school where she taught, Stanley exults, "Yep, it was practickly [sic] a town ordinance passed against her!" (101). Before he can rape her, he must penetrate her mask of the belle and confidently label her a whore. As much as the actual rape, it is this unmasking that Blanche fears and perhaps, to some degree, guiltily expects; in being judged and then raped by Stanley, she becomes a martyr to the same mainstream chauvinism in which she participated when judging her young husband's homosexuality.

It is easy to yield to the temptation to read the conclusion of the play as somehow inevitable and necessary. On a superficial level, Blanche's increasing delusion seems to legitimize her interment in the state asylum. However, one must not forget the trauma of being raped, nor should we overlook Stanley's desperation to eliminate her from the household, as well as Stella's betrayal. Not only is her ejection necessary to preserve his honor, but it is facilitated by the full disclosure of her recent illicit sexual behavior in Laurel. The play ends with Blanche serving as the scapegoat for Stanley's sexual offense, thus preserving the social order that has not changed since the height of Victorianism in America and especially in the patrician South. As with Lucretia Collins in "Portrait of a Madonna," it is Blanche's sexuality rather than her insanity that cannot be tolerated.

 Streetcar ends, however, without the social order's being fully restored. With the loss of her sister, Stella is left alone in the world with no remnant of her family and its culture. The breach of trust between her and Stanley will likely not be healed, at least not fully. Stella's clandestine letters to Belle Reve are a thing of the past; now she is fully immersed in the rough and heterogeneous lower culture of New Orleans. Recognizing her loss, she collapses not in the arms of her husband but the neighbor woman, Eunice, to whom she had felt herself superior earlier in the play. We see the beginning of an alliance forming between the two women, as Stella confesses to Eunice, "I couldn't believe her story and go on living with Stanley" (165), after which Eunice instructs Stella in the sort of day-to-day denial necessary for survival on the streets: "Don't ever believe it. Life has got to go on. No matter what happens, you've got to keep on going" (166). While the doctor and nurse from the asylum lead Blanche away, Stella recognizes her own complicity in destroying Blanche and says, "What have I done to my sister? Oh, God, what have I done to my sister?" (176). Just as Blanche spends her life reliving and coming to terms with her guilt for precipitating the suicide of her husband, Stella is likely to spend the rest of her life reliving this moment, foregoing Eunice's advice and obsessing over the possibility of Stanley's guilt, internalizing it as her own, and idealizing Blanche as a pure martyr, worthy of worship and emulation. Stella learns her own survival skills the hard way, just as Blanche and Eunice have, and the role of the innocent is no longer available to her without further moral compromise. Whether or not she dons the mask of the belle, it is certain that, like the belle and the minstrel, Stella will have to develop a double consciousness that will make her depend, not upon her husband, but upon herself for empowerment.

WORKS CITED

Baker, A. Houston, Jr. *Modernism and the Harlem Renaissance*. 1987. Chicago: U of Chicago P, 1989.

Cash, W. J. *The Mind of the South*. 1941. New York: Vintage, 1991.

Holloway, Karla F.C. *Moorings & Metaphors: Figures of Culture and Gender in Black Women's Literature*. New Brunswick, NJ: Rutgers UP, 1992.

Jacobs, Harriet. *Incidents in the Life of a Slave Girl*. 1861. Rpt. in *The Classic Slave Narratives*. Ed. Henry Louis Gates, Jr. New York: Mentor, 1987.

Wilhelmi, Nancy O. "Destructive Power Games: A Study of Blanche DuBois and Amanda Wingfield." *Tennessee Williams Literary Journal* 2.2 (1991): 33–40.

Williams, Tennessee. *The Glass Menagerie*. 1944. Rpt. in *The Harcourt Brace Anthology of Drama*. 2nd ed. Ed. W. B. Worthen. New York: Harcourt, 1996. 849–871.

———. *Memoirs*. New York: Doubleday, 1975.

———. "Portrait of a Madonna." *27 Wagons Full of Cotton and Other One-Act Plays*. 1953. Rpt. in *The Theatre of Tennessee Williams*. Vol. 45 New York: New Directions, 1981.

———. *A Streetcar Named Desire*. New York: New Directions, 1947.

Wright, Richard. *Black Boy: A Record of Childhood and Youth*. New York: Harper, 1945.

HAROLD BLOOM

Afterthought

Ever since I first fell in love with Hart Crane's poetry, almost sixty years ago, I have wondered what the poet of *The Bridge* and "The Broken Tower" would have accomplished, had he not killed himself. One doesn't see Crane burning out; he was poetically strongest at the very end, despite his despair. Williams identified his own art, and his own despair, with Crane's. Tom Wingfield, Blanche Du Bois, and even Sebastian Venable are closer to self-portraits than they are depictions of Hart Crane, but crucial images of Crane's poetry intricately fuse into Williams's visions of himself. One of the oddities of *Suddenly Last Summer* is that Catharine is far closer to an accurate inner portrait of Hart Crane than is the poet Sebastian Venable, who lacks Crane's honesty and courage. Williams's obsession with Crane twists *Suddenly Last Summer* askew, and should not prevent us from seeing that Williams's self-hatred dominates the depiction of Sebastian.

The aesthetic vocation and homosexual identity are difficult to distinguish both in Crane and in Williams, though both poet and playwright develop stratagems, rhetorical and cognitive, that enrich this difficulty without reducing it to case histories. Tom Wingfield's calling will become Williams's, though *The Glass Menagerie* presents Wingfield's quest as a flight away from the family romance, the incestuous images of the mother and the sister.

Blanche Du Bois, much closer to Williams himself, risks the playwright's masochistic self-parody, and yet her defeat has considerable aesthetic dignity. More effective on stage than in print, her personality is a touch too wistful to earn the great epitaph from Crane's "The Broken Tower" that Williams insists upon employing:

> And so it was I entered the broken world
> To trace the visionary company of love, its voice
> An instant in the wind (I know not whither hurled)
> But not for long to hold each desperate choice.

Williams, in his *Memoirs*, haunted as always by Hart Crane, refers to his precursor as "a tremendous and yet fragile artist," and then associates both himself and Blanche with the fate of Crane, a suicide by drowning in the Caribbean:

> I am as much of an hysteric as ... Blanche; a codicil to my will provides for the disposition of my body in this way. "Sewn up in a clean white sack and dropped over board, twelve hours north of Havana, so that my bones may rest not too far from those of Hart Crane ..."

At the conclusion of *Memoirs*, Williams again associated Crane both with his own vocation and his own limitations, following Crane even in an identification with the young Rimbaud:

> A poet such as the young Rimbaud is the only writer of whom I can think, at this moment, who could escape from words into the sensations of being, through his youth, turbulent with revolution, permitted articulation by nights of absinthe. And of course there is Hart Crane. Both of these poets touched fire that burned them alive. And perhaps it is only through self-immolation of such a nature that we living beings can offer to you the entire truth of ourselves within the reasonable boundaries of a book.

For all his gifts, Williams was a far more flawed artist than Crane, whose imaginative heroism was beyond anything Williams could ever attain.

Chronology

1911	Thomas Lanier ("Tennessee") Williams born March 26 in Columbus, Mississippi, to Cornelius Coffin and Edwina Dakin Williams, one-and-a-half years after his sister Rose Isabel was born.
1911–1919	Family moves often, then settles in St. Louis, Missouri. In 1919, brother, Walter Dakin, is born.
1929	Graduates from University City High School and enters the University of Missouri.
1935	Suffers a nervous breakdown. Play he collaborated on, *Cairo! Shanghai! Bombay!* is produced.
1936–1937	Enters and is later dropped from Washington University, St. Louis. Enters University of Iowa. First full-length plays, *The Fugitive Kind* and *Candles to the Sun* are produced. Sister Rose undergoes lobotomy.
1938	Graduates from University of Iowa with a degree in English.
1941–1943	Takes various jobs in different cities.
1944	*The Glass Menagerie* opens in Chicago.
1945	*The Glass Menagerie* opens in New York and wins New York Drama Critics Circle Award.
1947	*Summer and Smoke* opens in Dallas. *A Streetcar Named Desire* opens in New York and wins the New York Drama Critics Circle Award and the Pulitzer Prize. Meets Frank Merlo,

who becomes his long-time companion.

1948   *Summer and Smoke* opens in New York. *One Arm and Other Stories* is published.

1950   *The Roman Spring of Mrs. Stone*, a novel, is published. *The Rose Tattoo* opens in Chicago.

1951   *The Rose Tattoo* opens in New York, wins the Antoinette Perry (Tony) Award for best play.

1953   *Camino Real* opens in New York.

1954   *Hard Candy: A Book of Stories* is published.

1955   *Cat on a Hot Tin Roof* opens in New York; wins New York Drama Critics Circle award and Pulitzer Prize.

1956   First collection of poems, *In the Winter of Cities*, is published. *Baby Doll*, a film, is released and nominated for Academy Award.

1957   *Orpheus Descending* opens in New York.

1958   *Garden District* (*Suddenly Last Summer* and *Something Unspoken*) is produced Off-Broadway.

1959   *Sweet Bird of Youth* opens in New York.

1960   *Period of Adjustment* opens in New York.

1961   *The Night of the Iguana* opens in New York.

1962   Awarded a lifetime fellowship by the American Academy of Arts and Letters.

1963   *The Milk Train Doesn't Stop Here Anymore* opens in New York. Frank Merlo dies. Williams falls into depression.

1966   *Slapstick Tragedy* opens in New York.

1967   *The Two-Character Play* opens in London.

1968   *The Seven Descents of Myrtle* opens in New York.

1969   *In the Bar of a Tokyo Hotel* opens Off-Broadway. Converts to Catholicism. Nervous collapse causes him to stay hospitalized for three months in a hospital in St. Louis.

1970   *Dragon Country: A Book of Plays* is published.

1971   Revised version of *Two-Character Play*, called *Out Cry*, opens in Chicago.

1972   *Small Craft Warnings* opens Off-Broadway.

1974   *Eight Mortal Ladies Possessed*, a collection of short stories, is published.

1975   *Memoirs* and a second novel, *Moise and the World of Reason* are published. *The Red Devil Battery Sign* opens in Boston.

1977	*Vieux Carré* opens in New York.
1978	*Where I Live*, a book of essays, is published.
1980	*Clothes for a Summer Hotel* opens in Washington, D.C. Mother dies.
1981	*A House Not Meant to Stand* opens in Chicago. *Something Cloudy, Something Clear* opens in New York.
1983	Tennessee Williams dies in February at the Hotel Elysée in New York City.

Contributors

HAROLD BLOOM is Sterling Professor of the Humanities at Yale University. He is the author of 30 books, including *Shelley's Mythmaking*, *The Visionary Company*, *Blake's Apocalypse*, *Yeats*, *A Map of Misreading*, *Kabbalah and Criticism*, *Agon: Toward a Theory of Revisionism*, *The American Religion*, *The Western Canon*, and *Omens of Millennium: The Gnosis of Angels, Dreams, and Resurrection*. *The Anxiety of Influence* sets forth Professor Bloom's provocative theory of the literary relationships between the great writers and their predecessors. His most recent books include *Shakespeare: The Invention of the Human*, a 1998 National Book Award finalist, *How to Read and Why*, *Genius: A Mosaic of One Hundred Exemplary Creative Minds*, *Hamlet: Poem Unlimited*, *Where Shall Wisdom Be Found?*, and *Jesus and Yahweh: The Names Divine*. In 1999, Professor Bloom received the prestigious American Academy of Arts and Letters Gold Medal for Criticism. He has also received the International Prize of Catalonia, the Alfonso Reyes Prize of Mexico, and the Hans Christian Andersen Bicentennial Prize of Denmark.

JACQUELINE O'CONNOR teaches English at Boise State University. In addition to authoring *Dramatizing Dementia: Madness in the Plays of Tennessee Williams*, she has written several articles on Williams as well as other essays.

JOHN M. CLUM teaches at Duke University. He is the author of *Still Acting Gay: Male Homosexuality in Modern Drama* and has also published other titles and numerous essays. He edited *Staging Gay Lives: An Anthology of Contemporary Gay Theater*. Additionally, he has directed more than sixty dramatic and operatic productions and written his own plays.

NANCY M. TISCHLER, a professor emeritus of English at Pennsylvania State University, is the author of the first critical study of Williams's work, *Tennessee Williams: Rebellious Puritan*. She has co-edited, with Albert J. Devlin, *The Selected Letters of Tennessee Williams*.

BERT CARDULLO has taught at the Tisch School of the Arts at New York University. He has authored several titles, such as *Theatrical Reflections: Notes on the Form and Practice of Drama*. He is the editor of *What Is Dramaturgy?* and of other titles and also has done translating. Additionally, he has been a regular film critic for *The Hudson Review*.

LINDA DORFF, now deceased, taught at the School of Theatre at the University of Houston. She edited a book of interviews, *Working with Tennessee*, and produced and directed a documentary film for public television, *Tennessee Williams' Dragon Country: The Late Plays*. Also, she was an advisor to the Hartford Stage Company's Williams Marathon.

D. DEAN SHACKELFORD has taught English at Southeast Missouri State University, where he also has been a director of undergraduate studies. He has published articles on Tennessee Williams, Flannery O'Connor, Harper Lee, Countee Cullen, and others.

VERNA FOSTER teaches English at Loyola University. She has published *Name and Nature of Tragicomedy*. Also, she has published numerous essays on modern and Renaissance drama.

ANNETTE J. SADDIK teaches English at Eastern Michigan University. She is the author of *The Politics of Reputation: The Critical Reception of Tennessee Williams' Later Plays*. She wrote several entries to the *Tennessee Williams Encyclopedia* and also has published articles on Williams and book reviews of publications about his work.

FRANK BRADLEY has been chair of the Department of Performing and Visual Arts and artistic director of the Wallace Theatre at the American University in Cairo. He has written on American drama and theater semiotics and has directed theater productions in universities throughout the United States and Egypt.

PHILIP C. KOLIN teaches English at the University of Southern Mississippi. He authored numerous books, including *Undiscovered Country: The Later Plays of Tennessee Williams*. He also edited the *Tennessee Williams Encyclopedia*, and wrote and/or edited other works on Williams as well. Additionally, he is the general editor for the Routledge Shakespeare Criticism Series and the cofounder of the journal *American Drama, 1945–Present*.

GEORGE HOVIS teaches American literature and creative writing at Murray State University. He has published essays on various topics related to Southern literature. Aside from Southern literature, he is interested in creative writing and American literature overall.

Bibliography

Bak, John S. "'Sneakin' and Spyin' from Broadway to the Beltway: Cold War Masculinity, Brick and Homosexual Existentialism." *Theatre Journal* 56, no. 2 (May 2004): pp. 225–49.

———. "'Stanley Made Love to Her!—By Force!': Blanche and the Evolution of a Rape." *Journal of American Drama and Theatre* 16, no. 1 (Winter 2004): pp. 69–97.

Bibler, Michael P. "'A Tenderness Which Was Uncommon': Homosexuality, Narrative, and the Southern Plantation in Tennessee Williams's *Cat on a Hot Tin Roof.*" *Mississippi Quarterly: The Journal of Southern Cultures* 55, no. 3 (Summer 2002): pp. 381–400.

Bloom, Harold, ed. *Tennessee Williams's* Cat on a Hot Tin Roof. Philadelphia: Chelsea House Publishers, 2002.

———. *Tennessee Williams's* The Glass Menagerie. New York: Chelsea House Publishers, 1988.

———. *Tennessee Williams's* A Streetcar Named Desire. Philadelphia: Chelsea House, 2005.

Boxill, Roger. *Tennessee Williams*. New York: St. Martin's Press, 1987.

Bray, Robert. *The Glass Menagerie*. New York, NY: New Directions, 1999.

Conlon, Christopher. "'Fox-Teeth in Your Heart': Sexual Self-Portraiture in the Poetry of Tennessee Williams." *Tennessee Williams Annual Review* 4 (2001): pp. 59–69.

Crandell, George W. "'Echo Spring': Reflecting the Gaze of Narcissus in Tennessee Williams's *Cat on a Hot Tin Roof.*" *Modern Drama* 42, no. 3 (Fall 1999): pp. 427–41.

197

————. "Peeping Tom: Voyeurism, Taboo, and Truth in the World of Tennessee Williams's Short Fiction." *Southern Quarterly: A Journal of the Arts in the South* 38, no. 1 (Fall 1999): pp. 28–35.

Crandell, George W., ed. *The Critical Response to Tennessee Williams.* Westport, Conn.: Greenwood Press, 1996.

Fleche, Anne. *Mimetic Disillusion: Eugene O'Neill, Tennessee Williams, and U.S. Dramatic Realism.* Tuscaloosa: University of Alabama Press, 1997.

Fordyce, Ehren. "Inhospitable Structures: Some Themes and Forms in Tennessee Williams." *Journal of American Drama and Theatre* 17, no. 2 (Spring 2005), pp. 43–58.

Gilbert, James. *Men in the Middle: Searching for Masculinity in the 1950s.* Chicago: University of Chicago Press, 2005.

Griffin, Alice. *Understanding Tennessee Williams.* Columbia, S.C.: University of South Carolina Press, 1995.

Hayman, Ronald. *Tennessee Williams: Everyone Else Is an Audience.* New Haven, Conn.: Yale University Press, 1993.

Holditch, Kenneth and Richard F. Leavitt. *Tennessee Williams and the South.* Jackson: University Press of Mississippi, 2002.

Kang, Yuna. "Sexing the Fairytales: The Melodrama of Tennessee Williams." *Journal of Modern British and American Drama* 15, no. 1 (April 2002): pp. 33–57.

Kataria, Gulshan Rai. *The Faces of Eve: A Study of Tennessee Williams's Heroines.* New Delhi: Sterling Publishers, 1992.

Kim, Ki-ae. "Death and Rebirth in *The Night of the Iguana.*" *Journal of Modern British and American Drama* 15, no. 1 (April 2002): pp. 59–78.

Kolin, Philip C. "Tennessee Williams: The Non-Dramatic Work." *Southern Quarterly: A Journal of the Arts in the South* 38, no. 1 (Fall 1999).

————. *Williams:* A Streetcar Named Desire. Cambridge; New York: Cambridge University Press, 2000.

————. *The Undiscovered Country: The Later Plays of Tennessee Williams.* New York, NY: Peter Lang, 2002.

Kolin, Philip C., ed. *Confronting Tennessee Williams's* A Streetcar Named Desire: *Essays in Critical Pluralism.* Westport, Conn.: Greenwood Press, 1993.

————. *The Tennessee Williams Encyclopedia.* Westport, Conn.: Greenwood, 2004.

————. *Tennessee Williams: A Guide to Research and Performance.* Westport: Greenwood, 1998.

Murphy, Brenda. *Tennessee Williams and Elia Kazan: A Collaboration in the Theatre.* New York: Cambridge University Press, 1992.

O'Connor, Jacqueline. "The 'Neurotic Giggle': Humor in the Plays of Tennessee Williams." *Studies in American Humor* 3, no. 6 (1999): pp. 37–48.

Paller, Michael. *Gentlemen Callers: Tennessee Williams, Homosexuality, and Mid-Twentieth-Century Drama*. New York: Palgrave Macmillan, 2005.

———. "A Room Which Isn't Empty: *A Streetcar Named Desire* and the Question of Homophobia." *Tennessee Williams Literary Journal* 5, no. 1 (Spring 2003): pp. 23–37.

Pawley, Thomas D. "Where the Streetcar Doesn't Run: The Black World of Tennessee Williams." *Journal of American Drama and Theatre* 14, no. 3 (Fall 2002): pp. 18–33.

Presley, Delma Eugene. The Glass Menagerie: *An American Memory*. Boston: Twayne Publishers, 1990.

Savran, David. *Communists, Cowboys, and Queers: The Politics of Masculinity in the Work of Arthur Miller and Tennessee Williams*. Minneapolis: University of Minnesota Press, 1992.

Schvey, Henry. "Tennessee Williams." *Theatron* (Spring 2004): pp. 4–38.

Shackelford, Dean. "'The Ghost of a Man': The Quest for Self-Acceptance in Early Williams." *Tennessee Williams Annual Review* 4 (2001): pp. 49–58.

Shelton, Lewis E. "Elia Kazan and the Psychological Perspective on Directing." *Journal of American Drama and Theatre* 14, no. 3 (Fall 2002): pp. 60–88.

Siebold, Thomas, ed. *Readings on* The Glass Menagerie. San Diego, Calif.: Greenhaven Press, 1998.

Siegel, Robert. "The Metaphysics of Tennessee Williams." *American Drama* 10, no. 1 (Winter 2001): pp. 11–37.

Single, Lori Leathers. "Flying the Jolly Roger: Images of Escape and Selfhood in Tennessee Williams's *The Glass Menagerie*." *Tennessee Williams Annual Review*, 2 (1999): pp. 69–85.

Spoto, Donald. *The Kindness of Strangers: The Life of Tennessee Williams*. Boston: Little, Brown, 1985.

Thompson, Judith J. *Tennessee Williams's Plays: Memory, Myth, and Symbol*. New York: Peter Lang, 2002.

Tischler, Nancy M. *The Student Companion to Tennessee Williams*. Westport: Greenwood, 2000.

Vannatta, Dennis P. *Tennessee Williams: A Study of the Short Fiction*. Boston: Twayne, 1988.

Zeineddine, Nada. *Because It Is My Name: Problems of Identity Experienced by Women, Artists, and Breadwinners in the Plays of Henrik Ibsen, Tennessee Williams, and Arthur Miller*. Braunton, England: Merlin, 1991.

Acknowledgments

"Babbling Lunatics: Language and Madness" by Jacqueline O'Connor. From *Dramatizing Dementia: Madness in the Plays of Tennessee Williams*: pp. 61–75. © 1997 by Bowling Green State University Popular Press. Reprinted with permission.

"The Sacrificial Stud and the Fugitive Female in *Suddenly Last Summer*, *Orpheus Descending*, and *Sweet Bird of Youth*" by John M. Clum. From *The Cambridge Companion to Tennessee Williams*, edited by Matthew C. Roudané: pp. 128–146. © 1997 by Cambridge University Press. Reprinted with permission of Cambridge University Press.

"Romantic Textures in Tennessee Williams's Plays and Short Stories" by Nancy M. Tischler. From *The Cambridge Companion to Tennessee Williams*, ed. Matthew C. Roundané: pp. 147–166. © 1997 Cambridge University Press. Reprinted with permission of Cambridge University Press.

"The Blue Rose of St. Louis: Laura, Romanticism, and *The Glass Menagerie*" by Bert Cardullo. From *The Tennessee Williams Annual Review* 1998: pp. 81–92. © 1998 by *The Tennessee Williams Annual Review*. Reprinted with permission.

"'I prefer the "mad" ones': Tennessee Williams's Grotesque-Lyric Exegetical Poems" by Linda Dorff. From *The Southern Quarterly* 38, no. 1 (Fall 1999): pp. 81–93. © 1999 by the University of Southern Mississippi. Reprinted with permission.

"'The Transmutation of Experience': The Aesthetics and Themes of Tennessee Williams's Nonfiction" by D. Dean Shackelford. From *The Southern Quarterly* 38, no. 1 (Fall 1999): pp. 104–116. © 1999 by the University of Southern Mississippi. Reprinted with permission.

"Desire, Death, and Laughter: Tragicomic Dramaturgy in *A Streetcar Named Desire*" by Verna Foster. From *American Drama* 9, no. 1 (Fall 1999): pp. 51–68. © 2000 by *American Drama Institute*. Reprinted with permission.

"Critical Expectations and Assumptions: Williams' Later Reputation and the American Reception of the Avant-Garde" by Annette J. Saddik. From *The Politics of Reputation: The Critical Reception of Tennessee Williams' Later Plays*: pp. 135–150. © 1999 by Associated University Presses. Reprinted with permission.

"Two Transient Plays: *A Streetcar Named Desire* and *Camino Real*" by Frank Bradley. From *Tennessee Williams: A Casebook*, edited by Robert F. Gross: pp. 51–62. © 2002 by Routledge. Reprinted with permission.

"The Family of Mitch: (Un)suitable Suitors in Tennessee Williams" by Philip C. Kolin. From *Magical Muse: Millennial Essays on Tennessee Williams*, edited by Ralph F. Voss: pp. 131–146. © 2002 by the University of Alabama Press. Reprinted with permission.

"'Fifty Percent Illusion': The Mask of the Southern Belle in Tennessee Williams's *A Streetcar Named Desire*, *The Glass Menagerie*, and 'Portrait of a Madonna'" by George Hovis. From *The Tennessee Williams Literary Journal* 5, no. 1 (Spring 2003): pp. 11–22. © 2003 by *The Tennessee Williams Literary Journal*. Reprinted with permission.

Every effort has been made to contact the owners of copyrighted material and secure copyright permission. Articles appearing in this volume generally appear much as they did in their original publication with few or no editorial changes. Those interested in locating the original source will find bibliographic information in the bibliography and acknowledgments sections of this volume.

Index